The Best Day Of My Life

TRUE STORIES TO INSPIRE, MOVE AND
ENTERTAIN – TOLD BY A CROSS-SECTION
OF THE UK'S CELEBRITIES AND
COURAGEOUS EVERYDAY PEOPLE.

COMPILED AND EDITED BY
GILES VICKERS JONES AND HUMFREY HUNTER

JOHN BLAKE

Published by John Blake Publishing Ltd,
3 Bramber Court, 2 Bramber Road,
London W14 9PB, England

www.johnblakepublishing.co.uk

www.facebook.com/Johnblakepub   facebook

twitter.com/johnblakepub   twitter

First published in 2008 by Pennant Books
This edition published in paperback in 2012

ISBN: 978-1-85782-819-1

British Library Cataloguing-in-Publication Data:

A catalogue record for this book is available from the British Library.

Design by www.envydesign.co.uk

Printed in Great Britain by CPI Group (UK) Ltd

1 3 5 7 9 10 8 6 4 2

© Text copyright Giles Vickers Jones and Humfrey Hunter 2012

Papers used by John Blake Publishing are natural, recyclable products made
from wood grown in sustainable forests. The manufacturing processes
conform to the environmental regulations of the country of origin.

Every attempt has been made to contact the relevant copyright-holders,
but some were unobtainable. We would be grateful if the
appropriate people could contact us.

The Best Day
Of My Life

To Christopher Vickers-Jones and Thea Hunter

Contents

Foreword

In May 2007, we sat down over a couple of beers and started kicking around a few ideas for books we could do together. A few pints later the idea for *The Best Day Of My Life* was born. A few pints after that, it was nearly forgotten. But luckily we'd written down enough to be able to remember our main objective: to produce a book full of true stories which were special to the people who wrote them and which would become special to those who read them.

Then we set a few ground rules which we would break only in exceptional circumstances, such as no weddings, no births and no sporting events. Inevitably, we broke them and the stories about these things which have made the book are particularly good, for reasons which will become clear when you read them. But a word to those wives and husbands who will be irritated to see that their loved one chose to write about a day other than their wedding: you can blame us. It was our decision, not theirs.

We decided early on to do the book in conjunction with a charity so that contributors would have a good reason to open up to us. Profits from this edition will go to AfriKids, a truly remarkable child rights organisation which works to improve life for Ghana's most vulnerable and disadvantaged children. AfriKids' work ranges from the more traditional children's projects including foster homes, schools and street child centres to more groundbreaking initiatives which tackle complex cultural issues including child trafficking, child labour and the spirit child phenomenon. Its aims are to listen to what the community knows it needs, empower them to make the necessary changes themselves and to ensure absolute sustainability. For more information, please see www.afrikids.org and read the story in this book by Georgina Fienberg, who founded AfriKids.

As the stories began to arrive, we noticed something very interesting, which was that they were not all about a single day in isolation. Some were – and are brilliant for it – but of the rest many refer to one precise day as either the end of an especially difficult period of their lives or the moment when months or even years of hard work began to pay off. We decided very quickly that those stories were just as valid and they are now among the most poignant of them all for obvious reasons.

There are some incredible bits of work in this book and we don't just say that because we had the idea and put the thing together. The stories are extraordinary and we are sure everyone who reads them will find something in there to either inspire them, make them smile, make them cry or even just help them pass a few pleasant minutes on the loo.

On a serious note, wherever you read these stories, remember that each and every one is true and reveals something very personal about the person who wrote it. So please don't rush through and only pick up the superficial details. Re-read the stories and be sure to take everything in because that is how you will get the most out of them. These stories are a truly unique insight into some extraordinary days and lives. We are very proud of them.

Enjoy the book.

Giles and Humfrey

Lara Agnew

Teacher & Mother

I plan everything in my life. I always catch myself doing it and, when I do, it nearly always ends up not going the way it was supposed to. Even so, I still put a great deal of time and energy into organising things and people. I'm always prepared to work for things, and I love nothing more than putting a big tick on my long lists.

Meeting Ross was not planned. I was 23 and about to embark on my very grown-up life as a teacher. The last thing I needed in tow was a student. Ross was 19, a fresher, new to university life and played rugby. In fact, as I write this, it would be easy for me to make him sound unappealing, but he had a very endearing side which made me throw caution to the wind (very unlike me!) and take a chance on him.

Seven years later, Ross asked me to marry him. I instantly started planning what flowers I would have in my bouquet. By the time we were married, I was 30 and my biological clock was ticking very loudly. I knew Ross wanted children at some point but he wasn't ready yet and I understood that.

In February 2004, on my birthday, Ross announced that he was 'ready'. I was ecstatic. I was sure that in a few months' time I'd be trying to think of reasons to give my friends to explain why I wasn't drinking to conceal the early stages of my pregnancy. We planned weekends away and talked excitedly about preparing for a baby. When a few months passed, and I was not blooming, or even sprouting, I started recording the lengths of my cycles to see if I could determine roughly when I was at my most fertile. I found there was a pattern and so there was always a lot of activity around that particular time of the month.

After almost two years, we were very worried and decided to talk to our GP about running some tests. A couple of factors were suggested that could be affecting our chances, but no single cause could be identified. Each month was beginning to feel like an emotional rollercoaster: two weeks' build-up until ovulation, a flurry of hopeful activity and then the bitter disappointment when I was not pregnant. It was draining, both physically and emotionally, and the frustration made Ross and me snappy and bad-tempered. We knew that the odds were not in our favour after two years of trying for a baby.

We were both becoming very despondent and I seemed to bump into pregnant women and babies everywhere I turned. This just reminded me of the fact that I didn't have a baby of my own and didn't know if I would ever have one. I smiled and celebrated with friends as they started their families but cried when no one was looking because I wanted that to be me. After a lot of soul searching, we decided to try IVF.

It is a long process: each IVF cycle involved sniffing one hormone to down-regulate my ovaries and numerous scans to determine when to start the hormone injections to restart the egg production. This was followed by two weeks of daily injections that I administered myself. More scans followed to monitor how my ovaries were responding to ensure that the eggs were collected at exactly the right time.

When the eggs were ready, I had to inject another hormone exactly 36 hours before the eggs were collected. The egg-collection process was very intrusive, carried out under sedation, and left me feeling very sore. The eggs were then placed with a sample of sperm to fertilise.

After three to five days, some of the eggs had fertilised and developed into embryos. The two most established embryos were then transferred back into my uterus. On both our first two cycles, we reached this stage and then endured the two-week wait before we could do the pregnancy test. Both times the test was negative.

Ross and I struggled to stay positive, and the treatment made me tired, uncomfortable and extremely emotional. I could tell that Ross wanted to take my pain away but he felt helpless. After those first two failed attempts, we started to discuss how many more, if any, cycles we would try. I felt like a pincushion, and each unsuccessful attempt was exhausting, and unrewarding. But neither of us was prepared to give up so we decided to try once more.

Shortly after the embryo transfer during our third cycle, I felt sure that things had not worked out. I told Ross it was happening all over again and that we were not going to be having a baby. We did what we always do when we have to cope with something: Ross watched a lot of sport on TV and I cleaned and busied myself in the kitchen. Over the next few days, I didn't say anything to Ross, but secretly I allowed myself to have a glimmer of hope – I couldn't help it.

On the morning of the test, I went to the loo at 5 a.m. and came back to bed clutching the stick. This time there was a faint blue line on it. I turned all the lights on and just sat staring at it. Was I willing it to be there? Was I so desperate that I had started hallucinating? I woke Ross and he thought I had really gone mad as he had come to terms with the disappointment a few days earlier.

That day was bizarre; I bought another three tests on the way home from work and did them all. Every one was POSITIVE – I really was pregnant. A few days later, I did another two tests … oh my God, still pregnant! The next few days passed in a blur of glowing happiness. I felt like I was carrying around a very special secret that only Ross and I knew. Every morning when I woke up, I would touch my tummy, and smile to myself.

3

My pregnancy went really smoothly. I loved carrying my baby and felt like the luckiest girl alive. It was hard to believe that millions of women had done – and would do – this; it felt as if I was the only pregnant person in the world.

At 38 weeks (after a curry!), I woke up at four o'clock in the morning lying on a wet mattress. I turned to Ross, who is famous for his deep sleeps, and told him that I thought my waters had broken. He instantly jumped out of bed, scrabbled around for his glasses and started pulling on clothes in a wild frenzy. This was not at all how we had discussed he would react. After a call to the labour ward, Ross drove me in for a check-up. They confirmed that my waters had broken, and that I would 'probably' go into labour over the weekend. If not they would see me on Monday morning. We turned and headed back home, me squelching with every step and feeling like an incontinent old woman.

We sat looking at each other at 8.30 a.m. on a Saturday morning. Then I did some cleaning and Ross watched sport on TV, adopting our usual coping mechanisms. We watched a film – my choice (as you'd expect!), a romantic comedy and a real treat. Ross went for a run, went shopping for food and drink to take to hospital and we played scrabble. During the scrabble game, things began to happen, slowly at first, but soon my triple word scores were a distant memory. Ross decided he needed two watches, one to time each contraction and one to measure the time between them. He was also still trying hard to beat me at scrabble which I thought was slightly unfair given that I was bouncing, rolling and grimacing on the birthing ball at the time.

In the labour room, the midwife settled us in and told us to 'make ourselves at home'. This room was the place least like my home I had ever been in. Ross still managed to find a comfy armchair and sat down for a rest as I fell to my knees with another contraction. 'Get over here!' I spat at him. That was the last even vaguely civil comment I made to him for the next few hours.

As my labour progressed, I could hear music and snippets of the conversations that Ross and the midwife were having, but, overall, I was totally high on the gas and air in the hope that it would alleviate the pain. Ross kept me going with Ribena from a straw and bore the brunt of my anger and pain. I swore A LOT but in general this was one of those rare occasions where everything went as I had planned.

Just after midnight, while 'Sitting on the Dock of the Bay' by Otis Redding was playing, I gave birth to our son, Noah Peter Mackean Agnew, weighing 7lb 4oz. I was elated, tired and very emotional. Ross was elated, tired and very hungry. So he opened a packet of pork scratchings and shared them with the midwife while I stared in amazement at what we had achieved. This was the beginning of a new life and a whole new chapter in ours.

Ben Anderson

TV Presenter

I'd been told to go home and I was not expecting the trip to have a happy ending. I'd packed my bags, crossed the border into Rwanda and checked into a small room in the eaves of a beaten-up old hotel. Seven hundred rebels had occupied the base we needed to get to, outnumbering us 33 to 1.

I'd spent three weeks training with the Advance Force Rangers of the Virunga National Park in the Democratic Republic of Congo for a TV programme and I've never met a greater group of men. Their commander, Ellie Mundima, promised me that, if I completed my training and won a green beret, he would take me to meet one of the 29 mountain gorillas left in Congo. I'd passed, but the presence of the rebels, ruthless murderers led by an indicted war criminal called Laurent Nkunda, meant we couldn't travel to the gorilla area.

When Ellie heard how many soldiers there were, he looked down. 'You cannot fight a mountain,' he said, and told me to go home.

If it's true that you find the greatest heroes where there are the greatest obstacles to overcome, Ellie certainly proves it. His unshakeable optimism would give him a quixotic air, were it not for the very real dangers that he faces. He's been the victim of at least one assassination attempt, when poachers killed his bodyguard. And over five million of his countrymen are thought to have died as a result of the war in Congo which started in 1996. Yet I've never met a more positive man.

I asked Ellie about the fate of the gorillas and the lines on his forehead flinched. He told me that they would probably be killed for meat. If the rebels saw one of the babies, they might kill its entire family so they could take the tiny creature away and sell it on the black market.

I'd completed a three-month training course in three weeks, with Ellie taking me for runs every morning, teaching me jungle survival, first aid and endless military drills. He also gave me an AK-47, which he taught me how to use and ordered me to keep within arm's reach at all times. I should have been ecstatic to have succeeded. Instead, I was going home early, a little disappointed that I wouldn't see a gorilla, but mostly depressed to have seen first-hand what the rangers were up against. Their cause seemed hopeless.

Then I got a call from the rangers. According to local villagers, the rebels had left and the post was empty again. The rangers told me to get back immediately so we could go and check on the gorillas.

Our plans had changed so many times that I didn't allow myself to get too excited. I knew there was a strong chance that we'd find nothing or that rebels would force us to flee again. Or we could find an entire family killed for their baby. The rangers love the gorillas and I didn't want to see their reaction to discovering an entire family butchered. With only three families left in the entire national park, such a loss would surely tell them they were defeated.

We arrived at the base after a couple of hours of driving and there was no sign of the rebels.

As we had done so many times over the last three weeks, we stood in line and cocked our guns together. All we now had to do to make our guns ready to fire was flick the safety catch off. The ritual made everyone become deadly serious. But I also knew this

7

was the last time I would do it with these men, and I knew I was going to miss them.

After five hours of walking, we found a huge area of flattened leaves, which Safari, one of the trackers, told me had been a bed the night before.

There was only one flattened area, so it must have belonged to one of the three lone Silverbacks in the park. Gorillas eat a huge amount and don't travel far in a day, so, dead or alive, he had to be close.

Soon everyone stopped and motioned to the rest of the group to crouch and be quiet. I was told to take off my beret and remove the gun from my shoulder.

'Don't point at him, don't make sudden movements. Make eye contact with him for a few seconds then look to the ground, so he knows you are not challenging him. If he charges, just lean forward and remain still.'

I moved towards Ellie and, beyond a huge branch, in a small patch of brilliant sunlight, I saw the thick shiny coat of the gorilla. His head looked three times the size of mine. His shoulders were the size of watermelons. He looked at us and one of the rangers made a quiet grumbling noise, like an old man being disturbed in his sleep, and he went back to eating.

If we had both stretched out our arms, we could have made contact. He stared into my eyes, as if he was searching for my intentions. It felt like we were communicating and I was reluctant to look down, as ordered.

When I did, I dipped my head forwards theatrically and then slowly looked up at him again, finding it impossible not to grin. I hadn't even dared to imagine that this moment would really come. I turned to Ellie and whispered, 'When the rebels came I thought I would never see the gorillas.'

'Even if they kill, they can't end all. There must remain some,' Ellie said triumphantly.

'And you kept your promise.'

Ellie laughed and broke into the shining, permanently optimistic smile that I'd seen so much of over the last three weeks.

'Yes of course. Yes,' he said, as if the outcome had never been in doubt.

The gorilla, one of only three lone males in the entire national park, was named Kareka by the Rangers. Three weeks after I left, Nkunda's rebels killed the other two.

There are now less than 700 mountain gorillas left in the world, and perhaps less than two dozen left in the Virunga National Park in Congo. But, on that one day at least, Ellie showed me what a glorious place it could be.

Gemma Atkinson

Actress

The best day of my life so far was the arrival of my nephew, my sister Nina's first child, Hadley. He was born quite early and we knew he was going to be premature so when the time came we were sitting around waiting for the call. Finally we got the call that she was in labour. I spoke to Nina and she was crying on the phone saying she couldn't give birth because she was petrified. She didn't want to go through with it because she was so scared but I spoke to her calmly and said, 'You have to do it – either way Hadley's popping out so get in there, push him out and you can come home.'

So we went up to the hospital and sat in the waiting room. We sat and sat and sat waiting for news. Eventually my sister got wheeled through. She wasn't very well and looked awful. She was all pale and her hair was stuck to her face but she had little Hadley in her arms so she was smiling. He was tiny and everyone joked about him being a true Atkinson because he slept the whole time. He wouldn't wake up and he only woke up when I went over and started stroking his face. I was the first person he saw because the nurses and Nina herself said he hadn't really opened his eyes until that moment and that's really special for me to know. He's now 10 and I see him all the time. I pick him up from school and take him to football matches and he's a top little nephew.

Matt Beaumont

Author

The best day of my life? I've had loads. I don't think I'm particularly blessed, only averagely so. I actually believe that most of us have had several best days of our lives. The thing about best days is that, when one comes along, it feels better than all the previous bests by virtue of its freshness, the very fact it's the one we're having *right now*. It will stay the best of the best days until another one comes along, hopefully soon. Here, in chronological order, is a vaguely representative selection of mine:

Five days in July 1967: a camping trip with five classmates. Six boys in a jerry-built tree house in a forest, the nearest teacher (in fact, the *only* teacher) in a farmhouse over 200 yards away. We lit fires, swam in dirty streams (in our underpants!), rolled in mud and assaulted haystacks. The teacher even let us take the wheel of his Morris Minor van. For heaven's sake, we were eight years old! I still get giddy at the memory.

Today this would breach so many health and safety directives it would be the focus of a public inquiry. And if I gave up the teacher's name, he would be hounded out of his retirement home and placed on a Home Office blacklist. Don't worry, sir, I'll *never* talk.

11

July 1969: for one day and one day only, Malibu sunshine and Bondi surf on Whitby beach. None of us had surfboards and, even if we had, we wouldn't have known what to do with them. This being Yorkshire and us being practical folk, we would have fitted them with legs: excellent ironing boards. With or without surfboards, though, those waves were still the most exhilarating and terrifying things I'd ever seen. The Beach Boys were probably playing on a radio somewhere, but I didn't notice.

May 1975: running away from school. Standing on the A1 at Scotch Corner with my thumb in the air, waiting for (I imagined) an 18-wheel Mack truck to pick me up and carry me to (I imagined) Badassville, South Dakota, where I was going to begin living my personal road movie. I got as far as Pontefract, but for a moment back there...

Incidentally, I believe that every great day has its obverse, the bloody awful day. (If you believe in that sort of rubbish, you'll say it is all part of some great cosmological balance.) The obverse of my running-away-from-school day followed hot on its heels, the day after in fact. It was my return to said school. Parents, *never* send your child to a boarding school. They are not run by nice people.

October 1976: Middlesbrough 3, West Ham United 0. I'd been to football matches before and I've been since. This one, an autumn fixture in a season when Boro competed for nothing in particular, stands out in my memory like a French manicure on a bricklayer. Most of the previous times I'd seen my team, they'd been prosaic at best. This time, though, it was like watching Real Madrid. OK, Real Madrid playing in clogs and lost in a miasmic smog of chemical discharge from ICI Billingham. But West Ham did have Clyde Best, who, in the fug, looked vaguely like Eusebio. It could have been a Real–Benfica European Cup tie, then. For the record, the goals came from Armstrong, Foggon and a beardy Souness.

November 1978: the Clash, Middlesbrough Town Hall. Two golden memories set in Middlesbrough? I suspect that's two more than it has ever been awarded. This was one of many times I saw the brilliant Clash, but this show was definitely the best. They were promoting their second album, which wasn't their finest. Maybe that meant they had to work twice as hard and play twice as loud to compensate. Who knows? Whatever their motivation, they were possessed and they blew me away. And they literally blew the glasses off my face, which were crushed beneath 500 bouncing pairs of DMs. *Hooray!* They were vile glasses.

31 December 1993: New Year's Eve in balmy St Lucia. Like, *duh*, of course it was good. But believe me, I'm not a big one for parties, especially New Year parties. For a start, parties involve dancing. To say I have two left feet is an insult to left feet everywhere. I *hate* dancing. But for a full 60 minutes I achieved a nirvana state of drunkenness where I dumped my inhibitions at the foot of a palm tree and *believed* I could groove like MC Hammer (ridiculous pants, but, admit it, the man could dance). Miraculously – and this was what made the moment so special – Maria had reached an identical state of grace. 'You didn't tell me you could dance,' she squealed delightedly. I should point out that Maria is, among other things (one of them being my wife), a dance teacher. Consequently, she has Very High Standards – which, for a glorious hour, she tossed wantonly to the wind.

October 1999: the birth of Holly. I swore to myself that I wouldn't mention my kids in this piece. But when your daughter is born within a couple of hours of a publisher saying yes to your first novel, well, that's a pretty amazing day and it would be dishonest to ignore it. I didn't actually get the call telling me about the book deal in the labour room. No mobile phones allowed, you see. I had to wait till I got home. There I was, staring at my gorgeous baby, my agent in my ear telling me that, given a fair wind and a decent royalty rate, I might actually be able to afford to keep this vision in Disney Princess outfits.

Tomorrow: I just know it's going to be an amazing day.

Dave Berry

TV Presenter

My name is Dave Berry and I'm a 23-year-old TV presenter from South London. Well, actually I'm 29. But everyone in my industry lies about their age. In fact, the only reason I've come clean is because once you've read my story you won't have to be Columbo to work out the truth.

It was 14 September 1988 and I was celebrating my ninth birthday (see, I told you it wouldn't take long). The whole shebang started with the arrival of my friends at my house. They were all there: Paul Heyes, Jack Kennedy, Aiden McConville, Andrew Clark and the black kid in the A Team jumper whose name I could never remember.

My mum and dad, God bless them, had even bunged my little sister a glo-worm sleeping bag to keep her quiet when I opened my presents. So, in a nutshell, I was ready to rumble. Now, in 1988 in Charlton, Southeast London, there were three things that made you a cool kid: 1) being able to do an 'olly' on a skateboard; 2) having the ability to complete Chase HQ on the Sinclair Spectrum 48K computer; and 3) owning a twin-cassette black ghetto blaster with graphic equalisers. I've never been the sporty type so the skateboard was out and the thought of waiting until I was 17 for the Spectrum to load its bloody game from the tape was never an option. So when

I opened my first present and it was option 3 – a big, black ghetto blaster – I was over the moon!!! We immediately stuck *Don't Be Cruel* by Bobby Brown in tape deck A (it had twin cassettes of course) and the party kicked off … *ghetto blaster … cakes … sweets … fizzy drinks … hit sister … sweets … pass the parcel … more sweets … Rocky IV on video … another fight with my sister … more cake …*

We only stopped twice – once to catch our breath and once to open my VHS-shaped presents from Uncle Michael and Auntie Francis. They were: *Indiana Jones and the Temple of Doom* (8/10), *Teenwolf* (7.5/10) and *The Boy Who Could Fly* (2/10). Pure heaven and on it went … *ghetto blaster … cakes … sweets … fizzy drinks … hit sister … sweets … pass the parcel … more sweets … Rocky IV … another fight with my sis … more cake …*

Then, after what seemed like only 20 minutes, it was time for my friends to go home, party bags in tow. After bidding farewell to Aiden, Paul, Jack, Andrew and the black kid in the A Team jumper whose name I can never remember, I was shattered, which is surprising seeing as I had just consumed 109 times my own body weight in such wonderful sugary snacks as French Fancies, Cola Bottles and Dib Dabs. However, as I sat quietly in the front room watching Harrison Ford bundle a small Chinese boy into the back of a silver Rolls-Royce Silver Shadow, I was feeling full and content. Just as the blonde one was about to eat a monkey's brain my mum dragged me away and into the back room.

As I walked through the door, I saw it. It was black and shiny in places, red and padded in others. It was sleek, sexy and sophisticated. My mum and dad had only gone and bought me … A FUCKING BMX!!!!!!!!

And I'll tell you this, dear reader, forgetting the time I fell off that bike and broke my nose because I was riding as fast as I could while listening to 'Like A Virgin' by Madonna on my Sony Walkman (yes, the one with orange foam on the headphones), I always said that if ever I was to write about the best day of my life it would be the day I saw that BMX for the first time. It was … So, thanks, Mum, Dad, Kate and the black kid in the A Team jumper whose name I can never remember. You're the best.

Manish Bhasin

TV Presenter

Presenting *Football Focus* alongside a certain Mr Blair … or Sven … or what about the two months I spent in Australia and the West Indies covering the cricket … or even the day I got married? They were all contenders. But I'm sure anyone would agree the following day was pretty special.

It was during the 2006 World Cup in Germany. The BBC put us up in a pretty lavish hotel in the centre of Berlin. It really was every football fan's dream. I was practically living with the likes of Peter Schmeichel, Alan Shearer, Gary Lineker, Alan Hansen and Martin O'Neill for a whole month!

A couple of days into our stay, there were rumours of a living legend staying at our hotel. I refused to believe them until I saw him for myself. I didn't have to wait too long. Early that afternoon, I was leaving my room to go to the gym as the gentleman in the room directly opposite was leaving his. I could only see his back as he walked up the corridor. I wonder if that's … nah, can't be, I thought. Then I remembered the rumours. Is it *really* him? Any more dithering, I thought, and he'd be in the lift … although his pace wasn't quite what it used to be … but then again it was 40 years since he last kicked a ball in anger.

'Pele?' I enquired hopefully.

The man turned around. There he was, the Brazilian icon.

He smiled. 'Yes.' After casting his eyes on me, he simply said, 'Aah, London Dorchester.'

I couldn't believe it. He remembered our meeting a few weeks ago when I interviewed him about his autobiography. Instead of the expected handshake, he gave me one of his famous Pele hugs. I was pretty staggered. Not only was the man living opposite me but he also greeted me like an old friend. We spoke for about 15 minutes before going our own ways.

A couple of hours later, my wife Anushka arrived from the UK to sample the atmosphere of the tournament and update me on our wedding plans (which, incidentally, was a week after the Final). Understandably, she was a little sceptical when I told her about my rather illustrious neighbour – until we met again in the corridor. After a brief chat, Pele obliged to have a photo taken with us. In fact, he was keen to have his son in the photo too. It made our day. But it was to get even better.

The rest of the afternoon I spent preparing and presenting a highlights programme from the nearby studios. Usually, the evenings would end with a group of presenters and pundits digesting the day's results with a drink or two in the hotel bar. When I walked in, there was a quiet buzz. Pele was sitting by himself as if waiting for someone. In one corner, among others, were Messrs Lineker and Shearer. As I arrived, the pair were debating whether or not to welcome the footballing great and to ask him to join them for a drink (thinking about it now, what a lethal strike force that would've been if the three of them were still playing). I left them to it and sat with some of the production team. After a few minutes, Pele got up. The whole room seemed to take note of his every move. He casually looked around and, after seeing me, he walked across, put his hand on my shoulder and departed with a 'Goodnight my friend', blissfully unaware of the two former England captains standing a few yards away.

Alan looked at me with raised eyebrows. 'Look at you … Mr Big Time, eh?' he joked.

I laughed it off, looking a little embarrassed. Inside, I was pretty chuffed.

Jeff Brazier

TV Presenter

When you first begin to consider the greatest day of your life, you are instinctively drawn towards the landmark occasions in your life that stand out in the memory. The birth of both my boys, Bobby and Freddy, nine months of wondering what sex they were and not even checking for a good minute after, due to the miracle of childbirth reducing my legs to jelly, what would be any parent's first thought. There are also career achievements certain to rank highly; we work most of our lives with different incentives, to climb proverbial ladders, get promoted, win the contract or take over the world so any steps towards our targets make great memories. Signing my first professional footballer contract with Leyton Orient, now that was a feeling I'll never forget; and getting released two years later, that's something I can't forget either!

My first presenting job on C4's *Dirty Laundry*, the auditioning, the agonising wait for any feedback and the pride I felt in watching my first show on a Saturday morning. The excitement when I received the phone call from my agent to tell me to pack my bags for Australia to present *I'm a Celebrity, Get Me Out of Here* with Kelly Osbourne, the joy at winning *The Farm* and being instantly met by my son Bobby after not seeing him for three weeks was like heaven, and getting to present on *The X Factor* grand final twice was monumental for me; being in front of 13 million viewers was a buzz I will never forget. I am very fortunate to have played at Newcastle United's stadium in front of 52,000 supporters against my boyhood footballing heroes with my family watching, what a mixture of emotions that was! (I don't like to mention the result!)

Come to think of it, I've done a lot of things that I can be very proud of but memories do not make up a day and that begs the question: how can you define one particular day in your life that stands out from the others? A favourite day typically would have to involve a mixture of fun, excitement, adventure and one outstanding moment to finish it all off but I think my favourite day contains so much more than that.

In March 2001, I had been selected from thousands of applicants to appear on the third series of the reality-TV show *Shipwrecked* filmed in Fiji over a three-month period; it's within this, the best experience of my life, that all my best days were spent. The audition was a tense and nervy weekend at an outward-bound centre with 100 other hopefuls and the tasks we were put through were designed to test our physical and mental strength of character and to predetermine who would go well with who and also more importantly who would wind everyone up! I don't think I was part of the latter but I certainly impressed Andi Peters with my party trick, so, after a 48-hour period of massive highs and lows, I was finally told I was going to the island and I have never felt excitement like that before. The prospect of going to Fiji and living on a paradise island for three months was huge – you couldn't pay for a holiday like that!

I threw a big party at a local bar in Romford and invited all my friends just before leaving for the island. I can remember floating round the room so excited talking about the months ahead with all my friends. I'd had an idea to do something that would help me through the lonely moments when I would be missing friends and family, so I took a Polaroid of my mates and got a big drawing pad to stick them in accompanied by a message of good luck from that individual; to this day, that is still my proudest possession.

Before leaving for the island, I did all the things I loved and knew I would miss; the strangest one I recall was eating tricolore, my favourite dish of avocados, sun-dried tomatoes and mozzarella! I remember meeting everyone at the airport full of anticipation; we arrived at our destination a few days later, a neighbouring island called Dravuni, inhabited by Dravunians, a simple living community untouched by Western influence and seemingly better off for it too. These people taught us a few hunting and camping techniques and the hardest thing to do was shimmying up a tree to fetch coconuts; you needed Dunlop rubber on your feet and shins, not to mention more muscles than I actually had at the time to get higher than halfway.

Our first few days were spent telling the pretty girls in our group to stop sunbathing; unfortunately, some were quicker than others to realise that we had to be self-sufficient, living solely off what grew on the island – in other words, we were in trouble! I hadn't even camped before, too much football and not enough scouts as a kid. I had a feeling before they even pushed us in the shark-infested waters to swim to shore that we were going to be as close to the true meaning of 'shipwrecked' as a production company could legally inflict upon us!

How does a favourite day come out of all of this uncertainty and hardship? Well, the first few weeks of grafting, team-bonding and constant hunger built the rest of the experience into more of a learning curve and enlightening adventure than any of us 'kids' could have imagined. The three meals a day of yam and coconut dulled our tastebuds so much in the first seven weeks that, when rice was made available, we mixed it with coconut milk and we thought we were living like kings. The first few weeks of sleeping on the beach in our sleeping bags getting walked all over by crabs made us into near-expert hut builders when the rain came, and the early arguments and petty squabbling caused by the shifting group dynamics and pressure of our self-dependency made us mature very quickly and appreciate the strength of our newfound friendships, seeing as we all relied on each other to get through the tough, lonely and hungry moments we were all experiencing.

In my opinion, for every challenge we face, there is a positive result at the end of it; for everything we lacked, we gained in other ways, and, for everything we take for granted at home and went without, we learned to appreciate at a level I never thought possible; that is why the best day of my life was spent on this island and this is how a typical day was spent on our island, Yakuve levu.

Many times I would instinctively wake up before sunset and spring to my feet excited about what I was about to witness; we all slept in a row of sleeping bags under the bright moonlight and a blanket of stars in the northern hemisphere. I had discovered something so priceless I kept it to myself at first; I would walk from the south beach through to the camp area then out to the other side of the island where the sea was always noticeably rougher and noisier. Some weeks earlier I had stumbled across a single coconut tree on the end of the long point that divided two beaches. I often enjoyed sitting beneath the tree taking a moment to take in the view and consider life on the island and the life that was waiting for me back home. On this occasion I tiptoed and zigzagged barefoot across the rock pools and climbed up to a grassy mound at the end of the point; then I sat sitting against my tree waiting for the most perfect thing I've ever seen. Every morning was different, sometimes, depending on the clouds, the sky would be a mixture of beautiful reds and oranges; if you looked left, you'd see a beach curving round into the rocky and mountainous east corner of the island and, right, you'd see a single coconut tree bowing down to the water again crashing into another beach, one of six we had to choose from. This understandably became a daily ritual, as I knew I wasn't going to be seeing this out of my bedroom window at home very often!

That was a special start to the day; the next task was not considered so special at the time but looking back I'd say otherwise. On leaving the point, I would join the rest of the group in a very good mood. In the camp area, jobs would be delegated for breakfast duties and on this particular occasion I was elected alongside a few others to go and dig up the yam for today's speciality … yam with yam on yam. We would take a washed-up dustbin pierced by a long branch with two people either end round to the plantation area and dig up as much yam as we thought we needed for the day. It sounds easy but we were using a shovel and we were on a steep hillside digging into tough terrain trying not to chop the yam in half, and, oh yeah, the earth was swarming with ants and, as I never wore any shoes, they weren't very pleasant on the feet. However, there was a lot of banter and satisfaction when returning to the group feeling like the provider and I could then sit and watch the wood collectors make their fire and the cooks slaving away, endeavouring to make the perfect yam dish. It didn't taste very nice but, when the rice came a few weeks later, we had the most memorable mealtimes I'll ever experience – talk about being grateful for what you've got.

After breakfast, a few of us went to check the net we had received from the Dravunians as a gift; we stretched it in a channel between two islands the day before and we were optimistic we would have caught some impressive fish to have for lunch. I was one of three that swam out to investigate, and this was a nervy moment because we knew sharks swam in those waters – not massive ones but in my book a shark's a shark! We had snorkel sets too and when we got close we dived; as I held a net bag open, one of the Aussie lads, Geordie, a farmer from Brisbane, stuffed the barracuda inside. We got halfway along and realised there was a 2ft shark stuck in the net, so we rose to the surface to quickly talk tactics and decided we would have to kill it because it was distressed and injured from being tangled up overnight. We went to shore, got our cooking knives and headed back feeling a bit like cavemen! When we got back, it had already died, so thankfully no gruesome hunting methods were required and it was at this point that I could actually understand where the insanity in the *Lord Of The Flies* book originated from. We cut the shark out of the net and guided it back to land; by now, the rest of the group were eagerly awaiting our catch and gave a massive cheer when we revealed what we'd be cooking. It turned out that the ammonia in the shark's skin tasted a bit like urine and, although shark was good meat, it just wasn't a good taste, and we agreed next time we got a shark in the net we would let it go.

We had built a boat previously and I had the honour of naming it after my brother Spencer; because of his disability, the group were very kind, and so this day the HMS *Spencer* set sail for a neighbouring island to see if there was anything we could take back in the way of food. I was on the boat with five others and we were all paddling with coconut-tree branches; it took a fair while to get there against the wind but we weren't disappointed with what we found, as the production company had left us a jar of sweets, a pineapple (half-eaten by a crab) and two goats! Getting them on the boat and back to our island was one of the funniest things I've ever seen; the noises these poor animals were making went right through you and, if it wasn't for our crazy Sicilian Salvo, a stripper from London, and his rope skills, we would have left them there. The best thing about this adventurous part of the day was that, for the first time since landing on the island five weeks earlier, we were actually away from there; it felt as though we had been freed and we cracked open a few nuts to celebrate being outside of the bubble.

For me, the group was a mixture of very different characters, some you got on with better than others; when you're at home, you can avoid people, turn the phone off, close the curtains, but, here, you were in the same company for most of the day so it was a pressure-cooker situation on many an occasion.

We enjoyed a peaceful look at our familiar surrounding islands from this different and welcome angle before returning to the group rejuvenated and again popular because of our plus-two on the boat.

There wasn't time for much before the sun went down but I took a walk with my good friend CJ, a schoolteacher from Manchester and told her all about my trip; we often collected shells to make bracelets as the production people had kindly given us some string to thread them all together. It was a beautiful thing to do as the sun went down, chatting to a friend, enjoying our time on the island and talking about how much our trip would change us as people and influence what we did when we got home; we also discussed quite regularly what chocolate bar we would eat first on our return!

When the darkness crept in and the crew went back to their comfortable beds on the neighbouring island, we would be left to create our own entertainment. Fortunately for us, there were lots of characters around to make things interesting and Geordie had brought his guitar as his special item, which, due to its popularity, proved also to be the group's special item. We would sit round a fire on the beach talking about our lives, what we wanted and what we had, telling stories and singing songs; luckily Geordie had quite a few in his repertoire and we sang our hearts out under the stars on many a night.

This evening was particularly special because Randy, an actor in the making from LA, brought a bottle of Southern Comfort and it didn't take the whole bottle to have an impact on all of us; with nothing in us except the odd helping of yam, we were all easily guilty of being the biggest lightweights on earth! It was amazing how 16 teenagers could be alone on a big island in the middle of the Pacific and still feel so safe and content, despite the distance from home and the emptiness in our stomachs.

My evening ended with my favourite people, lying next to each other looking up at the stars in a neat line of sleeping bags with only faces visible; we would take it in turns to remember a song, and everything was somehow nostalgic and each song remembered was like something on a jukebox from years before. We were without money, machinery, gadgets and phones! But were these things missed? It was like I forgot they ever existed.

We are unbelievably versatile as human beings and we can adapt to whatever situation we find ourselves in. With this in mind, this particular day always reminds me of the huge lesson I learned six years ago on my own little paradise; it's not the success or materialistic things in life that define us, it's what's inside our hearts and our heads that makes us special.

Amy Brookbanks

Showbiz Reporter

Being a showbiz journalist is perhaps the greatest job in the world. I often think about what would have happened if I hadn't fancied my chances on this circuit. There's nothing else I could do, or even want to drag myself out of bed to do. It's a constant stream of free bars, copious amounts of champagne and those delicious, cute little canapés. So trying to narrow my career so far down to just one amazing moment has been extremely difficult. I could mention the day I was interviewing five hunky, naked male celebrities in bed, rubbing shoulders with my childhood sweetheart Mark Owen or the hilarious day I had trying to recreate the iconic *W Magazine* photoshoot of Posh and Becks with Jade Goody and her boyfriend Jack Tweed – thinking about the best day of my life was extremely difficult.

I have had some fantastic, unbelievable moments in my career so far, some of the best days I will take to my grave with me, as any good journalist should do.

I've met heroes, Hollywood icons, numerous members of the naughty Brit Pack bunch and rubbed shoulders with my childhood sweetheart Mark Owen (did I mention that already?).

But none of that beats the moment I discovered I was being posted to Cannes, in France, to cover the prestigious, world-famous 60th Cannes Film Festival.

Cannes is a list of a who's who from the movie world, people with big money, loads of cigars and caviar. I never dreamed I'd be there, but, despite the glamour, glitz and chaos, I couldn't help but wonder if there might just be a KFC or McDonald's …

I was being sent to capture exclusive stories on stars like U2, Pamela Anderson, Jude Law, Brad Pitt, Leonardo DiCaprio and just about anyone else I could get my hands on.

I was a Cannes virgin and totally bewildered by the hundreds of exclusive events promising world-famous talent, huge intimidating bodyguards ensuring no-invite-no-entry and paparazzi-coated red carpets. I was starting to think it would be me, not the celebs, having tears and tantrums – this was going to be hard work. You should know, by the way, that journalists aren't invited to these events, we gatecrash.

Between you and me, journalists use all sorts of tricks to get into these parties – one girl I know carries a champagne glass everywhere, whips it out of her handbag and walks to the door pretending she had been outside smoking a cigarette.

Another lingers behind a tall, hunky man with an invite and manages to squeeze under the net. Me, I just make sure I look like I belong. That works in London though; surely Cannes would be more tricky?

As soon as I arrived, I started working. I knew Paris Hilton, Jude Law and George Clooney were around somewhere and I couldn't wait to find them!

I began by walking down The Coisette, the strip by the sea lined with the top hotels and countless beach parties, which is always packed with celebrity spotters. It was like shopping on Oxford Street at Christmas. But I was unprepared for what was set to become the most awesome time of my life. I was there to report, but just kept wondering, Do some people in the world really live like this?

It was the first night, and there were two huge premieres in town.

It took me two hours to apply my immaculate 'look like a celebrity' make-up and squeeze into my glitzy gown. The hottest tickets were the Vanity Fair party at the glamorous Hotel du Cap and the Soho House party at Château de la Napoule. I used my trusty London methods of sneaking into parties and it worked – rule Britannia! It wasn't long before I was drinking with Leonardo DiCaprio, Jessica Simpson, Pamela Anderson and Gerard Butler and I managed to make small-talk with Jude Law.

My favourite night was the Soho House party; Prince William was on the guest list and everyone was talking about it. It was so exclusive the press were banned and there were no cameras allowed. I was nervous yet so excited about sneaking in. It was a bit different from my local nightclub, I've never seen anything like it in my life – it was held at Napoleon's castle!

Organisers had imported £15,000 worth of furniture from the UK. It was hard to see who was there as the rich and famous congregated by the sea front by candlelight, but that didn't stop me searching for Wills. Unfortunately, he cancelled at the last minute. Perhaps he wasn't a fan of the menu. There was £16,000 of lobster eaten in four hours. I'd never eaten lobster (I was a huge fan of Sebastian in *The Little Mermaid*), but that was standard for Cannes: lobster washed down with champagne.

Even Jamie Theakston couldn't believe how plush the party was. He told me, 'I'm here for a holiday, and left my colleague Harriet to do the radio show by herself. She'll kill me especially when she hears how much lobster there is!'

I couldn't believe my eyes when US singer Jessica Simpson arrived with an entourage of 11 at a party hosted by Nike on the beach. She turned up with her friends and her mum and dad. I'd never go partying with mine, but Jessica was having a ball sipping the champagne and cocktails.

Five minutes later, Jude Law walked in with a much more

manageable entourage of just three. He sat on a table next to Jessica's. I resisted the urge to run up to him and tell him how much I loved him. But then I couldn't contain myself any longer. I rushed over and Jude was more than happy to chat. He kissed me on the cheek (I haven't washed it since!) and told me how much he loved being at Cannes. He said it was the best year ever. I pulled out my camera as Jude wrapped his arms around me for a picture.

I spent my days hanging out at posh London members club Century. I heard this was where all the celebrities had lunch. They were right. I sat down next to Gerard Butler, star of the hit movies *P.S. I Love You* and *300*. He was unshaven but still looked gorgeous. He was on his way back to his yacht to freshen up, but he wasn't partying like the other celebrities. 'I'm off the booze,' he told me. 'I'm here to work this year; I've got to read this new movie script before my meeting with Jim Sheridan [director of *Get Rich or Die Tryin'*] later. But I'm going to read it on the beach so I can ogle all the girls!'

I thought, Go, Gerard!

Baywatch star Pamela Anderson was whisked past me at exclusive club VIP. It was an amazing place and security was tight. Two doormen stopped me in my tracks as I tried to sneak past. I smiled sweetly, and asked again. He let me in!

Pamela still looked amazing for her age, but I only recognised her because of her tattoos. She wasn't keen to talk, she just wanted to dance, but I didn't mind because so did I.

My luck couldn't have got any better when I headed on to a yacht for the day to sunbathe and relax after chasing after the celebrities. If anything, it was an incredible opportunity to see how the rich and famous really live it up in Cannes. The richest actors stay in the yachts and they're notorious for showing off to each other at the festival. The bigger your yacht, the more important you are.

I was expecting a rowing boat or something but, as we entered the harbour, I didn't even think P. Diddy could afford to have one as big as this. It was £1.2 million. Even the fuel cost £300 an hour. Unsure of the etiquette, I asked him to drive slowly. I had a snoop around the yacht, and it even had bedrooms with en-suite bathrooms. The owner then treated me to lunch on a secluded resort, only reachable by speedboat. It was fascinating to hear all of his private tales of celebrity guests. I giggled to myself how I'd travelled on more vessels than Popeye.

I'm not sure whether it was the sun, champagne or the golden hot sand, but something brought the celebrities flocking to me with no pestering required. The rest of the trip was spent lounging on yachts, feasting on lobster and shopping in overpriced boutiques. All in the name of work of course. Mind you, I couldn't wait to kick off those stilettos, soak my bunions and rip off my false eyelashes for good. Being a celebrity is too much like hard work to me.

John Broome, CBE

Businessman

I've been lucky enough to have had many hundreds of best days of my life, from building up Alton Towers to building a beautiful home and family. The whole period of my life from the start of the theme-park businesses up to now has given me immense pleasure. In particular, the theme parks allowed me to strike a chord with people everywhere, to see smiles on people's faces, which has been an absolute privilege. Through the theme-park business, I've met many famous families, including the royal family with *It's A Royal Knockout*; I've met presidents, prime ministers and Hollywood stars. I am, however, a family man and as such I try not to mix my business with them and therefore keep them out of the limelight. I remember on this one occasion, however, some of the limelight filtered on to them.

It was quite common to use well-known pop stars to open up the rides and cut the ribbon and on one occasion we booked Kylie Minogue to open a ride: the Little Mouse at Alton Towers. She flew in by my helicopter to be greeted by thousands of fans as she was immediately recognised. There was a media presence of at least 200 who were given the customary two-hour notice of her arrival. We had to keep going round and round on the ride, in total I think about 20 times, to get the right photographs for everyone. She even mentioned it in her book as she hurt her back because we were both subject to continuous G-forces as we went round and round for the pictures. I thought Kylie and I might fall out after that and that all my brownie points had gone. However, I'd shown her around and given her the VIP treatment, and we were fine and went into a private room in a restaurant for a snack. We got chatting and I said, 'Come on, Kylie, I'll get our helicopter pilot to fly you back to London.' She agreed and we were off. Unbeknown to her, we were off in the opposite direction away from London because I'd said I just needed to pop into my house to get something. I said it was only 10 minutes away but it was really 70 miles. Although it was in completely the opposite direction from where she thought and she'd been told by her agent and entourage not to do it, I'd convinced her to get on to the helicopter and do the extra detour with me. She had a glint in her eye so I thought I would get away with what I had planned. We agreed that, when we arrived at my home, she'd have some tea and then be on her way. So we landed in the garden and I believe it was something like half-five in the afternoon. I left Kylie with my wife in the kitchen and I walked into the TV room. I opened the door and my three children, William, Anna and Georgina, were watching *Neighbours* at that time. On the television screen was Kylie Minogue, a big star on TV and in the music business to all generations. Jokingly, I said, 'See her on the screen, that Kylie Minogue, well, she's in the kitchen!'

Will, my son, said, 'Come on, Dad, stop messing about, *Neighbours* has started, don't disturb us.'

So I went back to the kitchen and asked Kylie to meet my kids just to say hello. I brought her to the TV room and complete silence fell as they looked at her. They looked at the TV set and then they looked again and I think one of my daughters actually fainted. They clearly thought this was some kind of miracle. They didn't even know that Kylie Minogue was opening the ride. After a pause of about a minute, the three of them crowded around her and she could tell that she

35

wasn't expected and this produced something of a highlight for her as well as for me, and she certainly enjoyed this impromptu occasion. All this time she was on television with *Neighbours* playing in the background which just added to the atmosphere.

To be able to bring a world-class celebrity not only to add to the theme park's profile but also on this one occasion to share it with my family in such an innocent and uncontrived manner did represent one of the best days if not the best day of my life!

Michael Butcher

Journalist

7 a.m., 29 July 2006

'We're goin' to the chapel and we're gonna get ma-a-a-rried' belts out
Bette Midler FULL BLAST from the CD player. Thanks, husband-to-
be Phil. I met Phil 18 years ago on a street corner in Islington. I was
on my way out to a club and he was on his way home after work. It
could so easily have been ships that pass in the night, but instead it was
love at first sight and we've been together ever since.

As I try to force my eyes open, I realise that staying out until 1 a.m.
the night before my civil-partnership ceremony wasn't such a bright
idea. Mind you, the very faint hint of a hangover is a small price to
pay for the memories that come flooding back. Did I really get a
cuddle down a dark alley from Hollywood star Juliette Lewis as we
posed for a picture taken by my friend and partner in crime Gary
Irwin? Yep.

'Gee, that's so cool that two guys can get married over here,' Juliette
gushed enthusiastically in response to Gary randomly ambushing her
outside a theatre with: 'Oi, Juliette, this is my mate Dolly [Gary thinks
I'm a bit like Dolly Parton]. He's getting married to his boyfriend in
the morning.'

Actually, that's the only concrete memory that comes flooding back. The rest is a bit of a blur, but included me and Gary crowing, 'I'm/He's getting married in the morning, ding dong the bells are gonna chime, etc. etc. etc.' on a bar crawl around our favourite Soho haunts. 'Just one quick drink' after work always ends up in the same places. There is also a vague recollection of me and Gary doing our show-stopping 'catch dance' to great critical acclaim in our favourite club, The Shadow Lounge. Think the final 'no one puts Baby in the corner' routine from *Dirty Dancing*. Then substitute me and Gary (you need to visualise two lightweight, nimble and highly lovable sumo wrestlers) for Patrick Swayze and Baby and cut out the difficult manoeuvres. You've got to see it to believe it.

I finally drag myself out of bed, get ready and then get really nervous. But why am I so nervous? After all, all I have to do is say my vows in front of 'bridesmaid' Vicky, her boyfriend Sean and our other witnesses, Chris and Graham, also known as the African Queens (they're from Zimbabwe originally). And, of course, civil partner-to-be, Phil. I've known Vicky since we worked together in what could have been difficult circumstances at *Now* magazine, but which has turned out to be an enduring and close friendship. Vicky is five feet tall and very loud. Except for when she goes silent and gives an absolutely terrifying, frosty glare known as 'The Lewisham Look'. I trust her with my life and we're a great double act. I am so proud even now to introduce Vicky as 'my bridesmaid' and it makes me laugh when I think of the overtones such an introduction carries of Dame Edna and her bridesmaid Madge.

And surely the thought of saying my piece in front of Chris and Graham, who've been friends for over 15 years, isn't causing my apprehension?

No, the reason I'm nervous, aside from the inherent fear I have of officialdom and legal procedures, is because of a certain Andrew Saxton's threat of turning up to demonstrate outside the ceremony with a huge 'NO GAYS' placard. I have to say at this point that

Andrew is one of my heroes and best friends. He's a talented journalist who for many years has fought the long, hard battle for equality. In case you for just one second think he sounds a bit dull and worthy, the best way to describe him is as a one-man whirlwind. There's always a commotion around him – and somehow riotous things just seem to happen in his presence. You couldn't hope to sing karaoke or go on a demo with a finer fella at your side.

He's also one of those people who are slightly dangerously unpredictable – a bit like a nutter on a train. So, despite his being one of the most right-on people on this planet, there is a minuscule chance of him turning up with the aforementioned placard as his excuse for a joke. He knows it would make me shriek with laughter and cringe with embarrassment in equal measure.

After a champagne breakfast at the Covent Garden Hotel with our small party, it's off to Camden registry office, feeling much calmer after the alcohol! The service is short, but full of emotion – the significance of two men legally tying the knot isn't lost on any of us. Nor is the double entendre/gaffe by the registrar in talking about 'taking each other's rings'.

Ceremony over, certificate issued, legally joined in partnership for ever, it just remains to be seen if the one-man whirlwind is waiting outside. Dread, panic and fear start to raise my heart rate.

But a cursory look outside the building reveals there is no Andrew – and no bloody placard. Phew! But, instead, there are another couple of friends – Annie and Stephen, who've turned up guerrilla-ambush style armed with champagne as a surprise. Andrew with his menacing placard, or Annie and Stephen with champagne? There's no contest for who is the more welcome. Panic finally over.

So, following the traditional photos on the steps and fortified by more alcohol, it's off to the bar at the Dorchester for yet more drinks before lunch. By the time we're ready for lunch at J. Sheekey, our merry band is very merry. The whole afternoon passes in a very leisurely and relaxed way, until the time comes to make a move back to our place. For more champagne and more chat. I'm sure weddings aren't supposed to be quite so relaxed and stress-free. The only stressful moment – the threat of Andrew and his placard aside – is when a narky neighbour moans on about something or other. If Sean ever needed a badge of honour, he earns it by getting in the lift with a potentially explosive combination of the moaning neighbour and a very irate Phil!

The day is so perfect that we feel a bit guilty for not having had all of our friends and family there to celebrate with us. Fast forward to the 'reception' on 2 December 2006.

But that's another story …

Jo Carnegie

Deputy Editor of *Heat*

I've had many great days in my life, but one that sticks out as truly magical was the time when I was eight years old. It was the middle of the school holidays and we were having an Indian summer. Bored of playing on scorching-hot tarmac and the brittle, faded lawns in our close, I asked my mum if I could venture further into the cornfields. The place were the Big Kids played. Every morning I would see them go off like excited explorers, armed with packed lunches and various camp-building paraphernalia, and not return until dusk. I was intensely jealous and used to spend hours sitting on the kerb in front of our house wondering what adventures they were having in those huge, swaying swathes of yellow that encircled our village.

To my surprise, Mum agreed and I set off with my friend Hayley who lived next door. We felt so grown up! Despite promising to stay near the edge of the fields, we soon got lost in the four-foot-high corn as we wandered through, occasionally chasing each other. Eventually, we found 'our' spot and it was better than we ever imagined. We made tunnels and camps and built houses complete with kitchens, gardens and bedrooms. Once we'd finished one area, we'd move on. Occasionally shouts and voices would carry across from other kids playing out there but, for most of the day, it felt like we were the only ones in our little world. It was wonderful.

I remember as the light was failing we came across an abandoned shed where a local tramp was rumoured to live. I think his name was 'One-eyed Bill' or something. We saw a bundle of black rags in the corner and Hayley made me go in to check them. I remember the abject terror and exhilaration when the rags stirred and something horrible ran out towards us and out the door. Looking back, the pheasant was more scared than us, but at the time we thought it was the ghost of One-eyed Bill – or worse – and ran back through the fields, screaming our heads off. We eventually reached the edge again and decided it was time to go home for dinner.

Compared to many people's definition of the best day of their life, it must seem mundane and ordinary, but, to me, that is what's so special. It signified a time of innocence, the simple, happy pursuit of childhood pleasures before life started to be about paying bills and meeting deadlines. I am 32 now and, whenever I am squashed under someone's armpit on the tube home from work, I think about that halcyon day. It puts a smile on my face.

Alan Carr

Comedian

I definitely know what the best day of my life is. Apart from the day I was born, obviously. Can you imagine if I hadn't been born? It wouldn't just be me who would have lost out, it would be you! Yes, you! No, the best day of my life would have to be when I appeared on *The Royal Variety Performance*. I couldn't believe it when I got the invitation; I was so excited I kept re-reading it to check that it was Alan Carr and not Jimmy Carr they wanted.

Then I checked that it was Her Majesty Elizabeth II attending and not someone shit like Princess Michael of Kent or that bloody Edward. If I'm performing, I want the real deal. I want A-list royalty; I want ermine, I want a crown, I want orbs. I mean, Dame Shirley Bassey was headlining so Liz had a lot to live up to when it came to making an entrance.

The venue wasn't the Palladium, which was probably the only disappointment, as it was at Cardiff at the Millennium Centre, where I would be performing alongside Sir Cliff Richard, Dame Shirley Bassey, Charlotte Church and Will Young. So not camp at all then really! The only way it could have been gayer would have been if Dale Winton, Lulu and Christopher Biggins joined the Village People for 'YMCA' as the finale – but, thinking about it, wasn't that the year before?

Of course I was nervous. This was before I had done any television. I was just a baby and at the sound check I realised I was the only one who hadn't had extensive reconstructive plastic surgery. I was 28 and I looked the oldest there. Also, *The Royal Variety Performance* was renowned for being a tough crowd. Hen parties and stag dos I can deal with, but the thought of a whole room of snooty Welsh people and the reigning monarch slow-handclapping terrified me. At least if Sir Cliff Richard dies on his arse he can wheel out 'Devil Woman'.

There wasn't much camaraderie that night – all the big stars stayed in their rooms – but Charlotte Church was lovely to me as she always is. I passed Cliff on the stairs and said, 'Good luck!'

He replied sharply, 'I've already been on,' which was a bit embarrassing, but to be fair I'd had the runs and had locked myself in a toilet and missed him. I can't be everywhere.

There were rumours Dame Shirley had demanded extra sequins for her dress and they had sent it back to India to have more sewn on and it was then in the process of being flown back first-class to Heathrow just in time for the show. Oh, the drama! Can you imagine getting them to fly a dress from another continent just for you? I wouldn't have minded so much but they looked pissed off when I asked them to get me a cheese baguette and a can of Tango and the canteen was only downstairs.

In the dressing rooms, everyone receives a goody bag full of posh presents, aftershaves, scented candles and sweeties. I was sharing a dressing room with the band McFly and we all opened our goody bags together. They are lovely lads, but I had to laugh when their manager told them off for eating too many of the 'luxury jelly beans' because the 'e-numbers' would make them get all excitable. Who says rock 'n' roll is dead?

Before long, it was showtime and it was a huge success. All my worries were for nothing. I never fluffed my lines, I never fell off the stage and more importantly I never mentioned Diana. The night before, I'd had the worst anxiety dream where I'd ended my set that night with the words: 'You've been lovely, I've been Diana the Princess of Wales.' The Queen would have loved that, wouldn't she?

Speaking of the Queen, I finally met her at the end and, although I'm not the biggest royalist, there is something about her. I bowed when she shook my hand and I said, 'Hello, Ma'am.' Well, that's what Will Young had done and he's posh so I followed suit.

Then she said, 'You were very entertaining!'

Oh my God, can I have that on my posters for my next tour? By Royal Approval, I am entertaining. Somebody pinch me!

Then I heard her say it to Il Divo, then to McFly, then to Charlotte Church, then to Ozzy Osbourne, then to these two acrobatic dwarves from Croatia whose act was to spin half-naked on what looked like a silver wheelie bin. Christ, if she thinks they're entertaining, she needs her head testing!

When she started saying it to the woman who sold the ice creams, I realised I'd been duped. She says it to everyone. It's a line she dishes out to every Tom, Dick and Harry. Damn it! Anyway, for that tiny moment I felt very special indeed; I felt proud and warm inside and I wasn't going to let Her Majesty's cheeky white lies spoil the best day of my life.

45

Lucie Cave

Features Editor, *Heat*

How can I possibly pick one day? The answer is: I can't. So I've whittled it down to two. The first is more serious (and, if I'm honest, a bit on the worthy side) and the second involves me and a famous midget …

The best day of my life (part 1)
Euston Train Station. Destination: An adventure/activity hostel in the Lake District. I'm wearing a pair of ridiculous orange baggy trousers. Well, they were cool at the time (they were Maharishi, it was 2001 and I'd seen Jennifer Aniston wearing some a few weeks before). I've recently started working as a writer for *Heat* magazine, having just finished a five-year stint as a presenter on youth channel Trouble TV. Directly opposite me, waiting for the same train, there's a group of about 18 teenagers all huddled together underneath a sign for Burger King. I'm standing with an equal-sized group of adults, and we're being eyed suspiciously. We're a motley crew of all ages – Anne is a 48-year-old teacher, there's Sarah, a 35-year-old photographer, John, a 36-year-old Irish lawyer who speaks fluent French, Jane, a 24-year-old nurse, Richard, a librarian from Scotland … etc. etc. Then there's Tony, a friendly 6ft Rastafarian – the mastermind behind the trip.

For the adults, this day is the culmination of months of training.

We've been meeting once, sometimes twice a week in a Camden youth centre, having volunteered ourselves as mentors for young underprivileged people in the area. There were no promises, we were told. Although there was little doubt these youngsters needed guidance in their lives, this was a voluntary thing for them too. And it was up to them whether they wanted to spend their time in this way, meeting with their assigned mentor, once a week for a whole year – that was going to be some commitment. But, if it worked, these kids would benefit from the company and opinions of someone they wouldn't normally come across in their social environment.

'It's not going to be easy,' Tony advised. Some of these kids were drug dealers, some had been raped, some dysfunctional, others simply in dire need of social skills. But, as mentors, we would never necessarily know what or why they were here. We would only have that information if they wanted us to. And there were rules. Once paired with a teenager, we were told we must meet on neutral territory – never invite them to our house or tell them where we live. 'They will test you,' Tony warned. 'They'll try to catch you out – and ask you things about your lives which they might use against you.'

Once paired up, we were expected to meet once a week. But Tony advised us the chances of them turning up would be rare. They'd be doing their damnedest to work out whether or not they could rely on us.

And that's what this weekend was about: trust building. Forcing the teenagers and adults out of their comfort zones – making us spend time together, sizing each other up and crossing the difficult age (and class) divide.

En route to the Lakes, it's adults in one train carriage, teenagers whispering, swearing and causing havoc in another. The idea that anyone from either group will ever have anything to say to each other seems unfathomable. A few of the youngsters recognise me from the TV and cheekily sidle over.

47

'Can you be my mentor?'

'Will you get me on TV?'

'Could those trousers be any more orange, Miss?'

I find out later from Tony that, rather than this being seen as a reason for me to be paired with one of these kids, it will go against me. The idea of a mentor relationship is one that's neutral, not premeditated.

What follows are two days of confidence-building exercises between the scary-looking teens and their apprehensive potential mentors. Every hour we're split into pairs, and these rotate to ensure that everyone gets a chance to bond. From guiding each other around a hilly verge wearing blindfolds to wading together through treacherous waterfalls, admitting our insecurities in discussion groups and overcoming debilitating fears of heights on high rope ladders, we're thrown in at the deep end in what is to become a weekend I will remember for the rest of my life.

Evenings are spent tentatively chatting, trying to coax the anti-social squirt in the corner to play team games and attempting to mix with people we've never mixed with before. Slowly but surely, the divide lessens (having to sleep in the same dormitories helps – once they've seen you in the morning with hair that looks like Swampy, there ain't much more to hide!). The kids are a mixture of overconfident scallys and shy, nervous underachievers. Some venture to the adults with inquisitive ease, but most start off thinking they're way too cool. One boy, James, fits neither camp. His acute lack of social skills results in his being left out in the cold by his peers as well as removing himself from all contact with the adults. I learn that he's in foster care – his mum, who he refers to many times, is an alcoholic; there's a deep scar across his face and he has a severe nervous twitch. James spends his first day trying hard to appear nonchalant, while barely masking his desperation to be liked. The last person he would be seen dead with is 48-year-old Anne – after all, she's the oldest, most unfashionable and squarest of the adults. Whenever she approaches and tries to introduce herself, he bristles and walks away muttering, 'Fuck off.'

As the weekend draws to a close, we're all told to find a place on the grounds of the hostel and write a letter back to ourselves which will be posted to our home addresses in a month's time. We must document what we've learned as individuals and about the time we've spent together. We've hardly spent 48 hours in one another's company – but so much has changed, so many barriers broken. And as I sit on my bed, looking outside the window, soppy as it seems, I actually choke back a tear at how much this weekend has affected me.

The image I see captures it all.

Seventeen-year-old James is lying on the grass, poring over his letter – laughing. Beside him, offering tips and suggestions with a calm smile on her face, sits 48-year-old Anne.

A few hours ago, James would rather have cut off his right bollock than do that.

The return journey is in complete contrast to the one getting there. Kids are clambering to sit with the adults, demanding to chat to them, poking and shrieking with laughter. When we part company, knowing that we'll meet again as mentors and mentees (Tony will assess who should be paired with who based on his observations from that weekend), it's like – as *EastEnders*' Peggy Mitchell would say – 'We're faaaamily'. All the more poignant when we remember some of these kids don't have proper families to go home to.

A few weeks later, I was paired with a young, shy girl called Leonie. I was surprised as I felt I hadn't spent as much time with her as I had with some of the others. Tony sagely told me that this was the very reason. Leonie was the only one who hadn't been impressed by my job.

As for James? He was paired with Anne. And, despite Tony's reservations, turned up – on time – for their meetings every day for a year.

Five years on, they're still in contact.

The best day of my life (part 2)

OK, so enough of the righteous. As features editor on *Heat* mag, I have to admit there are several contenders for the best day of my life, such as getting to spend the day as the Hoff's PA (must've done something right – he sent me flowers!), and being an extra in Ant and Dec's film *Alien Autopsy* (no, I wasn't an alien). But without doubt one of the funniest days of my life occurred pre-*Heat*, in the days when I was a kids presenter on Trouble TV. I had just interviewed an actress called Sheridan Smith who was in *Two Pints of Lager and a Packet of Crisps* at the time. We were in my hotel in London – and, although we both had commitments that evening (and cabs arriving in half-an-hour), we'd really hit it off so decided to go and neck a quick drink together afterwards.

As we entered the bar, we noticed a small bald man perched on a stool sitting opposite another equally stunted man (who looked spookily like a mini Lionel Richie). We recognised the first fella as Mini Me from *Austin Powers* (aka the actor Verne Troyer) and scuttled past him trying not to giggle. Pretending we couldn't decide where to sit meant we could scour the room, clocking several glimpses of him without the poor guy feeling like some strange species in a zoo. Eventually we landed at a nearby table (I won't go into the exact nature of our conversation but it had something to do with midgets and bedroom activities).

After a few minutes, a barman came over. 'There are two gentlemen in the bar who'd like to buy you both a drink,' he smiled.

'Oh my God!' said Sheridan. 'Is it Mini Me?'

The barman replied that the men in question didn't want to disclose their identity, but they insisted on paying for whatever we wanted. So, naturally, we ordered.

By this time the bar was filling up and we couldn't see the two little chaps any more. Instead, every time we glanced across the room, we were met by two pairs of eyes belonging to a duo wearing kilts (what kind of place was this?!).

50

'I hope it's not from them,' Sheridan said.

As the barman returned with our drinks, we again asked him to reveal our benefactor, but he refused.

'OK, can we write them a note to say thank you?'

He nodded and handed us a pen and a piece of paper from his note pad.

'To whoever you are, thanks for the drinks, we chose "Sex on the Beach" … love Lucie and Sheridan.'

We craned our necks as we watched the barman walk away to deliver the note – but the room was so packed we didn't have a clue who was on the receiving end. Mini Me and his mate might have fallen into their drinks and drowned by now for all we knew.

Just as we were about to go our separate ways, I noticed something waving at me from the edge of our table. A piece of paper was slowly making its way round the periphery, as if being guided from the ceiling by an invisible thread.

It was our note.

And there was a person holding it from below …

Suddenly, a hand appeared on the stool next to me and a tiny-but-very-sturdy-body hoisted itself up. Sitting bolt upright, thrusting a hand into mine, the little man spoke: 'I bet you didn't know it was me, did you?'

Stunned silence.

'The name's Verne.'

'Er, hello,' we answered with suppressed smiles. 'What are you doing in London?'

'Verne' proceeded to tell us he was in the UK playing a goblin in a Harry Potter film – which nearly caused Sheridan to choke on a peanut – before cockily asking if we fancied joining him for a night on the tiles.

'No paparazzi though,' he warned, looking nervously over his shoulders.

We politely told him we had prior engagements.

He casually asked if we'd ever been to the Playboy mansion before. It turned out he was quite a regular there. So not the small shy retiring type after all. He began telling us about all the glamour models he knew, while we sat open-mouthed.

Time for a change of subject. 'Verne, tell us, what else have you starred in – besides *Austin Powers*?'

'Well,' he began, before leaning in conspiratorially, 'I was *actually* the stunt double in a film called *Baby's Day Out*.'

Oh. There's our taxi.

Aaaah. What could have been, eh?

Sarah Cawood

TV Presenter

Getting into the Royal Ballet School has to be up there as the best day of my life.

I had decided not to go when I was 11 because I would have had to board and I wanted to stay at home with my parents and friends. I decided emphatically that I would go when I was 16. Being awarded a place was apparently not going to be a problem, even though 30 places are contested each year by thousands of young hopefuls and I still think that my unquestioningly pure self-belief and determination played a huge part in getting me in there.

In my diary on 16 April 1989, I wrote: 'I GOT IN!!! No one is more surprised than me! So this is how it went: orthopaedic first, then an academic interview. Then ballet class. All the others were prodigies with legs by their ears and I just wanted to cry (but I didn't). Then a rep class, then a character class, then after weeding out a few, the remaining 15 had to do another pointe class – it was agony such as I've never known! But I survived. Then we were stretched (oh dear! My extension!). Then we had interviews. By this time I had gathered I'd probably got in …'

I don't actually remember that much of the process itself and I'm really thankful that I have kept a diary since I was 11 as I can remind myself of these incredible memories just by digging a box out from under my bed.

The reason that getting into the Royal Ballet School remains the best day of my life is that it was an incredible twist of fate that started a chain of events that lead directly to the place I am now. A place I love, surrounded by people I love. I honestly wouldn't change a thing. Good or bad.

I attended Royal for a year before being asked to leave because technically I wasn't quite up to the standard they wanted: never mind about how much passion I had when I danced, it's all about technique. My heart broke that day. They say that for every Yin there is a Yang; I agree: if getting into the darn place was my best day, then getting kicked out was by far the worst …

My wise daddy said to me when I was asked to leave, 'As one door closes, another one opens.' He was so right (he often is!). I left Royal and went to Arts Educational Schools in Chiswick, another dance school. There, we were fully encouraged to be passionate about our art; we obsessed about our physical ability less and danced truly from the heart much more. If getting into Royal was the happiest *day* of my life. Then my two years at Arts were my happiest *years*.

But back to before that. I'm looking through all the letters and poems my friends wrote me as I got ready to fly the nest for Royal and I'm actually a little choked up. I'd like to share some of them with you. This is a snippet of a poem written by my best friend Joe (still my best friend today!):

'You've now got the key
To open all those doors
Now you will see
The dreams you had before

    Stardom is nearing
    Fame is at your feet
    All the top professionals
    With those you must compete

    We'll miss you, don't ever doubt that
    And I'm sure you'll miss us too
    But you know that everything you want
    Is waiting there for you.'

We always were a ridiculously soppy and sentimental bunch ...
Still are!

Anyway, back to that fateful day.

I was 16. The only things that really mattered to a 16-year-old in
1989 were boys, drinking, smoking and hanging out on the meadows
with your friends. I mention this only because I'm going to refer back
to my diary for the rest of that day:

'Saturday night was wonderful – I can cope with all this
attention – it's like a drug: once you've tasted a little, you hunger
for more and more. First I went to the Scotgate – no one there.
Then I went to the Raj: Sal, Katie, Joe, Miranda, Bek Bisset and Nel
were there. I said "I got in" and they gave an almighty squeal! If I
could immortalise any moment of my life it would have to be that
one. Then we all left to go and meet the boys on the meadows: I
got a round of "for she's a jolly good fellow", it was wonderful ...

Anyway, life is looking up, except that I'm SHIT SCARED about
leaving. I suppose we all have to leave sometime, I just wish it could
stay this way forever ...'

From the mouths of babes, eh?

So, that was the best day of my life. It's been really lovely to
remember it and all its finer detail. I love that I took myself *so* very
seriously back then, everything was very dramatic and any event

could be soundtracked by a soft rock ballad (well, it *was* the 80s!). So, I will leave the last word to one final diary entry and the insightful lyrics of one Mr Jon Bon Jovi:

'OH PLEASE GOD LET EVERYTHING WORK OUT. I don't want to leave home anyway but I have to realise that I will never be famous if I carry on living at home, I've just got to "Stick To My Guns" ...'

'So you wanna be a cowboy
Well you know it's more than just a ride,
Cos you gotta know the real thing,
If you're gonna know the other side,
Ain't nobody riding shotgun,
In the world tonight,
And when you spit you better mean it,
You better make 'em all believe it,
If you're gonna be the one ...'

Chico

Singer

I've lived such an amazing and varied life it would be impossible to pinpoint what exactly is the best day of my life but I've had some incredible experiences that will always stay with me so I have picked this story.

I woke up at 4 a.m. and looked out of my shale into the beautiful Thailand sky. It was a magnificent night so I strolled outside and sat in a hammock gazing at the stars and as dawn approached I saw the most incredible sunrise. It was truly magnificent and was made that much more beautiful by the 11 orange-robed men walking past by the shore carrying big clay pots. I thought I was dreaming – I'd never seen this before mainly because normally I'm just coming in at that time from a crazy night out. But this was different so I thought I'd go and investigate. I approached them from the side and I tried to ask a question but no one answered me, so I asked the next and the next. But still I got no answer so I thought, If you can't beat them, join them. The only difference was I wasn't going to be quiet, so I took my place at the back and started to sing, 'Hey ho hey ho, tell me which way to go, 11 orange monks with their pots and curly cheeky Chico, hey ho.' It must have looked mad.

Anyway, we journeyed into the jungle, up a hill, down a hill,

57

through this secret passage and still no one turned around or batted an eyelid or even spoke to me. It felt so strange yet serene and then all of a sudden like a hidden treasure I saw this magnificent temple that just took my breath away. My head was going at 100 miles an hour when all of a sudden an old monk appeared in front of us. With his tattooed head he reminded me of a grandmaster out of a Bruce Lee movie, and I was a Bruce Lee nut when I was young so you can imagine how I felt. I was transfixed by him and as he was with me the other monks surrounded him. He looked at me, I looked at him, he looked at them, I looked at them and any Thai I'd learned had just vanished from my brain. I thought, OK, when in doubt smile, and boy did I smile. I must have looked like a Cheshire cat or more like a gurning monkey.

Then the monk pointed at me and said, 'Tarzaaaaaaaan, Tarzaaaaaaaaaaan.' Then they all joined in together: 'Tarzaaaaaaaan Laaaaaabooooooo,' which is the Thai name for Rambo.

So I beat my chest and let out the Tarzan howl! Everyone started laughing and they all started feeling my biceps and chest in admiration. They took me in and gave me some delicious food. I asked the chief monk all kinds of questions through a translator and there was so much love and compassion coming from him.

We did a little meditation, he blessed me and I was on my way. I really felt something strange and beautiful going inside me, as though there was an electric current going through my body that lifted me and made me feel like I could fly, something I also experienced with my spiritual master Mawlana Sheikh Nazim. I just felt free, I bowed to all of them and said, '*Cup coon macup*' (thank you) and left.

As I walked back to the beach the sun had risen into its full splendour. When I got to the sea I dived in and just contemplated life and humanity as a whole, people, cultures, creeds and faiths. One thing really remains in my mind from that day. What I learned was, when you take away the garb, the external stuff, the colour, the skin and so on, all that remains is what's inside and inside is the heart and inside the heart is love. Love is what I felt, love is what I received and after that love is what I promised to give and live by, the best religion of all.

Later on in my life when I'd experienced so many diverse cultures from temples to mosques, ashrams, churches and synagogues and spoken to many gurus and spiritual masters, the essence of all they spoke about was love. Now I know one thing for sure: I searched for God and there was no place I could see Him until I looked deep within and realised He lives within me and that's what that Buddhist monk was trying to tell me. God is truth and God is love, so, whoever is reading this, may love, health, joy and laughter follow you wherever you go and may you find God within too.

Peace,

Chico

Brendan Cole

Dancer

My dance partner Camilla Dallerup and I had been dancing for most of our lives. We teamed up as amateurs in 1996 and turned professional in January 2000. As a dancer you can define your success, firstly, on the results you get as a competitor (which we were doing OK with), but, more importantly, the invitations you receive to certain events around the world.

Not long after turning professional, while climbing steadily up through the ranks, our defining moment would come with an invitation to dance at a major event in Tokyo, Japan. We were young and in love and this trip could potentially make or break our career and ultimately our dance lives. This would be the chance to prove our worth and potentially set up our business for years to come. To put it into perspective, being invited to Japan as a ballroom dancer was not only a huge honour, but also a real sign of acceptance in the dance world. Big organisers in Japan only tended to invite the top-six ballroom and Latin couples to demonstrate at their events and Camilla and I were only just squeezing into the top-12 couples at the time. We had a lot to prove! Our fear didn't end there. On arriving at the hotel, we were told the event was actually the Prince Mikasa Awards. Along with the organiser, we were greeted by five of the top-six professional ballroom and Latin dance partnerships, here to demonstrate at the same event. Not only did we have to prove our worth to the organiser and in front of HRH Prince Mikasa, but we also had to do so standing alongside pairs that had already proved themselves time and time again in this kind of situation. This was our chance!

After waking up in our hotel room, a combination of anticipation, a spring morning in Tokyo and a sense of this potentially being a sign of things to come, I decided to go for a walk and take it all in. The setting was a picturesque Japanese rock garden, typical of what you might expect to see in an old film. A pond filled by a 10-foot flowing waterfall, morning sunlight beaming through shoots of bamboo and the red leaves of Japanese maple trees, winding paths through a garden groomed to perfection and tranquillity enough to make any anxiety simply disappear. The memory of that morning will always be burned in my mind as the emotions were so high and the setting was unlike anything I had ever seen. The excitement of the day to come was building with every moment that passed, just being there was such an achievement yet the outcome could mean the difference between huge success and a long struggle ahead.

Being able to stay focused on this day was extremely important. I am not someone that particularly suffers with nerves; however, with what was at stake, I found my nerves becoming increasingly present and my confidence disappearing. It's times like these that Camilla and I were at our best. Our strength lay in our passion for what we did, our fiery temperaments as well as our partnership and support for each other. Spending so much time together, we had an innate understanding between ourselves. We knew what each other needed at different times and felt like we could get through anything as long as we were there together. Well, we did just that and focused on the job ahead.

So time to get ready and head over to the magnificent ballroom for the first time. Walking in was one of the proudest moments I had ever felt. We were extremely excited if anxious, and we were greeted by our lovely hosts and the excited audience with such respect that we could be nothing but happy for being there. All couples were to do three dances each, one after the other over the scheduled hour, but the next petrifying news was really going to test us as professionals. We were to open the show with our Samba. Having danced all our lives, this should not have been a problem but that extra pressure was proving too much. My legs started physically shaking, as the evening opened and I stepped up to the floor as our names were announced.

The ballroom was the biggest I had ever danced in and the spotlights were extremely harsh and shining right into our eyes. It was hard to get our bearings within the room but we could just make out the audience anticipating our performance. The opening choreography was a series of reverse Samba rolls to get to our position before the music started. You could hear a pin drop as we commenced our dance and no doubt the knocking of my knees. Samba is a dance that requires a great deal of control of the legs and feet as you flex into your knees … and mine had none. Panic was setting in! However, as we hit our centre position and the music started, the crowd erupted and my nerves began to settle. The audience were fantastic and we were feeding off of their energy. As we finished our dance, one small problem was not knowing where we finished within the room due to the bright spotlights and trying but not being able to find an exit. So, I decided to walk us straight through a small gap in the front row which unfortunately was exactly that … a small gap in the front row. After our struggle to remove ourselves from the floor through the audience, our organiser greeted us, with a smile on his face and some extremely kind words: '*Domo arigato* [thank you very much], very, very good.'

The evening was a huge success and the beginning of a great friendship between him and us that would last our entire professional partnership together and until this day. Without a doubt, an incredible day.

Jenny Colgan

Author

I thought about writing about my first wedding, when the howling storm blew out all the braziers, and we all had to stumble about the castle grounds in the dark searching for our supper, hungrily following the sound of the bagpipes.

Or I thought about having my second wedding (to the same chap), when we were waiting in Vegas for our car to turn up, and the lady on the phone said, 'Are you sure you can't see it? It's a pink Cadillac with Elvis in it. Oh, and a baby seat,' just as it swung in in all its unmistakeable pink Cadillac-y glory, Elvis posing in the front and, yes, a baby seat.

Or the days my babies arrived, of course; but those are everybody's miracles.

So this is a just a lovely day I had a couple of years ago that for some reason has always stuck in my memory.

I always get impossible at the end of books, as everything goes faster and faster and I just need to get it finished. *West End Girls* was a particular pain in the arse as it was the first book I'd written after Wallace arrived, and, like most new mothers, all I really wanted to do was stare at my amazing baby and, if at all possible, bore the pants off other people about how amazing my amazing baby was.

My husband Andrew was out working in the garden with Wallace, who was then about eight months old. Every time I glanced out of the studio window, they were doing something useful – moving earth with Wallace perched proudly on top of the wheelbarrow with his serious face on, or chopping wood, with Wallace hopping and giggling in the bouncer Andrew had rigged in the nearby tree. October is gorgeous where we are in France; the days are sunny and warm but the evenings are crisp and chilly.

Taking me quite by surprise, the book finally, FINALLY tumbled to a halt that afternoon – I thought I had a few days to go, but no, there it was. Everything had worked out nicely and I could type THE END (which I always do).

As usual when I finish books, I had a little snivel. It sounds ridiculous, but when you've spent a year or so with a bunch of people, even ones you've made up in your head and even ones who deep down you know can't really exist (in my line of work, for example, the really handsome and also humble and single man who has a knack of turning up in the right place at the right time), you do miss them when they waltz off, all problems solved and all obstacles removed, into the sunset.

So I tottered a bit blearily into the sitting room where Andrew was laying the fire and trying to stop Wallace from crawling into it.

'I've finished!' was all I could say, before bursting into tears.

'That's fantastic,' said Andrew as it certainly was for him, not having to live with a whingy end-of-book writer any more. 'I'll open some champagne.'

'OK,' I said, then on impulse went and changed into my red party frock. So then Andrew changed into his good shirt.

We drank the champagne and decided to put some music on. And then we did some dancing, and put Wallace to bed and ate good steak for supper. Later, our close friend Joaquim drew up in his car. We're used to having our friends wander in and out, and he'd had a hard day at the harbour. We realised that perhaps we're *too* open with our house when he wandered in and grunted at us, before slumping down on the sofa, turning on the television and falling asleep without noticing that we were drinking champagne, I had an evening dress on, the fire was roaring and we were actually dancing. So we just looked at each other, laughed our heads off and went to bed early.

That was it. That's all there was to the day. It was delightful, though nothing amazing happened. But the reason I wanted to remember it was this: one day I know our boys will be all grown up, and I won't have a baby to bounce on the tree in the autumn sunlight; there will be no books to finish because no one will want to read them any more; the red cocktail dress will not fit, or be too old and worn.

So I just wanted to record an ordinary day that had books and champagne and dancing. And – and I think I have just realised I am really writing this for my twice-wed husband – I want you to know how much I have always loved you. And I hope this scrap helps keep us warm on that never-thought-of future day, when we have had our last dance, because there will be a last time for all of these things. And then the howling winter wind blows in, and turns the fire cold.

James Corden

Writer & Star of *Gavin & Stacey*

I've been asked to write about the best day of my life – I would like to think you already know this as I feel sure it will say something about it on the cover of this book. If it doesn't say anything of the sort, I can only imagine there was a mix-up at the publishers. These things happen, but it's a pretty big mistake and I would hope the culprit has had some harsh, stern words shouted at them and has probably become the talk of the office. If I made a mistake like that, I would probably bring in a tub of mini muffins for my fellow employees and try to win back some respect. Trust me, it works every time.

Anyway, I digress ... the thing is, I was asked quite a long time ago to write this chapter and the minute the request was made I knew instinctively what this day was, where I was, what I was wearing, everything! This doesn't, though, make it any easier to write. See, I don't know where to start. How to completely tell this story in the way I feel would do it justice. So, after putting it off and putting it off, I now find myself lying on my living-room floor trying to take my mind back to that time. And, if I think about it, I think of where many of my happy times took place ... school.

Now, to fully tell you about the best day of my life I kind of have to fill you in on one of the worst. I was walking home from school on quite a grey day, I was listening to Arrested Development on my walkman and was, I imagine, walking like I was in some music video. You know the ones where people stride purposefully towards the camera in time to the music? Well that was me, all the way home. Sometimes it would be the sound of Take That in my ears, but today I distinctly remember the beat to 'Mr Wendal' kicking in when my dad pulled up alongside me in his car and asked if I wanted a lift. Of course I jumped straight in, but rather than talk to my father about his day or tell him something about mine, I just carried on listening to my music.

We got home, and Dad said he had to tell me something. I went into the lounge where my mum and two sisters were sitting. I remember asking my older sister how she got home so fast.

'Dad picked me up,' said Ange.

'And me,' said my younger sister Ruth in her incredibly cute little voice.

At that point Dad came in and sat down next to Mum. I wish I could remember exactly what he said, or how he even began to tell us, but I can't. I can't remember anything about that moment, except one thing. Dad told us that he had been called up to fight in the first Gulf War.

'But you're just a musician in the Air Force,' said Ange, saying exactly what all of us were thinking.

'Yeah, you just play the saxophone. What are you gonna do?' said Ruth, also echoing our thoughts.

Dad told us that he was going to be a stretcher bearer and that he would be leaving in three weeks. At that point I remember standing up off the floor (we had furniture, I just often preferred the floor) and dramatically sweeping out of the lounge and up to my room. I had done this half for effect and half so that my mum wouldn't see me crying. The big problem with sweeping out of a room in times like this is that the moment you get out you often feel unsure of where to go! I also found myself suddenly with lots of questions for my father: 'Will you have a gun? What will you eat? Where exactly is Bahrain?' But, rather than go back and ask, I just went to my room and got into bed. I got out pretty quick though, 'cos what with today's news Mum had gone all out for tea and we had turkey burgers, chips and beans. A dream dinner for any schoolboy!

Three weeks came and went pretty quick and the day for Dad to leave arrived. I remember this day so vividly. We were all stood in the kitchen and Dad was dressed like an action man. His normal work clothes were navy blue but now he had all this camouflage gear on. It wasn't much good in our kitchen – I mean, if anything, it made him stand out more.

We said goodbye and Dad went down the line hugging all of us. There were so many tears, Mum was trying her best to be strong but, the minute Ange went, Ruth went, then Mum was gone and that made me go. Dad remained strong but when he held my mum he was sobbing so much he held her in his chest and beckoned the three of us to put our arms around Mum; it felt like ages that cuddle, the whole family just clinging on to each other. I'm sure this sounds quite dramatic, but the thing about war is that it is just that! Everything feels like a drama. It's the unexpectedness of it. No one actually knows quite what they're letting themselves in for so you really only have the worst-case scenario to think of.

Dad left, and life kind of got back to normal, but to tell you the truth I was never really myself during the time he was away. I couldn't cope with it. I had never bunked school before, although I had pulled sickies where I'd fake to Mum that I had some Ferris Bueller-type illness. But, this time, for two days I just didn't go in. I wandered around the shops, had a bag of chips and just wandered around some more. If anyone reading this is thinking of bunking off from school, I would recommend getting a mate involved in the whole scam. It's actually quite boring on your own!

The whole time Dad was away, I couldn't talk to him on the phone. He'd ring every couple of days, and Ange, Ruth and Mum would speak to him, but I would just burst into tears if I heard his voice. I just couldn't ever really adjust to where he was and what he was doing and pretend like it was normal. We would send airmail letters to each other, and these were hugely exciting to me. We would always try to write jokes as a P.S. on the bottom.

Some days it was fine, it wouldn't feel any different to if he was away anywhere, and other days you would really feel it in our house. I remember being in the kitchen eating Frosties one breakfast when they said on the news that a scud missile had been intercepted over the base where Dad was stationed in Bahrain. I just stopped eating and looked at Mum, who had gone pale, and she walked over, put her arm around me and said it was good news 'cos it hadn't worked and everyone was fine. I was down all that day; in fact, it had now got to a point where they were all pretty much down days in our house. The family friends had stopped rallying around Mum quite as much as they did and it seemed people had forgotten all about it.

We were moving into month five when I remember coming downstairs and seeing Mum sitting on her own in the lounge. I was watching through a gap in the doorway, and she was just sitting there, not crying or anything, just sitting, like the weight of the world was on her shoulders. She looked so alone.

'You all right, Mum?' I asked.

'Yep,' she replied and briskly left the room. It wasn't all right at all.

All a bit down this, isn't it? So I'm gonna skip forward to the good stuff. The day we were told that Dad was coming home was incredible, amazing! So amazing that I don't actually remember where I was or who told me or anything. All I remember was being told he'd be home in three days! Those three days went, on the one hand, really slowly but, on the other, incredibly quickly. Before I knew it, we were in the car on the way to RAF Uxbridge. We got there and there were loads of families there, all waiting for loved ones to return.

Mum was talking to lots of other mums, and me and Ruth just sort of hung out together. Someone had tried to set up some kind of buffet in the mess, but to be honest they shouldn't have bothered. It consisted of lots of little bowls full of crisps. Rubbish crisps at that, and two bowls of peanuts. Now that's fine, but a spread such as this should never ever be referred to as a buffet. You're just getting people's hopes up for sausage rolls and the like. Just place them out and say nothing about it, that way people will be thankful, instead of complaining about the spread!

This disappointment didn't last long though, because suddenly there was a rush of activity, people all racing to get outside and the sound of whoops and cheers was starting to get drowned out by the noise of a roaring engine and the odd beeping of a horn. I ran to the front of where people were standing and could see a big blue and white coach pulling in to where we were stood. It drove past us a bit and I ran along the side of it looking up to see if I could see Dad. I couldn't see him anywhere so I kept running and so did all the other kids, looking up at every opportunity but all I could see was a mass of camouflage waving at various people. I started to worry for the briefest moment that he wasn't on the bus, that something had happened.

Then, just as the coach began to stop I saw him. He was right there in the window, looking straight at me. It was like there was no one else in the world. He was smiling and looked tanned; he didn't look like Dad in a strange way, he looked different. The coach door opened achingly slowly and Dad was one of the first off.

He looked at me and said, 'Hiya, son!' and with that he held his arms out and I ran towards him. He threw his arms around me and I remember squeezing him so tight. My face pressed into his shirt. I remember so clearly the smell of his clothes. He smelled like the inside of the bag you have your stuff in when you come back from the beach. I kept holding him tightly as I heard him calling to Mum and Ruth. They came over and at first I refused to let go. Then he picked Ruth up in his arms and held a hand out to Mum. I stepped away and I saw Mum put her hands up to his face and just stand looking at him. They both smiled and almost began to laugh at the sheer joy of it all. Dad pulled Mum closer and tenderly kissed her on the forehead, and she just sighed the biggest sigh of relief. She shut her eyes and kissed him on the cheek; Ruth leaned in and gave him a kiss on the other cheek. And Dad just pulled them both closer to him smiling all the time.

And that, right there, that moment. That was the best day of my life.

Tracey Cox

Writer & TV Presenter

Nothing like being cleared of a life-threatening disease to count as one of the best days of your life. Even the ponderous question of how to celebrate such an event was taken care of. An hour after I'd heard the good news, I was due to film a pilot for a TV show, *The Friday Night Project*. We filmed the show then got mindlessly sloshed at the Electric in Notting Hill, joyous there were still brain cells left to be annihilated by alcohol. Nothing new there then … but I'm skipping ahead of myself.

This particular dodge with death (and I've had a few – nearly fell off a cliff once and had some cancer scares) was quite unexpected. As I suppose most are.

'Sorry I must have misheard you. Can you spell it?' I said to my doctor. She has a glorious French accent and I have the attention span of a two-year-old on the phone, so it does make for confusion. Even 'I'm afraid you need your left leg removed' and 'Your leg is fine' sound remarkably similar.

'B. R. A. I. N. T. U. M. O. U. R.,' said Alix, patiently spelling out each letter.

Even then I remember thinking, Damn it, why don't I sound like that?

'Oh,' I replied. 'That's what I thought you said.'

'Don't worry, *please*,' she said. 'I've got you an appointment with a specialist on Tuesday – it's late Thursday and everywhere is shut now for Easter or I'd take you today. But if it is a brain tumour, they'll just remove it and everything will be fine.'

'What's the likelihood it is one … of those things?'

'Well, it's the most likely cause of the result of the test.'

'Like *how* likely?'

'Um. Ninety per cent? But, even it is, you will be fine. Honestly.'

'OK,' I said, rather cheerily actually – *that's* how reassuring my doctor is – hung up the phone and went back to typing my column.

Two minutes later, I stopped and thought, Holy shit! I've just been told I have a 90 per cent chance of having a brain tumour. So I picked up the phone and called my agent who also happens to be one of my best friends.

'Apparently I've got a brain tumour,' I said calmly.

'Er, what, why? How?' said Vicki.

I'd been to the doctor the week before to get some blood tests because I wasn't feeling quite right. Hormone tests were part of this and one of them revealed that the pituitary gland in my brain wasn't working. The gland is supposed to secrete a certain hormone which is crucial to all sorts of body functioning but mine wasn't even squeezing out the odd drop. In 90 per cent of cases, the cause for this is because something is pressing on the gland. That something being a brain tumour. Or, to be more precise, a pituitary adenoma.

'But what are the symptoms if your pituitary gland isn't working?' Vicki asked sensibly. 'Have you had headaches? Blurred vision? Nausea?'

'No. The symptoms are loss of an appetite for food. And no interest in sex.'

And then we both giggled.

'Bloody hell!' she said. 'If this is you with a decreased libido and

73

appetite, you're going to turn into an obese nymphomaniac when they fix it.'

I felt a sudden sense of relief.

They've mixed up the blood tests, I thought. It's not me. It couldn't be. I'm a greedy, randy little bugger.

'You'll be fine, really,' she said. 'I'll come with you to the doctor on Tuesday though.'

'Thanks, Vic,' I said. Bless her.

Having decided the test clinic had mixed up blood samples and I definitely didn't have some *thing* growing in my brain, I decided to milk what was, after all, a potentially brilliant way to get lots of attention.

'SUSPECTED BRAIN TUMOUR – POSSIBLY DYING,' I typed as the heading for my email. That should get them sitting up and paying attention.

'Apparently I have a brain tumour because something is pressing on my pituitary gland and stopping it from functioning, The symptoms are not wanting to eat or have sex. (Yes really.) Clearly they've mixed up the blood tests but because it's the Thursday before Easter I can't find out for sure until Tuesday. Which means four days of wondering whether I'm going to die and what scarves to wear because they're bound to shave my head. Anyway, nothing to worry about. Apparently brain tumours are incredibly common. Who would have thought, eh? I didn't know that, did you?'

I sent it to all my friends and family, then sat back waiting to see what everyone would do. I was quite pleased with myself actually. I mean, most people would be in a lather of panic after hearing something like that. Not me. I just thought it was funny.

Until the next day.

Easter Friday was spent fielding off constant, frantic, panicked phone calls. Every time I'd sit down to tuck into my Cadbury's by-God-they're-delicious Easter egg, some bastard would ring me. Which was terribly flattering and made me feel extremely loved and protected. But I quite like sucking rather than crunching chocolate and this was seriously interfering with my egg consumption. Besides, no one was seeing the funny side. In fact, they were all *so* worried that suddenly I was.

Then I did the absolute worst thing anyone diagnosed with anything serious should ever do: I looked it up on the internet. The first thing I saw was the word 'blindness'.

'The tumour can press on the optic nerves causing loss of peripheral vision and, in some cases, blindness.'

Then I read that removing the tumour is difficult because it's near the optic nerves. Fucketyfuck. One slip up and I'm blind.

That night I woke up in the middle of the night, sweating and terrified because I dreamed they'd done the surgery and told me they couldn't save my vision. I sat bolt upright in bed, opened my eyes and (of course) it was pitch black and I couldn't see anything and for one awful, heartbreaking, heart-stopping moment I thought it was real. And, bugger it, I was all alone.

My appointment was for 10 a.m. Tuesday and I was there at 9.30 a.m., ever so quietly going slightly round the bend. At precisely 10 a.m., I got taken into the endocrinologist, a no-nonsense Eastern European woman, bristling with efficiency, hands steepled in front of her ample bosom. She wasn't smiling though, which had to mean she suspected she was going to have to give me bad news. Vicki, thank God, was outside in the waiting room.

The specialist nodded sagely when I told her what the doctor had said, read the reports, then proceeded to ask a copious amount of questions. When did my periods start? Did I eat healthily? How long had I smoked for? Blah blah bloody blah and all the time inside I'm screaming, 'For God's sake, woman, get to the point. Do I have a sodding brain tumour or not??!!' After half-an-hour, I said as much. 'Look, I'm sure it's terribly important whether I eat broccoli or not but I'm really worried here. Do you think I have a tumour or not?'

She pulled herself up, fixed me with a withering, icy gaze and said, 'That's what I am trying to find out. Let me do my job.'

Another 30 minutes later, she sat back to deliver the news. 'Lucky for you,' she said (a bit sniffily, I thought, I hadn't kicked up that much of a fuss!), 'I have seen a case like yours before. I can see why your doctor thought you had a brain tumour and most doctors would be sending you straight for an MRI.' Pause.

Jesus Christ woman, this isn't *The X-Factor*!

'But I'm sure you don't have one.'

Turns out, a combination of the type of contraceptive pill I was on, my particular brain chemistry, a reaction to Zyban (a drug I'd be taking to help give up smoking) and (ewwww!) my age was responsible for the hormone's lack of secretion. Nothing pressing on it, after all. Most particularly, nothing beginning with B and T.

The whole appointment took over an hour and I emerged to see Vicki looking so ashen-faced I felt like bustling her through the door to get a check-up herself. We hugged and did a silly little jump up and down thing that teenage girls always do in movies and you think to yourself, Oh puhleeze, no one does that! Then we had champagne and then, I guess, life went on. I went to film the TV special, got drunk, woke up with a hangover and went to the gym. Just as before.

Except for one thing. There's a saying that's always struck me as brilliantly perceptive: 'Good health is a crown that only the sick can see.' Or perhaps also those who thought they might become sick. Because I am now acutely aware of what's perching on *my* head.

Lewis Crofts

Author

Ⓜ y teeth were covered in glucose fur and my tongue picked out soggy lettuce from behind my gums. Ian's floorboards were hard underneath me. I tried to roll over but my hip-bone complained and I slumped back, turning my head away from the light. I gulped and flapped like a fish on the deck of a boat.

In the bed above me, Ian broke wind next to my head and I realised lying on the floor was a bad idea as a fog of flatulence swirled out from underneath his covers and across the room. I was then reminded that the previous evening's festivity – the launch party for my first novel – was perhaps the only time a London literary event had substituted fine wines with Nethergate's Old Growler.

Once up, I went into the kitchen and stared out the empty fridge. I checked the cupboard, pulling down a plastic container marked CAFE. At the bottom lay one split tea-bag dying on a bed of its own leaves. I grabbed my coat from the back of the chair and walked down the stairs and out into the street. My knees cracked into action and I raised the coat's collar against the wind; my wrists clicked like cheap castanets.

The previous evening's rain had turned into morning sludge, saturating papier-mâché *Evening Standard*s and sucking the brown off tyres and out of gutters. I felt for my wrist, loosening the strap and corrugated skin. It winked 68.72 at me and then faded away.

The sun – veiled in cloud – gave no indication of the time; no more than the empty streets and the urban hush broken only by a dog sniffing around rubbish. The shops were silent but for the rattling at the back of the baker's and the sliding and slamming behind the butcher's.

A dull double-thud came from a glass door across the street. I walked over to the far pavement, pressing my face against Erotic Garden's glass, misted with condensed sweat on the inside. The door smacked into my cheek and I was swept to the side as a tangle of limbs and denim was thrown into the street. A man folded and lay still in the middle of the road. I took one step towards him and then stopped as he sprang up, pulled his trousers straight, checked for his wallet and hobbled away down the street.

I walked past four newsagents, stacks of papers sitting untouched outside their locked doors. I waited at the bus-stop, head in hands and my stomach turning. The saliva tap started to run in my mouth, collecting in a viscous puddle between my trainers. The bus pulled up. It coughed fumes at me and I stepped inside.

'Single to Tesco's, please.'

'Two pound, mate.'

'Cheers, drives.'

'You look awful.'

'Cheers, drives.'

I couldn't manage the stairs so I stayed on the ground floor, rocking, swaying then stumbling as the bus pulled away. My stomach was begging for coffee, water, bread, tablets, anything to settle its hydrochloric hell. Head down, I walked to the back of the bus and collapsed in a corner-seat, pushing my chin up to suck at the shaft of air coming in through the tilted window. I opened my eyes.

Opposite me sat a young woman: her hair was pulled to one side in a precise parting; her pin-striped dress ran perfect parallels over her thighs and down to her knees; her thin arms were comfortably folded and her shoes were pushed together in faultless symmetry. It was as if she had been created in a geometry class.

Our eyes met and she turned away, looking out the window. I leaned forward and squeezed my palms against the sides of my skull. I caught a suspicion of her perfume and leaned back, partly bewitched, partly nauseous. She shifted in her seat, moving inches away from my acrid stench. She glanced up again and caught me staring. Cautiously, she scanned the other empty seats, contemplating a move. I closed my eyes, graciously giving her the opportunity to withdraw without causing offence. The aftermath of an Old Growler bulged in my lower gut as I tried to count how many I had drunk at the launch party.

I heard her rummaging and I tilted my shivering body away, squeezing my buttocks together and tensing my stomach muscles. The saliva tap started to run again and, slyly, I brought a sleeve to my face to absorb the spit. Longing to exit my hideous world, I opened my eyes again.

I looked more closely at the woman; her mouth was moist with freshly applied lipstick and her eyes glinted with the reflections of vehicles passing outside; her neck was bent gracefully forward as she looked down at a book.

I rubbed my eyes and focused in on the familiar cover. I registered my own name in the bottom corner and smiled.

She looked up and frowned. 'Is there something wrong?'

'Not at all. Not at all.'

'What do you want then?'

'Nothing.'

'So, stop looking at me.'

'Sorry.'

She read to the end of her paragraph and I flinched as she bent the corner of the page. She picked up her bag and moved to the front of the bus.

Two stops later the bus approached Tesco's. I pressed the bell and went to stand by the doors.

'What is it?' she said irritably.

'Just one thing before I get off.'

'What?'

'What's the book like?'

She looked at me bemused.

'You gettin' off or what?' shouted the driver. 'I ain't got all bloody morning.'

I stepped down on to the pavement and the doors fizzed closed behind me. The stench of Old Growler announced itself to the outside world. As the bus pulled away, I looked back and caught sight of the woman. She nodded at me through the glass and returned to my book.

James Crossley

Former Gladiator

From the age of eight, I was obsessed with superheroes. Most mornings I would run into my parents' room and rip off my PJs to do impressions of the Incredible Hulk, Spiderman and Superman.

I would go to the movies and watch their films over and over again. I saw *Ghostbusters* eight times and when I was 12 my mother took me to see *Rocky I, II* and *III* in a six-hour bonanza. We took sandwiches and drinks and I sat glued to the cinema screen as the Philadelphian southpaw underdog came good.

That's it, I said, I want to be a boxer.

No chance, I was told!

I was disappointed but quickly found the next best thing for me was to get the body of a boxer. So bodybuilding seemed like a good compromise. My father took me to the local gym and I started lifting weights, always thinking about one day being one of these superheroes.

This became an obsession: training every day, monitoring my food, sleep and workouts, watching training videos and reading magazines every night when I got in from school.

One thing I always did was set goals and at 13 years old I wrote in a training diary that I wanted 16-inch arms at 16 years old, 17-inch arms at 17 years old and so on. I also decided I would match my body weight in stone with my arm measurement – this peaked at 20 when I weighed in at a monster 20 stone with a 20-inch arm measurement!!

I would be listening to the *Rocky* soundtrack every workout in a quest to become my own little (or big!) superhero, sacrificing going out, drinking, partying and focusing on one day being that underdog I so admired.

After three years I was ready for bodybuilding shows. At 15 it was Mr York, at 16 Mr NE Britain, at 17 Mr England and at 18 Mr Britain.

On 23 May 1993, I was backstage at the Junior Mr Britain competition when two gentlemen approached me. I was in my posing pouch covered in oil and fake tan (just like a Saturday night out) and knackered from the gruelling muscle tensing of the pre-judging. They told me they were from LWT's hit show *Gladiators* and they were very impressed with my height and physique. I had seen the show and loved it, muscle-bound superheroes being challenged by members of the public. They were looking for a new tall blonde young superhero and said they would like me to come to London the following week to audition for the show, which was filming the next month. This was everything I had always wanted.

The following week I turned up at a school in Peckham for my 'trial'. It was a morning of tests of fitness and agility. I knew this opportunity could turn into something big so went in totally mentally focused, even though I was so big that climbing ropes wasn't going to come naturally. I literally went for it until I threw up.

After I finished, the producers huddled together while I was swigging water and mopping off the sweat from three hours of trials. Then Nigel Lythgow, the head of LWT, walked up to me and said, 'Welcome to the team, you shall be known as Hunter.'

Jason Cundy

Broadcaster & Former Footballer

It was February 1997 and I was playing for Ipswich Town. I was 27 and at the peak of my fitness. Ipswich were challenging for the play-offs, I was newly married and life was good. Then one day (in the shower) I noticed that one of my balls had changed shape and size. The density of it was different; it was bigger, harder and heavier than the other one. I knew something was up straight away. I went to the doctor and was sent for an operation. They found a tumour on the Monday. On the Tuesday I had the operation to remove the ball, then I had to wait 10 days to find out whether the tumour was benign or cancerous. Up until this stage I was convinced the tumour was going to be cancerous because I'd done some research into the symptoms of testicular cancer. I'd looked on the internet and spoken to doctors and I knew the chances of it being cancerous were quite high. The moment you're told you have cancer is not one you forget quickly. I'd gone in with my wife Lizzie, we'd sat in front of the doctor and he said, 'OK, it's cancer.' I was silent as Lizzie broke down in tears. We'd been married less than a year and all of a sudden she thought she was going to be on her own for the rest of her life.

We then had to go through a series of tests and the biggest question was whether the cancer had spread. Of course, if it had spread, there would be all sorts of complications with my treatment, depending on how far it had gone. This was the most tense part of the whole thing. I had to go for x-rays and blood tests and the build-up to that was possibly the worst day of my life. I was naturally terrified. But when the blood tests and lymph node tests came back negative – meaning the cancer hadn't spread – it was a huge relief because it was so much easier to treat and my chances of surviving increased considerably. Knowing the cancer hadn't spread made going into the treatments and the care after them much more bearable. I didn't feel that much fear, I just wanted it to be treated.

Lizzie took it worse than I did, but I think it's much harder for the loved ones watching on. When you're dealing with the situation, as I was, you're in complete control and you know exactly how you feel. Other people don't know how you feel and they fear for you. My mum always said to me the only time she felt happy was when she was around me and could see I was handling it OK. When she wasn't with me, she worried that I was covering it up or putting on a front and hiding my feelings. But, once I found out it hadn't spread and was treatable, I knew there was a way forward and that I could handle it.

Looking back now, I always wonder what would have happened if it had spread. I might not be around. There are still young men dying of this disease but luckily for me I caught it at stage one. By stage three it's spread to the lungs, the brain, the heart and is all over the body. At that stage it will kill. Luckily for me I was diagnosed early, treated early and the outcome was successful.

I tried to get back into playing for Ipswich that season because we were in the play-offs against Sheffield United but I couldn't. Chemotherapy involves powerful drugs and, although I didn't particularly feel ill, I felt nauseous and lethargic; the wind was really taken out my sails. That was the only time I really felt ill. When I tried to get myself back to some sort of fitness, as I needed to for playing professional sport, it took me a long time. In fact, it took me ages, probably six to eight months after being diagnosed and having the operation, to get back to the fitness levels I had before. So it took its toll but fortunately there were no long-term effects.

I went on to play the rest of the following season for Ipswich successfully; we got to the play-offs again but Charlton beat us that year.

I retired two years later at 29 with a knee injury, which comes with the territory when you're a professional footballer. But I'm still here today with my wife and family and that's what matters.

Liz Cundy

Fashion Expert & Broadcaster

The date was Sunday, 14 May 2000; I was eight months pregnant and Ipswich Town, who my husband Jason used to play for, were in the play-off finals. We were watching the game and Ipswich were doing terrifically well. It was a huge game and I was having a fantastic day.

As Jason played for Ipswich, they're a big part of my life. We know all the players and I know all the wives, the chairman David Sheepshanks and the manager George Burley really well. George was Jason's best friend so we were really rooting for Ipswich Town. We got all the family round, had some food and wished George good luck before the game.

When Jason played for Ipswich, he'd got into the play-offs three times but he hadn't made it into the Premiership so it was a really big day for us. It was very exciting and Ipswich were playing incredibly well, and I was thinking, This time they could do it. We were slightly sad that Jason wasn't playing but we love Ipswich so we were really wanted them to win.

We were sitting there and I suddenly got a little bit of a twinge in my tummy. I thought it was nothing as I had another couple of months to go. So we carried on and as the game went on I was getting excited as Ipswich were winning and everyone was cheering and shouting and we were getting really involved in the game.

Before I knew it, I was half hanging off the couch, thinking, God, I'm not feeling too comfortable here. But I was ignoring how I was feeling because Ipswich were winning and doing brilliantly. Matty Holland was playing well, Jamie Scowcroft, all our old buddies were doing well.

Then I got these really crazy pains. I thought, Hang on, this might be something but just keep quiet, there's only another 40 minutes to go, I'll hold on. It's nothing, I've got another month and a half. It's just me being excited.

Anyway, the game went on. Ipswich were winning and we were cheering and going mad. Suddenly I'm thinking, Hang on, this baby is coming. I looked at Jason and said, 'I think the baby's coming.'

He looked at me and said, 'Can you hang on for the full 90 minutes? We have to watch the football.'

By now I was clinging on to the couch and actually feeling the biggest pain I've ever felt in my life. I was holding on but I had one eye on the football and thinking, This baby's on its way. Everyone around me was ignoring me because they were watching the football. Before I knew it I was lying on the floor. I was in bits. I said, 'Jason, this baby's coming.'

He looked back at me and said, 'There's only 10 minutes to go, hold on!'

On the one hand, I was holding on for dear life and, on the other, I was watching the football and Ipswich were winning. They were going to make it through and I thought, I can't leave it, but in my mind I was thinking, This baby's bloody coming!

Finally Ipswich won, they got through to the Premiership and with that I was gone. The pain was out of control. They had to carry me into the car. They whizzed me to the hospital and I gave birth in about 10 minutes flat. I had James, lovely James who we weren't supposed to have because Jason had testicular cancer and we were told we couldn't have any more kids. We had this wonderful baby boy and I got to watch the football and Ipswich went up to the Premiership. Now that was a special day.

Ann Daniels

Polar Explorer

I first became involved in Polar exploration quite by chance. At 32, as an ordinary housewife and mother of baby triplets, with no outdoor experience whatsoever, it was an unlikely change of path. However, a chance hearing of an announcement on the radio changed my life forever.

Pen Hadow and Caroline Hamilton were putting together a North Pole relay and asked for ordinary women to apply for selection. Although I had never carried a rucksack in my life before and had no real thought of being selected I sent off an application form and soon found myself on Dartmoor with over 200 other 'hopefuls'.

I appeared to be the only character that had never had walking boots on her feet before and the other women all seemed to be outward-bound instructors or hardy outdoor types. We walked hour upon hour across a dismal Dartmoor with heavy rucksacks on our back and I spent the whole weekend in pain and agony. At one point in the dark and under cover of torrential rain, I gave way to tears and cried from the horror of it all.

Although I hated every second, somewhere along the way I caught the dream. This could be my one opportunity in life to do something special and change my life forever. I had two choices.

Either give up completely or work hard to make the dream happen. I chose the latter.

Thankfully, no one was thrown out at this stage and we were all invited back for four days 'OF HELL' when the final team of 20 would be chosen.

I had nine months and my already hectic life became even more manic. I took the children to the crèche in the local gym each morning for an hour. On an afternoon when they slept, I did press-ups and circuits in the back garden. Friends taught me how to read a map, pack a rucksack and cope with the great outdoors and finally when the next selection weekend came up I was ready.

The hard work paid off and I was overjoyed to be selected for the final ice team.

The expedition was a relay, five teams of four women together with two guides went in relay format to the North Pole. I was on the first leg of the journey and I set off for the Arctic, full of fear, excitement and apprehension, unsure of what to expect.

However, it was on this expedition I fell in love with the Arctic and its magnificence. Nothing, not the cold in my fingers or the exhaustion from pulling a sledge over huge ridges, could suppress my awe at this fantastic wilderness. The colours ranged from the brightest white through to the darkest of blacks from the inky ocean. The sun shone on the ice ridges and glinted crisp blues and pinks. For someone who had only had an experience of Dartmoor, it was mind-blowing. Even wiping my own bottom with ice wedges became a huge thrill.

Each team did their bit and on 27 May 1997 team echo planted the Union Jack and stood on the North Pole triumphantly. For me it was the start of a wonderful new career.

I wanted to do a real expedition without guides and five of us got together and organised an expedition to walk across Antarctica to the South Pole. We planned it ourselves and walked over 700 miles across the most inhospitable continent in the world to reach the South Pole on foot, the first all British women's team to do so.

I began to guide last degree expeditions to the North Pole and soon decided to put together a whole expedition to the North Pole, from beginning to end.

I approached two of the South Pole team, Caroline Hamilton and Pom Oliver, who agreed to join me. The expedition entailed walking in terrible temperatures over 500 miles across the moving Arctic Ocean to the North Pole, pulling all our own equipment.

We left from land and the temperatures were so much colder than we had ever experienced before, between -40 and -54 for the first 27 days. It was horrendously painful and all consuming. Everything froze, our clothes, our eyelashes, even our brains. We found we could only do one thing at once and function at a very slow pace.

We pulled all our own equipment, food and fuel in sledges weighing almost 300lb and travel during the day was excruciatingly slow and hard. In the early days we completed just one nautical mile a day. The ice ridges were huge and never ending and it took three of us to lift one sledge over each ridge. If the days were bad, the evenings were worse. As soon as we lit the cookers, the tent filled with steam and we couldn't see each other at all. We sat hunched up on our sleeping bags unable to see, unable to talk. We ate silently and as quickly as possible until it was time to crawl into our sleeping bags. After five days, the bags froze solid and we literally had to chip our way into them each evening and lie on solid ice until we fell asleep exhausted.

On our seventh day, we had travelled only nine miles and went to bed disheartened. We were woken early as the ground around the tent began to break up and we only just managed to pack up and abandon the area before it all gave way and swallowed us up.

Shortly after our escape, the air became ominous and dark and while we looked for a place to camp a severe gale hit us and we couldn't pitch the tent. We crawled under the material on the ground to take shelter. For three days we lay there unable to move, with only a small amount of chocolate and water to sustain us.

After three days, the storm died and we began our journey once more but the cold had taken its toll on our bodies. Caroline's fingers were frostbitten and she couldn't do anything with them, not even go to the toilet by herself. Caroline and I became very close during those days. Pom's feet were also seriously frostbitten and painful and walking became a problem.

We had two more storms to contend with, and on day 37 of an intended 75-day expedition we had travelled just 69 miles of the 500-mile journey.

Thankfully, Caroline's hands healed but Pom's frostbite got steadily worse and wet gangrene set in. She could hardly walk. She put her boots on in the morning and wept with the pain but still skied for eight or nine hours to keep the expedition alive.

On day 47, Pom unfortunately had to leave the expedition on the resupply plane.

It was a devastating blow. Caroline and I had over 300 miles to go in less than 30 days. Each day we skied longer and longer to gain miles. If the cold had been our enemy, the warmth suddenly became the problem. Temperatures rose and there were more and more areas of open water and thin ice. So much so that we had to swim across stretches of open water. We skied over 15 hours a day to increase our mileage.

In the evening we only drank tepid water because we didn't have the time to boil the water for a hot drink. Many other disasters occurred during the journey and it wasn't until our penultimate day when we only had 18 more miles to complete that I began to believe we would make the Pole.

Finally, after 80 days on the ice, we reached the North Pole, exhausted but triumphant and planted the Union Jack. Against the odds, we had become the first women in the world to walk to both the North and South Poles.

I went from housewife and mother of triplets to driving forward a world-record-breaking expedition to the North Pole. Besides the birth of my four children, it was the best day of my life and taught me that with the right opportunity and support anyone can achieve more than they thought possible.

Model

The best day of my life started in December 2004 when I got a call from my agent asking if I'd be prepared to fly over to Iraq to visit the troops. Morale was really low so they were looking for people to go out and cheer them up. It was obviously still dangerous and they were saying we could have danger money for going over there but I was so excited by the idea I wasn't really bothered about the money so I agreed to go. Leilani, a model colleague of mine, was also asked, as was ex-footballer John Barnes so we all flew out there together.

We went from a military airport and we had to wear bulletproof vests and these horrible helmets throughout the whole of the flight. We landed at the airport in Iraq in the middle of the night and it was really weird as it was completely deserted. I've never seen anything like that before – I'm used to seeing airports where people are coming in and out all the time, but obviously since the war people don't fly to Iraq any more, so it was completely dead, with no one around at all and a really eerie place to be in the middle of the night.

We got out of the airport and were taken into some armoured trucks. There were no streetlights and it was pitch black as we drove off to where we were going to stay. There were lots of bridges over the road and as we came up to them the driver kept swerving into the

94

next lane. I asked the driver why and he said it was because the Iraqi civilians throw rocks off the bridges to try to hit the cars and by changing lanes they don't know where they come out in the tunnel. At which point Leilani and I looked at each other, obviously both thinking, What have we let ourselves in for?

We got to the army base and went to bed. The next day we were each assigned a bodyguard for the whole time we were there and we had to wear bulletproof vests and helmets, so we weren't looking very ladylike and feeling very unattractive – I mean, we were meant to be out there looking sexy for the soldiers not wearing big old helmets and vests!

During our visit, we did lots of different things including flying a plane and I even got a chance to control it for three-quarters of an hour! I thought I was doing a great job and the pilot said I was really good. But when we landed I asked a couple of boys how I did and they said it was horrific – bumping all over the place! The next day we drove tanks and all sorts, it was brilliant fun.

Then we went to visit the boys who served on the front line. These were the ones who saw the most traumatic things, people being blown up and worse. It was great to see them and to try to give them a morale boost. It was fantastic to see that we had an impact on them and that one day made the whole trip worthwhile.

The last day was probably the best and also the most exciting day of my life. We got in the truck on our way to the shooting range to go and shoot some weapons and started driving along in a convoy when all of a sudden Leilani's and my bodyguard jumped on top of us and started screaming. What the hell is going on here? I thought. And then among all the confusion someone got out of the car to look around.

'What's happening?' I asked.

'We've just been shot at!'

'No way!'

Everyone got really scared but I was really excited, and they kept saying how strange I was!

We finally got to the shooting range and saw all the soldiers there who then showed us the different weapons that they use including the grenade launchers. They asked if we wanted to have a go, so Leilani and I got on the floor and started shooting these big rifles. It was great fun, although being really small the power of the rifle sent me flying backwards!

Before we left they said they had some grenade launchers and that we could have a go with them as well, but not too many shots as it was £50 per grenade. So we had two gos each. There was a target quite a way up ahead which they told us to aim for, so I did and it blew up. Everyone was really pleased for me, saying they couldn't believe I'd done it, clapping and telling me I was amazing. What they didn't know what that I was actually aiming for the other target! Well, they didn't need to need to know about it. They kept saying how good I was all night and Leilani was gutted!

That last night we went with the troops to where they go for their downtime and a few drinks. We all ate and drank and John Barnes gave his talk, which was great, questions and answers including stuff about Paul Gascoigne and other players. He also fancied himself as a bit of a rapper so he started rapping along to bit of Ludacris. Next thing I knew I was pulled out of the crowd grinding and dancing with him on a stage in front of hundreds of people. I've never been so embarrassed! That was the perfect end to the perfect day. Experiencing all I did and giving something back by helping the troops made me feel really good and I still get messages to this day. I've never had a day like that before. Just amazing.

Emma Donnan

Journalist

Most of the best day of my life was spent on a train. On my own. Sitting staring out the window at the passing countryside, with nothing but a book and several glasses of wine for company. Maybe not most people's idea of a perfect day, but it was the sense inside me of freedom and nothing but adventure and the unknown ahead that made it that way.

The idea to head off to France, with just a bag on my back and no real plans, had come to me over a couple of months. It began with the stereotypical end of a long-term relationship the week before Valentine's Day, and developed with a skiing trip to France where a holiday fling reminded me how much I liked all things French.

I was 24 and ending my first step on the career ladder as a journalist on a local paper, and knew, once I headed for the nationals, there would be no time to pause for breath for a good few years. So before I knew it I was handing my notice in and was at my village station, rucksack on back and parents waving goodbye.

I had simply a vague notion to head to Montpellier on the South coast of France and see what happened. And as the train pulled out of the station, with me surrounded by commuters on their way to another mundane day in the office, I was braced to feel complete and overwhelming fear at what I was doing and I suppose a tiny bit of me did. But only in that nice kind of way, where you get a bit of an adrenaline rush, and a few butterflies, but nothing paralysing or painful. In fact, I felt more the urge to giggle, wondering what the hell I was doing, but at the same time kind of proud of my own madness.

All of my friends had been at pains to tell me I was crazy while also expressing their envy. So many of them said, 'I wish I could do that,' which frustrated me at first – of course they could. We were all young people, mostly back living with parents after university, and still finding our feet as to what career path we were taking. To me it was the perfect time to head off on an adventure.

Then I realised they didn't really mean that. They meant they would like to, but in a kind of fleeting 'wouldn't it be nice' way, but really they preferred the safety of home. Or knowing the security of their future or job was in hand.

But anyhow, there I was with my one-way ticket off on my journey.

It was an hour's travel into London, then a struggle on the underground with my rucksack – note to other would-be travellers, hairdryers and hair straighteners are just a luxury too far when balanced out against their travelling weight! Then it was the Eurostar, and a further six hours on the fast TGV overground trains on the other side. But the whole way, as we rushed under the sea and through the empty French countryside, all I was dealing with was a sense of euphoria.

I chatted to my fellow passengers, tentatively tried my rusty French on the train bar manager, and had read the guide to Montpellier so many times I could chant it off by heart.

Then finally I was there.

As I staggered out of Montpellier Station 12 hours after I had set off, there was barely light to see where I had arrived. So plans to explore were set aside, and I had dinner in a trusty McDonald's before checking into my hotel. Booked as the cheapest from my guidebook on the train hours before, it was easy to see why. The grubby-looking bed in my rickety old room and communal bathroom were hardly the welcome I was hoping for.

But lying in bed half-an-hour later, flicking on the light every few minutes to check for stray cockroaches, I felt a huge rush of happiness. I had no idea what would follow the next day, let alone in the following months, but that was the idea. I had faith in myself and the unknown, and was ready and waiting to go with whatever lay ahead …

Stella Duffy

Author

We live in a society that teaches little girls to fantasise about their wedding day. The lovely dress, the beautiful shoes, the pretty flowers, the dancing, the people, the party – the attention. In many ways, as women, we are trained up from an early age to see ourselves at the centre of our wedding-day story. At the age of 5, 10, 15, no girl really cares that the figure waiting at the other end of the aisle, the other person destined to say 'I do', is necessarily fuzzy. For most little girls, though, that person – whoever he may be – is a he. It was for me when, as a four-year-old and my sister's bridesmaid, I pictured myself in her place. It was for me again when, a little older, another sister and several cousins married within a couple of years. By the time I was in my mid-teens, though, I was starting to suspect that the other person saying 'I do' might also be a woman, and, by the time I was in my late twenties, I knew I wanted that person to be Shelley.

Two women, two great dresses (neither matching nor meringues), two gorgeous bouquets, two stunningly beautiful pairs of shoes. Two brides and 180 people on the last day of summer in 2005. It was actually a couple of months before it became legally possible for us to be civil partners and, while we have since taken advantage of that great and hard-won step forward, for me, the 'real' wedding was this one – where we spoke our vows in front of all those people we care for and about, where we planned for several months how best to give our loved ones a great party, where we were witnessed, as a couple, by our peers. Witnessing has always been how people married. Whether they were jumping over a broom, or handfasting, or tying a (literal) knot, long before religious leaders became involved in wedding ceremonies, a couple were always united simply by the fact of them saying so in public and asking that their declaration be witnessed.

The other reason we wanted a party for all our loved ones is that, five years earlier, at the age of 36, I'd been diagnosed with breast cancer and had surgery, radiotherapy and chemotherapy, combining the best of Western medicine with an array of complementary therapies. The year of being ill was hard work, often very depressing, and yet also, ultimately, quite amazing – as staying alive always is. That year, 2000, we'd both said that, if I made it to five years, we'd have a big party to celebrate. We'd actually given each other wedding rings in front of a small group of very close friends to testify to our commitment (a small group being about as much as I could cope with at the time), and we especially wanted to do it again to include our wider circle of friends and our families. There is, of course, no magic to the five-year mark, or even being 10 years away from diagnosis – as my consultant says, every single day after diagnosis is what matters. The five- and 10-year markers are merely there to make it easier for statisticians. Being cancer-free for five years certainly can't guarantee it won't come back; nonetheless, it is a marker, and one which, alongside our 15 years together, we were keen to celebrate.

So it was a wedding day and a celebration. We both loved the dressing up and making a fuss. Our people made amazing efforts to come and be with us from all over the UK and the world; my parents were not there as they have both died, but not only did I feel them there with us in spirit (and carry their photo in my bag), my brother also spoke movingly and lovingly on their behalf, as did my father-in-law. We had friends from Spain singing and friends from London performing comedy, plenty of people crying (at all the right places), food and drink were taken in liberal quantities, and we danced for hours.

I still hope that in my lifetime I will legally be able to say I am 'married' to my wife, that our world will have grown enough to grant us the right to marriage as a stable, committed, long-term couple, a right that so many people take for granted, but until then our family and friends call that day our wedding, we call it our wedding, and we call each other wife – it's short, obvious, easy to say and precludes any of those embarrassing confusions that can come from the words partner or girlfriend. For both of us, one of the most touching elements of the day, were the half-dozen teenagers partying late into the night. The children of various friends, they have been born into a time and a culture where, while the wedding of two women might be unusual (for many people it was their first – it was mine and Shelley's first attendance at a wedding with no groom too), it is also just the same as any other. And I hope that our wedding gave them the gift of recognising – at a time in their lives when to know this is such a bonus – that we are all different, be it the difference of gender or sexuality or race or religion or class or accent or region or nation or whatever. And that, while those differences may be intrinsic to much of who we are, they also don't really matter a great deal in the end. What matters are friends and family and two people expressing their commitment, being witnessed in that love. It would have been great to know that at 14. It was certainly very good to know it on 24 September 2005.

Matt Dunn

Author

The first piece I ever wrote for public consumption was when I was 14 – a report to be read out at school assembly on a cricket match I'd played in (somewhat disastrously). But, while I was no good with the bat, I seemed to do somewhat better with a pen in my hand – to avoid complete humiliation, I'd put a couple of jokes in – and, when I nervously read it out, the other kids actually laughed. And laughed. And while in retrospect I found out that this may partly have been because my flies were, in fact, undone, hearing that kind of response to something I'd written was addictive. It was there and then I decided I was going to be a writer. And a comedy writer, at that.

But, while it took me 14 years to realise what I wanted to do with my life, once I'd actually left school, it took me a further 14 years to sit down and do anything about it. Life kind of got in the way. And, while it was all good material, I suppose, it wasn't until my mid-thirties, when I'd decided to take a sabbatical (or, to put it another way, was sacked) from my job as a head-hunter that I decided the time was right to, er, write.

The traditional route I'd planned to take – that of the struggling writer bashing away on an old typewriter in a draughty garret – wasn't quite the way it turned out, particularly when a friend offered me the loan of his villa on the Costa del Sol for three months. As three months turned into two years, the only thing I suffered for my art was sunburn. But eventually, finally, the novel was finished, and I duly printed it out and sent it off to a few agents.

After the usual thousand or so rejections, I finally convinced one that I was worth a shot, and after incorporating some of his editorial suggestions, or 'rewriting the whole thing', as I preferred to call it, it seemed that we had a bite: a publisher wanted to meet with me.

'What for?' I asked naively. 'To check I'm not a mad recluse, and don't look like the elephant man?'

'Pretty much,' replied my agent.

In a state of nervous excitement, I ironed my cravat, practised my air-kissing and headed off to London to see them. The meeting seemed to go well – they praised my book, and seemed to like me, so of course I *loved* them – and they promised to get back to me with a decision the following day.

I spent that night in a state of anxiety that even copious amounts of alcohol couldn't dull, unable to sleep, willing what could turn out to be either the best or the worst day of my life to arrive. For every would-be author, being on the verge of a publishing contract represents everything you've ever worked towards. Would that dread of being woken up by that nightmare thud of another rejected manuscript dropping on to the doormat finally be gone? I didn't dare to hope.

The following morning, I found myself wandering nervously up and down Oxford Street, glancing at my phone every 30 seconds to check I hadn't missed the call. And I was in Selfridges – torn between gazing at the shelf in the book department where my novel would hopefully go, and drooling at the flat-screen televisions, wondering which one I'd be able to buy with my advance – when my mobile finally rang.

'Congratulations,' said my agent. 'It's a "yes". You're going to be a published author.'

Never before, apart from perhaps with my first proper girlfriend, had the word 'yes' been so significant. All I could do was make like a goldfish, my mouth flapping open and shut silently, while my agent outlined the terms of the offer, which quite frankly I'd have accepted even if they'd asked for the donation of my vital organs in return.

'I'm having lunch with one of the editors from Granta, and Pierre's joining us,' he continued. 'Why don't you come over and meet us for a celebratory drink?'

One of the editors from Granta – only the most famous literary magazine in the world! And *Pierre*? Surely not *DBC Pierre*, another of my agent's clients, who had literally – in both senses of the word – just won the Booker Prize? Was this how my life was going to be now – an endless whirl of lunches with the literati? I mutely nodded my agreement – a pretty pointless gesture down a phone line – then ran out of the store, flagged down a cab and headed off to join them.

And that's how I came to find myself, half an hour later, sitting with my agent – a phrase I still take a childish delight in using – drinking champagne in one of London's most exclusive literary establishments, with an editor from Granta next to me at the table, a Booker Prize winner topping up my glass, and even a dog called Heathcliffe at my feet. But it wasn't until my agent stood up and proposed a toast, and the whole table joined in with the congratulations, that the reality of my situation finally sank in. I *was* going to be a published author. The thing I'd dreamed about since the age of 14 was actually going to happen, and soon my first novel, *Best Man*, would be there, fighting for space on the 3-for-2 table. As I rose to my feet to acknowledge their good wishes, I glanced down surreptitiously, and was pleased to note that this time, my flies were in fact done up. It surely was the best day of my life.

Richard Dunwoody

Champion Jockey

It was a Saturday in March in 1984. I'd been an amateur jockey riding over fences for just over a year. I'd had a few rides with a bit of success; four winners in my first season but progress was slow. Then, at the end of February I had a fall and was concussed which meant I was signed off for a week. During the time I was signed off, Hywel Davies, the main jockey at our yard, had a serious fall at Doncaster. He had very bad concussion and actually stopped breathing on the way to the hospital but they revived him, and he ended up having three weeks off.

While he was out I was given the rides on some of his horses. At a Saturday meeting at Hereford, I rode three horses which he would have ridden and with a couple of amateur races I ended up with seven rides on the day – three for my main trainer and four for others.

All I remember from the Friday night before was the boss, Captain Tim Forster, coming round for a chat. I was in the stables on 15 quid a week, and most of my time was spent grooming and mucking out the horses. I would muck out three in the morning, perhaps ride out three then go to the races and then back to the yard. That Friday night, the captain asked me, 'How many rides have you got tomorrow?'

'Seven.'

'You won't get through them, you're useless, you're too weak, you'll really struggle to get through the day.'

He was a very good boss to me but he had a very dry and very sarcastic sense of humour.

When Saturday came, I got a lift to the races because I couldn't afford the petrol in my own car. I went with a good friend and fellow jockey called Brendan Powell, who's now a trainer, and off we went to Hereford for the day. I'd probably ridden out one or two horses before I left and had been up since 6 a.m. Gill Kermack, the assistant trainer, came with us to make sure the horses from Tim Forster's yard were tacked up properly and everything was in order.

I finished third in the first race then won the next. I then finished third in the third race before winning three in a row. In the last race I was beaten only by a neck. Had I won it would have been a five-timer, an incredible achievement for an amateur jockey. I was gutted at the time. But, even so, it was an amazing day. All the horses just jumped and galloped for me. Some of them never ever ran that sort of race again. It was one of those days when it all worked perfectly and confidence did everything. I was seeing a stride early, that is, my judgement for take-offs at the obstacles was really accurate and the horses were running for me. It was a brilliant day.

After that we went and had a Chinese at the Peking Dynasty in Oxford where we always used to go on a Saturday night. I had a few too many glasses of wine and Brendan drove Gill and I home.

So why was it such a great day? Well, it was to get me the ride on West Tip because Martin, the brother of West Tip's trainer, Michael Oliver, was there and he recommended me as a result of it. West Tip went on to give me my first Grand National winner in 1986 and, by riding West Tip, I got my job with David Nicholson which in turn lead to me being Champion Jockey. You could definitely say that day at Hereford was the start of it all. That day meant I was going to become a professional jockey. When you're an amateur jockey you can go one of two ways. You either stay amateur and possibly become a trainer in time or you prove your worth and become a professional. That was the day when I finally knew I was going to become a professional jockey.

Mark Eccleston

Film Critic & TV Presenter

In September 2006, we bought one of the grottiest properties in London. A tired, terraced house that Shrek would have refused to live in.

The previous owners, Bill and Margaret, a red-faced couple in their sixties, had lived there all their married life. Although it had initially been her family home, over the decades Bill had turned the place into a museum to his hobbies, which included CB radio, car-boot sales, heavy drinking, DIY and vintage motorbikes. In the living room stood a tribute to the last three: a stripped-down bike engine that stood on a wonky homemade plinth.

Interior designers talk of picking a single décor theme which will 'tie' a property together. Bill and Margaret had gone for 'scary pub snug'. Downstairs was a series of dark musty rooms brightened up by a collection of bric-a-brac and humorous memorabilia – horseshoes, Guinness signs and a plaque that read 'Children passing this point will be eaten'. In the kitchen was a plate that featured a poem called 'A woman's place is in the kitchen'. For some reason a brass ship's wheel had been screwed on to a door.

And nothing seemed to work. Before we bought the place, we asked if there were any problems with the boiler. But Bill got all flustered and hustled us into another room. Now, plugging away at the pilot-light with the nagging feeling I could smell gas, it all made sense. A man with a number of qualifications in boilers was called. He shut down the gas supply and left. Perhaps he'd noticed the wiring.

No job, regardless of complexity, had been too big for Bill. He'd even had a go at rewiring the entire house – but like most things hadn't got round to finishing the project. In the living room a thick grey wire stuck out of the wall. Next to it he'd written 'Live. Danger' to avoid any mishaps. It was becoming clear that, with winter approaching, Bill and Margaret had decided to abandon ship in a hurry, leaving the brass wheel behind them.

Over the next three months, a selection of builders, plasterers, plumbers and tradesmen would set about renovating the house. Beams would be replaced, pipes would be ripped out and walls knocked down. Some of these jobs we'd asked to be done. Others were best seen as 'surprises'. Probably the worst of the bunch was a bloke called Pat, who was billed on the internet as a general tradesman. He certainly looked the part. A big burly character who drove up on the first day in a yellow Smart Car with his head poking out of the sun-roof. And he had plenty of power tools in big black plastic suitcases. I'd become very interested in power tools by now, so it was all very impressive. Pat may have had the power tools, but also had big sausagey fingers and was unable to operate them with any subtlety. When he left in the evening I'd go around filling in extra holes in the wall or wiping grouting off the ceiling.

Initially a genial man, a low dark cloud began to settle over Pat. Over the weeks the house slowly wore him down. The toilet was his Waterloo. There'd been a slow leak in the outflow pipe, which, despite Bill having wrapped masking tape around the trouble spot, had been happily dripping away for years. The leak was directly above the work surfaces in the kitchen below. The image of Bill sitting upstairs reading *Motorbike Collector* magazine, while downstairs Margaret, knowing her place, rustles him up a sandwich still haunts me now. Pat ended up completely gutting the bathroom, shoring up the flooring and throwing out the bath, sink and toilet – curiously, a job that he chose for Friday afternoon. We'd been living in the house as work went on and now our only toilet had been relocated to the front garden.

To be fair, there were a couple of good tradesman though. An electrician neighbour of ours who was originally from Poland. He'd pull the builders up for any shortcuts they'd made, cornering them with some ripe Polish phrases. Then there was an Albanian plasterer who'd end the day entirely covered in plaster, except his eyeballs, but the stuff that did end up on the walls was as smooth as glass.

The work progressed slowly and the bills racked up. The largest of them for sugar. But eventually the builders began to pack up tools, some of them mine, and head off. The house had revealed itself to be handsome in its own way, with a solid roof, and a sense of beginning. We were expecting twins in a couple of months. This would be a home, and the trials of its making forgotten.

Shutting the door on the last of the workmen. Then hugging each other. Now that was the best day of my life.

Jenni Falconer

TV Presenter

L ife is too short to wear ugly shoes – this has always been my motto, but sadly the cost of a truly fabulous pair of six-inch stilettos is far too great to warrant abiding by this mission statement. So, despite the fact that I always felt influenced by *Sex and the City*'s Carrie Bradshaw – who has the greatest array of designer footwear known to womankind – I could never practise what she preaches that shoes take priority over food, rent and practicality – and sometimes even men.

Tom Hanks, in *Forrest Gump*, said, 'Mama always said you could tell an awful lot about a person by the kind of shoes they wear,' and this is the reason I spent years longing for a pair of Christian Louboutins. These shoes are not something you simply wears on your feet, instead they are a passion, a personal statement, a source of authority, sexual independence and joy. They are the Aston Martin of the shoe world, the jewel in the footwear crown, the ultimate fashion statement, and, no matter how fat or miserable you feel, wearing Louboutins is supposed to wipe any misery from an insecure female mind and quite simply make you feel fantastic.

The only problem is the price tag. These shoes don't come cheap. So, I spent time saving – putting a pound aside on a daily basis, because, unlike the aforementioned Carrie Bradshaw, I was 21 and couldn't justify missing a month's rent on account of my shoe obsession. Besides, they say, the longer you lust after something, the longer you'll appreciate it once you have your hands on it, or in this case them – the six-inch, black leather, red-soled, pointed-toed wonders. For me, I would be lusting for 400 days.

The man himself, Mr Louboutin, is a foot saviour from Paris who takes pride in making a woman look and feel incredibly sexy in a pair of skyscraper heels. His designs are beautiful – with the magic lying in the position of the arch. The soles are red, giving the illusion that you are an A-lister walking along a red carpet. They are supposed to make you feel sophisticated, graceful and help you strut in a way that will drive men wild.

The days passed slowly, but eventually the time came and I was more than ready. I headed into town knowing that on this occasion, instead of browsing, I would be buying. The excitement was intense, I had really waited for this moment for so long. I had dreamed about walking in my very own Louboutins and the dream was about to become a reality … this was without doubt going to be the best day of my life.

On opening the box, I half-expected a chorus of angels singing and a shaft of golden light to come spilling out. There they were, highly polished, gleaming as a result of the sun shining through the window or possibly just the overhead fluorescent store lighting. They truly were magnificent – almost pieces of art. Now came my Cinderella moment – trying them on. My prince – who sadly just happened to be a French sales assistant called Nicole, rather than a swashbuckling hero – placed the shoes on my feet. They were obviously destined to be mine as the fit was perfect.

I stood up to wander to the mirror – I wish in this part I could say I glided elegantly, but, having never worn heels of this vast height previously, balance was an issue. In an attempt to look confident at my tallest ever – in these shoes I was well over six foot – I simply stood swaying and made the executive decision to admire the shoe from afar knowing that, with a spot of practice, walking would get easier. Besides, walking was not the point – owning a pair of killer heels was.

I left the shop, bag in hand, a beaming smile stretching from one cheek to the other, desperate to get home to reopen the box to look again in awe at my purchase. At this point I knew my life was complete … at least until I got my hands on the next pair.

Georgina Fienberg and Mama Laadi

Founder & Director of Children's Charity AfriKids

I awake slowly with the sense that I'm not alone in the room any more. Sure enough, as I squint into the gathering light of the African morning, a little head has popped round the door. I'm not surprised that it's Gifty, once again grinning from ear to ear, apparently thoroughly pleased to have just declared herself off school for the day, and yet with just a hint of trepidation about how I might react to this unilateral decision. I tell her off without being able to suppress a smile – safe in the knowledge that her freedom will only last until one of her 20 elder 'sisters' finds her and sends her in no uncertain terms towards school.

Mama Laadi's remarkable foster home in Northern Ghana has created a close and caring family of more than 50 from children in desperate need of help. It's an atmosphere of smiles, laughter and dancing and, even though most of the children have long since departed on their long journey to school, you can almost feel the sense of community and happiness in the unusual quiet that follows the great school departure. Sure enough, my breakfast is there waiting as usual. I've never seen Mama Laadi sleep; every evening she is tending to the needs of a handful of newborn babies and any other child that wants her attention; and yet with effortless grace the entire place runs like clockwork. At 7 a.m. she is already off for her daily chores, but not before seeing her kids off and making sure her visitors have everything they need.

Thomas, a major donor who has come to see the projects he has funded in action, also thinks this is a 'jolly good show', as he hungrily wolfs down an omelette and some Laughing Cow on toast. Brushing aside his lack of sleep in the stifling heat, he is all fired up and ready to go and 'see what there is to see, make sure we get it all done'!

Outside in the courtyard, Dramani, our driver, locally referred to as the Minister of Transport, stands proudly next to our slightly battered but perfectly polished truck. Ayingura, an extremely cheeky four-year-old, is 'driving' and predictably I find Gifty curled up under the tarpaulin in the back. Our country director, Nich, manages to detach her as she giggles uncontrollably, peeling each of her fingers off in turn.

Fifteen minutes later, we're rattling down the Sirigu road, the deep-red earth kicking up against the back of the truck spraying a fine copper mist across the right side of my face that no amount of wet wipes can remove.

We head off to a local rural village, where one of our project managers, Joe, is busy overseeing construction of a new community centre. Thomas is transfixed by the harsh and yet compelling rural African countryside – lush green vegetation delicately perched on unforgiving desert which is about to consume it; tiny children without clothes, smiling and playing; old men simply sitting and watching us pass with an expression that confirms we can never understand this place like the people who will live and die here over countless generations.

Thomas is looking very much the part in functional yet stylish khaki gear, and in his enthusiastic melee cannot decide whether to grab his camera, phone, binoculars or digicam. He'll soon know that none of them is necessary.

We meet Joe, proudly perched on his motorcycle, who leads us the rest of the way into the village, and as he does so a beautiful teenage girl jumps on the back of his bike; it's only when we all reach town that we realise who she is.

One year ago, we were alerted to the terrible plight of a young girl who had been cooking in her compound when a freak gust of wind disturbed her fire and set her alight. We found her in the regional hospital where she and her mother waited patiently for five months hoping and praying that she would recover. Covered in 60 per cent burns Asokipala Atingabono existed with the help of a straw fan, some painkillers and two very kind nurses. She has no father so her family relied on the support of neighbours to help them get by. In the oppressive humidity, her skin was seeping and bleeding, and her elbow had been fused at 90 degrees. She couldn't lie down and was in excruciating pain, and yet, when we found her, she was smiling. Emergency donations from the UK, including from Thomas, had ensured she had extensive hospital treatment in a Kumasi hospital shortly afterwards. Her treatment lasted 11 months, and involved numerous operations and skin grafts; and when she eventually left the hospital staff were in tears to lose their beautiful patient who had never once stopped smiling and laughing despite her almost unimaginable trauma.

And so suddenly and unexpectedly, Thomas was face to face with Asokipala, no longer the bandage-clad patient who inspired winces of sympathy, but a beautiful young woman with her life ahead of her. Her smile and demeanour are enchanting, and Thomas was lost for words for the only time I've known him to be. He took her hand and hugged her, and listened to her story as we sat under a mango tree in their compound.

For the rest of the day, Thomas was deeply pensive and clearly affected by what he'd seen. And as the unique and inexplicable scenes of African rural life passed him by that day, he never once reached for his camera. I think he'd come to realise what I had realised when I first came here – that, for all the wonderful photos you can take of a place like this, it's the inspiring, mysterious and dramatic encounters with the people which end up being all you ever need to take away with you.

And I remember clearly the effect it had on me; seeing yet another person realise that; it's why I remember that day.

Mama Laadi Awuni, who is mentioned in the previous story, is 36. She runs Mama Laadi's Foster Home in Bolgatanga, northern Ghana, where she cares for 50 abandoned and orphaned children. In her lifetime she has cared for over 250 of Ghana's most vulnerable children.

I was 16 years old and living on the streets of Bolgatanga, in the impoverished Upper East region of Ghana in West Africa. My parents couldn't afford to keep me or send me to school, so I slept under a market stall at night and worked at whatever I could during the day to raise the money to pay my school fees.

After being unable to afford the fees for three months, I was asked to leave school. I despaired at the thought of never sitting in a classroom again and asked God why he had forsaken me. Then, about two hours later, two pupils came and told me that the headmistress, Madeleine Ayamga, wanted to see me. She offered to fund my entire education, including polytechnic; which included paying for school fees, school uniforms, school shoes, books, pens, everything. I didn't know how to thank her.

As I returned home, full of joy but weak from hunger, I fell on the road. Some people came to help me and, because they were worried about my condition, took me to the local Catholic convent where the nuns showered me with their generosity. They fed me and even invited me to return to eat with them every day. I also met a priest, who offered me a job washing clothes so that I would have some money to help keep myself. I couldn't believe my good fortune. I was so grateful.

As I left the convent with a friend, we met a Dutch nurse named Sister Gerdie. She stopped and asked me where I was going, but it was the first time I'd met a white lady and I was afraid. My friend told me not to fear, that she looked after people, even those who did not have money to pay for medicines. Sister Gerdie wanted us to go to her house but I said I wouldn't go unless Madam Ayamga said it was OK. Surprisingly, she came to our school to seek permission. Sister Gerdie's interest in us gained my friend and I respect within the school. Once at her house she gave us each two yards of material to make a dress. It was the first time I had a new dress.

This day was the beginning of all things good in my life. On that very day I decided I would devote myself to helping others. I went to polytechnic to study nutrition and childcare and worked with Sister Gerdie in the villages, advising mothers about how to feed their children properly with the food available to them.

In 2000, Sister Gerdie was transferred to another part of Ghana. Soon after, the villagers started bringing beggars and street children to me for help. I used every penny of my salary to buy food and medicine for them because I couldn't bear to see others suffering – I knew what it was like to live and breathe poverty. I forfeited my own meals and numbed my hunger by drinking a spoonful of flour mixed with a glass full of water every evening before I slept. What I couldn't pay for I stole, because I had to do whatever I could to keep them alive. The debts mounted and I wanted freedom.

Freedom eventually came in the form of an AfriKids' volunteer named Claire. Within four hours of meeting me and the 12 children I was caring for, she brought us a bag of corn, a bag of rice, yams and fish. We had never seen such food before. Since that day, none of us has stolen food for our family. Last June, AfriKids built us a house. I now care for 50 children and am able to provide good food, medical care and a safe, loving home for them to grow up in. It is still a dream to me.

Without doubt the happiest day of my life was the day Madam Ayamga made possible the education that led to my work with children. There is a phrase I say so often that people have made it my nickname: 'Wonders never end.' They are still happening today.

Liz Fuller

5TV Presenter

I recently decided to do something very different for this New Year. I longed to seek out the less privileged and those in dire need. I travelled to India, searching out three orphanages in Delhi, and I visited all of them in one day.

The first two were in a slum area which was an eye-opener, most of the community had not seen a blue-eyed blonde walk through these back streets, and despite this I felt really safe. I learned that many of the extreme poor in India accept their lot and do not have jealousy in them towards the wealthy, so unusual and different to the Western world and culture where we are full of aspiration and hunger for achievement, and are often not happy for those successful. However, my first experience was not pleasant, I got the feeling my gifts would not get to the children and had the suspicion it was more of a struggle for survival for the people running the orphanage as well as the kids.

The final place I visited was the Asharan orphanage and – wow! What a fabulous job the couple do by running it. It's like a big extension to their own family, I got to spend three hours with roughly 20 kids ranging from an abandoned baby of two weeks to a fluent English-speaking girl aged 10. After turning up with a Santa sack full of Woolworth goodies, we blew up balloons, ate chocolates and laughed a lot; I really was like a big kid joining them. They got to practise their English and I in return fully appreciated their innocence and how fragile life is. Being able to see smiles on children with no family to love them was so touching.

In the West, we are often too hung up on driving the latest car and longing for the most desirable handbag, but this isn't what life is about. Spending my day seeking out those who have started life in a less privileged way has turned out to be the most meaningful day of my life.

Mike Gayle

Author

'**M**ate?' says my friend John, turning towards me.
'Yeah?'

'This is the best thing ever, isn't it?'

I look around at the rest of our friends all laughing and joking and then I glance across at the girls sitting a few yards from us and smile. 'Yeah. This is the best thing ever.'

It's late on a hot and sunny Sunday afternoon in August, I'm 17 years old and I'm on holiday in Guernsey with John, Mick, Rodney and Si, my best mates in the whole wide world. It's actually a camping holiday that has been organised by the comprehensive we all used to go to, together with the nearby girls' school. The holiday has taken place every summer for the last decade or so – roughly a hundred or so pupils from across the school years, all living out of tents in a field in the Parish of St Pierre du Bois. The boys and I had all gone the year before (the summer after our O levels) and had the time of our lives, and so when we heard that we could go again (even though most of my mates were in the world of work by this time) we were there like a shot. What could be better than a dirt-cheap holiday in the sun with your mates even if there were rules and teachers? The important thing was we'd rule the roost. There would be no one bigger. No one better.

We would be it. We paid our deposits in a flash and then just counted down the days until we were ready to go.

The holiday is everything we hoped it would be and more. Days hanging out at the beach, nights hanging out at the Golden Monkey (St Peter Port's only nightclub), a couple of altercations with local youths swiftly sorted out with the minimum of force, a day of impromptu bike riding around the island, a number of late-night bonfires on the beach, a modicum of illicit drinking and more girl-chasing escapades than you could shake a stick at.

But on the Sunday on the second week of our holiday we do something we've never done before: we do absolutely nothing at all.

The day starts, as usual, quite late, given that we were out at the Golden Monkey last night. We slope down to the main tent for breakfast but don't bother with plates as all we need are two slices of bread each and something to put in between them. We eat our bacon butties on the way back to the tent and then when we reach our destination pull our sleeping bags out of the tents and lie down and doze in the sun.

Our female counterparts (a mixture of sixth-formers and fifth-years) come over and ask us to come down to the beach or into town. Some of these girls are my friends' girlfriends, some are girls that the single among us have been working on the whole holiday and some are just friends. Every single one of them is young and beautiful and almost impossible to turn down and yet without any consultation we unanimously do just that. It's as though we are all feeling the same thing at the same time. It's as if we all know that there are a finite number of days left in our lives when we can sit and do nothing at all except hang out with our mates.

The girls choose to stay and the best day begins.

We lie down in the sun, eat ice cream brought by the girls, make stupid jokes that we think are the height of hilarity, attempt to build a human pyramid, offer younger kids cash bonuses to run our errands, make plans for the evening ahead, talk about our plans for the future, laugh until we literally think we're going to be sick and sing our hearts out to Si's U2, Cure and Smiths tapes but most of all what we do is nothing. We do nothing and we love it. We do nothing and we appreciate every moment of our youth.

And it's during one of these long moments of nothing (just after we've finished singing along to U2 but before we start singing along to The Smiths) that my mate John turns to me. 'Mate?'

'Yeah?'

'This is the best thing ever, isn't it?'

And I look around at the rest of our friends all laughing and joking and then I glance across at the girls sitting a few yards from us and smile. 'Yeah. This really is the best thing ever.'

Jacqueline Gold

Businesswoman

Little did I think 25 years ago when I first set up Ann Summers that I would one day be sipping champagne with the Queen in recognition of my achievements as a businesswoman.

I was thrilled when the gold-trimmed invitation landed unexpectedly on my desk inviting me to an exclusive reception for women in business hosted by Her Majesty at Buckingham Palace. The first person I excitedly called with the news was my father David Gold, who was over the moon for me.

Then my thoughts turned to more important matters – what to wear to the party which was just two weeks away on Valentine's Day 2007. Although it was a daytime event, I wanted to be glamorous and feel special, so I treated myself to a beautiful bespoke Ben de Lisi dress, in indigo-coloured chiffon.

In the days leading up to it, the press made a big fuss about the boss of Ann Summers being invited into the royal fold. I suppose the palace were quite brave to have included me but I would have been immensely disappointed if they hadn't. On the day itself, I went to the hairdressers, changed into my beautiful new dress and went off to the palace, where many of the 200 women invited were already arriving.

Once inside, there was a buzz of excitement as we were given champagne. I chatted to Birmingham FC managing director Karren Brady, interior designer Kelly Hoppen and *X Factor* judge Sharon Osbourne – so it was great networking. We were then ushered into a queue and shown how to curtsey when meeting our royal hosts. As I got to the front I could see there was the Queen, Princess Anne, Camilla Parker Bowles, the Duchess of Cornwall and Sophie, the Duchess of Wessex – obviously in pecking order.

I shook hands with the Queen. She took one look at my name badge and I could see she immediately knew exactly who I was because she had a twinkle in her eye and her body language changed as if to say, 'Next!' I was disappointed but thought, I am not going anywhere! So we had a chat about how great I thought the event was and how nice it was for women to be recognised for their contribution to business.

A less confident person would have moved on and, although I didn't, I wish I had talked to her more about Ann Summers because I am very proud of what I do. I don't mean to be immodest but I took a business aimed at the seedy, dirty-mac brigade and transformed it into a female-friendly company. I employ 10,000 people – most of them women. In 1979, there were four stores, now there are 135 across the country. I have tried to portray sex in a positive, fun way and to create an environment where women feel comfortable and now turnover is £156 million a year.

I then moved to Princess Anne, who was very well informed – perhaps because her daughter Zara Phillips has been to an Ann Summers party!

I said, 'I think this event is fantastic and hopefully will help inspire women to go into business.'

And she replied, 'Oh we won't be doing this every year, you know!' which seemed a little curt!

It was Camilla that I really warmed to – we had a lovely chat. At the time they were showing *The Verdict* on the BBC, a show in which

I was one of 12 celebrity jurors presiding over a real trial. The first thing she said to me was: 'I'm loving *The Verdict*; it is compelling viewing – although I am not sure who all the people are.'

I was thrilled she was a fan.

Then she said, 'Can you tell me what the outcome is?'

'Well, I am not supposed to because we have all signed confidentiality agreements!' I replied.

But she begged me: 'Please, I promise not to tell anyone.'

So I decided I could trust her and we had a really good giggle about it.

She was so refreshing, I really did like her. She is definitely very down-to-earth and more in touch than the rest of the royal family. She is just what the monarchy needs and I would definitely like to see her become Queen one day. I had my picture taken with her and I have it displayed on my mantelpiece at home.

I was on such a high when the event was over I didn't want to go home, so a girlfriend and I went for a drink and a meal together. The day made me recall fondly how Ann Summers, as it is known now, all started when I was 21. I got the idea after going to a Tupperware party. The women there knew I was doing work experience at Ann Summers, which was my father's company. They said they would love to be able to wear sexy underwear but didn't want to go into a seedy sex shop. That's when I had the idea for Ann Summers parties.

I think my father was worried about being accused of nepotism so he insisted I present my idea to the all-male board and convince them myself. I remember one board member saying to me, 'This isn't going to work, women aren't interested in sex.'

That said more about his sex life than it did about my idea!

Despite being very nervous and inexperienced, I felt passionate about it and did manage to persuade them to allow me to give it a go. And I am thankful for that because it gave me the chance to experience what will always be my happiest and most memorable day.

Phil Greening

Former England Rugby Player

Growing up in Gloucester, I hung around mostly with kids who went to the same school as me. My school was a … well, let's just say it was not particularly high up in the social-status rankings. My school was the place you were sent to if you got expelled from somewhere else. That kind of place.

Even though it was a bit rough, I absolutely loved my school and all the people in it. Pretty quickly I fell into a group of people who loved to fight and play up. In the group was a guy called Jermaine – or Ja as we called him – and we became great friends. We used to steal, fight, bully – you name it, we were into it and pretty much ran the place.

At 15, one of our pals' dads' invited me and Ja to play rugby. We thought we were tough men and he thought it might keep us out of trouble. He was right, we enjoyed it and I found myself loving it more and more every time I played. But still we continued to get into trouble and be lads about town.

Then one day I was asked to represent the county. My rugby career was taking off – Gloucester Rugby Club, one of the best teams in the country, had already shown an interest in me. But on the same day, Ja got arrested for GBH. It was then I realised I needed to make a choice. On the one hand, I had my friends telling me, 'Forget rugby, it's rubbish. Come and hang around with us,' and, as I began spending more time on rugby, that became: 'Are you with us or not?' I knew rugby was driving me and my mates apart, but, on the other hand, a major club had asked me to play for them. It was so tough. I was torn between my friends and a sport!

One day, me and Ja were in a friend's car going through town in mid-afternoon when he spotted a rival gang's car. There was a guy in the car who owed him money so a car chase ensued. Eventually, the car got stopped in the middle of town, right across a very busy street lined with shops and loads of people all around. Ja jumped out of the car and dragged the driver out of his seat and started hitting him. Then Ja got into the car and battered this guy. While he was battering him, Ja was shouting to our other friend to get me out of there as he didn't want me to be caught by the police who we knew would be there in a few minutes. Ja knew I was different and could get away from all this shit but he couldn't. It was his job for life.

The next day I decided to sign and play for Gloucester and I turned my back on that part of my life. Friends kept hassling me but I had to be strong and better myself. I didn't want to end up in prison or on that slippery slope for life. I wanted to be someone. I still kept in contact with Ja, and while playing on my league debut a year or two later I spotted all the gang in the corner watching. They'd all come to see me play! I was so chuffed.

Three years later I was selected to represent my country at the highest level. On the day which was to become the best day of my life – the day I won my first cap – I found a letter left in my room addressed to me. It was from Ja. A note wishing me luck. It was written on paper with the heading HMP – Her Majesty's Prison. Ja had been locked up. In the letter he said I had made the best decision of my life leaving all that behind and he wished he'd had the strength to do the same.

The emotions that were going through me that day were incredible: pride, fear, excitement, exhilaration, doubt – you name it, I felt it. As I walked out at Twickenham to hear 75,000 people roar, I couldn't have been happier or prouder. The roar was deafening, like nothing I have experienced before. I was the proudest Englishman in the world. I sang the national anthem with everything I had, tears streaming down my face as I stood there so proud.

The game itself was a blur in my memory. It all happened so quickly. Apparently, that's common in your first one. After the game the exhilaration and happiness that came over me was just mind-blowing. To have played with the legends in that room, even just to be in that room, was unbelievable. That night was the best I have ever had, even though I got so drunk I can't remember it.

But what I can remember is the day I made the decision to make something of myself. Not to listen to peers or blame others for not being able to change just because there is no chance for them. I knew that, unless I accepted responsibility for myself and my future, I'd be the one writing letters with HMP at the top.

Zoe Griffin

Journalist

The day you get a kiss from *The Pirates of the Caribbean* heartthrob Orlando Bloom has to be a pretty good one. On 25 February 2007 – the day of the 79th Annual Academy Awards – I also got winked at by George Clooney, tapped on the arm by Leonardo DiCaprio, had a chat with Penelope Cruz, lunched with Courtney Cox and Jennifer Aniston and got a free Mulberry handbag.

I woke up in a sumptuous, fluffy white bed at the Beverly Hilton and felt like a princess. All I had to do to open the windows was push a button by the side of my bed and the blinds rolled back.

I had a great view of the hotel pool. Sunlight was reflecting off the water and I had to blink to stop myself crying. I was so overwhelmed. How did a Hemel Hempstead girl like me, whose childhood involved fighting with my brother and sister for living space in our cramped three-bedroom semi, end up getting invited to the Oscars and staying in a four-star LA hotel? I wished I could have brought my mum and dad and friends from back home to share the experience.

Dad would have loved the gigantic room-service menu. Did I go for the buttermilk pancakes with maple syrup? Or push the boat out for a platter of corned beef hash, eggs, sausage links and fried bread? No – I am proud to say that I did breakfast LA style and had a virtuous egg-white omelette and a fresh fruit salad. (Just to make sure I had a chance of squeezing into my skin-tight Oscars dress.)

Breakfast over, I wrapped myself in a soft, white towelling robe and sauntered down to the spa. I was told Keira Knightley, Nicole Kidman, Oprah Winfrey and Angelina Jolie had all used it when they stayed at the hotel. My brief from the *Sunday Mirror*, where I was a showbiz columnist, was to live and breathe the whole Oscars experience. If Keira started the day with a facial, then Zoe could too.

It was one of the best facials of my life. The beauty therapist made sure I was thoroughly exfoliated, cleansed and moisturised, and then brought out something that looked like a vacuum cleaner. She said it was an 'oxygen machine', which blew out air rather than sucked it in. The therapist held the pipe over the left of my forehead for three minutes then moved it to the right before starting on my cheeks. After half-an-hour, I was buzzing.

The designer handbag brand Mulberry had invited me to a pre-Oscars lunch at an LA branch of the celebrity members club Soho House. I was worried about accepting the invitation because fashion parties are often full of the label's best customers – a bunch of skinny, blonde, snobby women – and thin on the ground in terms of celebrities. But my fears were allayed the moment I walked into the wood-panelled dining room of Soho House.

The lunch was for 20 people and five of them were famous. *Friends* stars Courtney Cox and Jennifer Aniston were at one end of the long rectangular table, *Dream Girls* actress Jennifer Hudson was at the other and *OC* star Mischa Barton was opposite Brooke Shields in the middle of the melee.

One of the Mulberry PRs introduced me to Brooke, who very kindly invited me to sit next to her for the lunch. Over a delicious meal of sea bass and steamed vegetables followed by a tangy lemon sorbet, Brooke told me she was moving to Canada to star in a new television series.

I was relieved to get a story in the bag before the Oscars ceremony had started, but there was a slight moment of panic when another Mulberry PR tapped me on the shoulder as I was leaving the dining room. Sometimes PRs can be quite controlling about events and I feared she was going to ask me what I was writing.

'You have to come back for a second,' she demanded. 'You can pick a free handbag.'

I was back in that room quicker than a fat kid chasing a Smartie.

'Have you been in Delta Airlines' room yet?' she asked. 'They're giving away free air miles.'

For a moment, I felt slightly guilty. I had already blagged designer clothes to wear to the ceremony, I'd travelled first class to LA, stayed in a beautiful hotel and I was about to have the evening of my life. Did I need any more free stuff?

Probably not, but I ended up pocketing 4,000 Delta air miles, a couple of pairs of Pussy Glamore lacy lingerie sets, a few boxes of Godiva chocolates and some Cowshed shower gel, moisturiser and massage oil.

I also got more stories. I visited the MAC cosmetics room and was invited to have a makeover. The make-up artist who saw to me had been at Jennifer Lopez's house earlier that day. He told me that Jennifer and her husband Marc Anthony were talking about doing a duet together.

I must have had a guardian angel watching over me, as I also managed to corner Penelope Cruz in the ladies. I was checking out my new smoky grey eye shadow and glamorous red lipstick in the bathroom mirror, when I saw that the *Volver* actress was standing next to me. I knew she had split from her then boyfriend Matthew McConaughey a few months before, and the *Sunday Mirror* would have wanted me to ask about it. I was amazed by how open she was, as she told me her job made it difficult to have a relationship. It was the first time Penelope had spoken so freely about her love life.

Jake Meyer waving a Union Jack at the summit of Mount Everest.

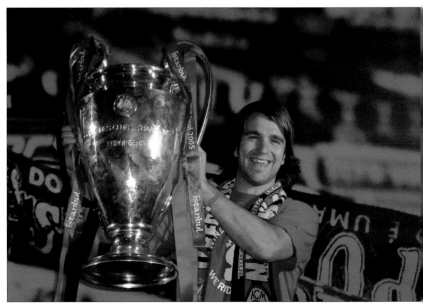

Above: Dan Rookwood holding the European Cup – three hours before it was presented to Liverpool captain Steven Gerrard in Istanbul, on 25 May 2005.

Below left: Ann Daniels in the Arctic.

Below right: James Crossley as Hunter the Gladiator.

Above left: Georgina Harland with the Olympic bronze medal she won in Athens, 2004.

Above right: Steve Kemsley as the voice of Wembley.

Below: James Haskell singing the National Anthem before his England debut.

Above: Lara and Noah Agnew on his first birthday, 24 June 2008.

Below: Orphan with face painted like a dog by Clare Wigfall.

Above: Mama Laadi with some of her adopted children.

Below: John Broome CBE with Kylie Minogue.

Above: Sharon Marshall and Morten Harket.

Copyright © Jules Annan.

Below left: Tracey Cox.

Below right: Lauren Henderson.

Above: Natalie Pinkham, Jarrod Cunningham and his wife Carrie at the Jarrod Cunningham SALSA Fashion Show on 17 March 2004.

Below left: Lucie Cave.

Below right: Stella Duffy on the left in green shoes, Shelley Silas in red shoes.

Above: Ben Anderson with gorilla.

Below: Paola dos Santos with orphans and street children in Nicaragua.

The only thing that could have made 25 February 2007 better was if I had tickets to watch the ceremony inside LA's Kodak Theatre. Instead, I stood on the edge of the red carpet with hundreds of other journalists. I had made an effort to dress up for the occasion in a skin-tight, sparkly gown from Ben de Lisi's couture range and I felt like Cinderella as the nominees, presenters and their plus ones sauntered past me.

However, it was a million times better than waiting on a red carpet in rainy London. I've reported on lots of Leicester Square premieres and you're lucky if you get one or two Hollywood actors.

At the Oscars, the first person I saw was gorgeous George Clooney. He was tall, toned and utterly charming. I asked him if he was still single and he winked at me. He said he was too busy with work and told me about some of his newest film ideas.

I also got a story from Leonardo DiCaprio. He said he had taken his mum as his date. I said he should have taken me and he tapped me on the arm in a playful way.

'Maybe next year?' I asked hopefully.

He grinned and walked away, but at least it wasn't a 'no'.

I got some quotes from Arnold Schwarzenegger and Jennifer Hudson. Arnie said, 'I'll Never Be Back,' when I asked if he was going to do another *Terminator* film. Jennifer, who later won an Oscar for Best Supporting Actress, said she had Burger King to thank for her success. She said working at Burger King was the kick she needed to make something of her life.

I watched Nicole Kidman walk down the red carpet on her own. She had got married to Keith Urban a few weeks earlier, so I reported it was strange that he wasn't by her side on such a high-profile night.

When all the stars had walked the carpet, there were a couple of hours to kill before the after-parties. I wanted to see who had won what so I went off with some other journalists to find a bar that was showing the awards. We toasted our hard work with a glass of champagne. I pushed the boat out and had a slap-up steak and chips meal – delicious.

But the highlight of the day came at Elton John's post-Oscars party. I was standing with some photographers on the red carpet; as yet again I didn't have tickets to go inside. Victoria and David Beckham walked up and I was less than a metre from the A-list couple. All the photographers were mesmerised by the Beckhams and nobody spotted a tall, rugged man with shoulder-length dark, wavy hair standing behind them. It was Orlando Bloom. The actor was too polite to walk behind the Beckhams and mess up the shots so he was shivering on the red carpet in the cold. I seized my opportunity, leaned over and squeezed his arm.

I couldn't believe it when he gave me a kiss on the cheek and said, 'Hi, gorgeous.'

Perhaps he thought I was somebody else, or perhaps he'd had a bit to drink. I didn't care – I had been kissed by Legolas from *Lord Of The Rings*.

After a day of getting pampered, getting free stuff and getting stories, I got a kiss from Orlando Bloom and instantly knew it was one of the best days of my life.

Ashley Hames

TV Presenter

It's not often that a day at the office can give you one of the best days of your life but the joy of working in television is that sometimes that can happen.

Up there with standing for parliament as Live TV's News Bunny, day one as the producer of *Topless Darts* and flying by helicopter over Sydney with Miss Nude Australia as the newly installed presenter of *Sin Cities* came the privilege of taking part in 2005's *Celebrity Poker Club*.

It's Thursday afternoon in a Cardiff studio and I'm about to become part of a tiny slice of poker history. I'm genuinely honoured. The cast of players includes Rodney Marsh, Dave Gorman, Johnny Vegas and rugby player Mike Tindall. Commentary is provided by Jesse May, the esteemed voice of poker, and last year's winner Victoria Coren who can be heard referring to comic Richard Herring as 'a small fish swimming through shark-infested waters'. Genius.

Poker is a game I adore, which I play regularly and that I have always loved watching on television. When *Late Night Poker* first appeared on Channel 4, the seed was sown.

I'm an obsessive, compulsive, addictive personality. I want life to be a reckless rollercoaster ride. I have attention deficit disorder and, just as fish need to swim in order to stay alive, I need action, risk, madness and unpredictability in order to function. That's what poker has and that's why it's perfect for me: no-limit Texas Hold 'Em was to become an occasional hobby, then a favourite pastime and now an expensive obsession.

When I arrive at Cardiff train station I find myself packed into a cab with Dr Raj Persaud – it turns out he's also playing in my heat. I feel slightly worried about playing poker with a psychotherapist. He looks at me strangely when I reveal that my previous jobs have included 'getting dressed up as a rabbit' and 'sort of presenting a kind of erotic show on cable TV'. I mentally chalk Raj up as a danger-man: he's already got me on the defensive.

We arrive at the studio where milling around backstage are Scottish football legend Ally McCoist, aristo-cad James Hewitt and Diet Coke enthusiast John McCririck. I'm interviewed by the presenter Helen Chamberlain and brazenly declare that 'I'm the only real celebrity here'. No one laughs and I'm beginning to feel nervous.

Round one begins – next to me is my old mate Dr Raj 'The Iceman' Persaud. Spencer from *Big Brother* is being told he has to scratch the Ray-Ban label off his shades as there can be no product placement. I love the cheap, paper-thin world of low-rent celebrity and I'm slap-bang in the middle of it. I can't stop smiling and I can't wait to begin.

Fast forward and I've made it into the final. As well as being a rank outsider in the fame stakes, resident bookie and former poker champ 'Mad' Marty Wilson has made me the field's underdog to take the prize. He writes me up as 6 to 1 – I persuade him to put me out to sevens and then immediately stick a tenner on myself to win.

As I'm interviewed beforehand, I mistakenly refer to ex-England cricketer Ed Giddens as Gittins. I apologise to him but I sense he's not happy. We've also been told to give ourselves a poker name – with due bravado I've chosen to call myself 'The Kamikaze'. Helen Chamberlain suggests that the high stakes and the pressure of the final table may inhibit me but I insist my fearless reputation will stand me in good stead. Commentator Vicky Coren appears to agree, describing me as 'an intrepid sex reporter who hangs out in crack dens and whore houses … he's not easily scared'.

There is some pressure though – 25 grand is up for grabs for whoever wins and I'm totally skint.

I become so immersed in the game all other thoughts are banished. With so many card combinations and unknown quantities, poker is a game that focuses you like no other. It's incredibly intense and no one's giving an inch.

The game is about six hours long now; there's five of us left and suddenly I've become chip leader. For those who don't know poker, that's kind of like being in heaven. I'm hot favourite for the bounty and my forthcoming unemployment is looking rosy.

But then, in several crucial moments, poker did what all great sports can do – it teaches you about yourself, in my case that I wasn't half as ballsy and reckless as I originally thought. Having set myself up as a fearless risk-taking kamikaze, I discovered I can also be a fairly conservative and frightened ex-public schoolboy. You guessed it, I limped out with a whimper, swearing quietly to myself.

Then it hits me. I suddenly realise that what I love about poker is exactly what I love about television – no matter how long you've been in the game, you'll never have it truly sussed.

Television and poker are like space – there's no finish line in sight. Both are endless and constantly evolving and at their best they perfectly combine technical excellence and creative flair. They are, in equal measure, both infuriating and exhilarating, with fortunes to be won and lost at the flick of a switch or the turn of a card. All this and more is what makes them so utterly compelling and brilliantly entertaining.

Along with sex, cigarettes and alcohol, television and poker are the true loves of my life. And this was the day they hopped into bed together and shagged for England. I feel like the baby conceived that day, and that's why it's the best day of my life.

Georgina Harland

Olympic Medallist Modern Pentathlon

Everyone dreads the ringing of an alarm at 5.30 a.m., but on 27 August 2004, it was a noise I had been eagerly awaiting for some time. Since I was an 11-year-old girl, in fact, I'd dreamed of competing at the Olympic Games; of following in the footsteps of the world's sporting heroes, on the greatest of all sporting stages. For so many, the Games remain just a dream, but, for me, in Athens, it was about to become a reality. This was a day I had thought about for so long, and now as I went through my normal competition preparations I found myself thinking about it again, and again.

Modern Pentathletes compete in five disciplines – shooting, fencing, swimming, riding and running – and it all has to take place in one day. So it was only a couple of hours later that I found myself walking out for the shooting event, into the largest competition arena I had ever experienced. Shooting is all about control, and I still felt controlled, still felt confident – I was consciously keeping my breathing steady to regulate my heart rate. I was suffering from an (all-too-familiar) sense of nausea but I forced myself to concentrate on the task in hand – and after a positive warm-up I felt prepared. But just as I released the first of my 20 competition shots the reality of where I was suddenly hit me, and was immediately followed by a rush of adrenaline. All the built-up nervous energy, excitement and tension that I had been containing for weeks escaped in a second; my heart was racing.

I could feel my whole body physically shaking each time my heart beat. There were only 20 seconds to bring it under control before I had to take the next shot – and it was too big a task. I was hoping to hit a centre 10 for my second shot, and I hit a three. My next two shots weren't much better; I knew then that my dream – of a gold medal – would probably have to wait for another day. But I knew too that I couldn't let the dream go completely; this was the Olympics. So I had to gain control again, had to do myself some sort of justice.

After the shooting, I was in 31st position out of 32. I slowly packed my bags. I wanted to go back and do it all again, but I couldn't. I had to move on and focus on the next event, the fencing.

In the fencing arena was a sea of home support: Union Jacks waving in the crowd, draped from the stands, painted on friendly faces. The crowd's incessant singing carried me through the next two events, the fencing and 200m freestyle swim. Their energy was electric and enabled me to put in two performances that moved me higher up the leader board, to 19th position, and on to the fourth event of the day, the showjumping.

This time, I wasn't going to let my emotions take control. There are 12 metre-high fences to clear – I had to focus on them and I had to relax. The horse wasn't allowed to know that this actually meant quite a lot to me! But once I entered the arena for my show-jumping round I became strangely unaware of my surroundings. In the stadium sat 10,000 people, but any noise from the crowd and all of their expectations of me vanished. My mind narrowed my focus, to the point that all I could hear was the horse's breathing. It was as if time stood still. It is a moment that will stay with me forever.

It was a demanding course, and with only two obstacles knocked down I had to be pleased with my round. But most importantly it moved me up to 14th position before the fifth and final event – my strongest – the 3000m cross-country run. The start of the run is handicapped, so that the leading competitor sets off first, followed by the competitor in second place, and so on – the delay between each competitor reflects the number of points between them. I found myself starting 50 seconds behind the competitor in third place, the first of the medal positions.

The Olympics gives something special to many people; to me, that day, it gave strength. I believed that anything was possible. As I left the start gate and began to chase down the athletes ahead of me I felt a surge of energy on every corner as British supporter after British supporter leaned over the barriers, shouting encouragement. It was suddenly only 800m to go and only two more girls stood between me and the podium. In those closing stages I searched for that last bit of energy to carry me forward and I recounted to myself the years of training I had done for this one day. I was not about to give that up and, with 500m to go, with a huge roar from the crowd, I moved into bronze position.

I knew silver was too far away but I was starting to falter. I had pushed myself beyond my body's natural limits; I had to hold on to that bronze position. I couldn't let my dream slip away now and as I crossed the finish line in third I raised my arms in celebration at what I had achieved. I remember looking instantly to the crowd for my family but they were lost among the sea of Union Jacks. This was not just my medal; it belonged to so many others, who had all been a part of what I had achieved. The day had been full of so many life-changing moments that when I was standing on the podium 15 minutes later I was just trying to take it in. It had been such a rollercoaster and had challenged every part of me both mentally and physically, and it had led me to despair a few times. But maybe that is what happens when a dream becomes real.

142

Kate Harrison

Author

It seems crazy now but, at the age of 18, I was desperate to earn my living. While my mates were visiting universities – and scouring the glossy prospectuses for top totty – I was counting the days until I could join the rat race.

Teenage hormones have a lot to answer for.

September came. My contemporaries were driven to all corners of the nation by their parents, with three years of fun ahead: getting pissed on snakebite, copping off with each other and attending the occasional lecture, all funded by full student grants. Meanwhile, I was making my first forays into the heady world of journalism.

I'd pictured myself as a fearless Watergate-style reporter (my hair even had an authentic Dustin Hoffman flick). But principled investigation wasn't quite what my new boss had in mind. He combined the crumpled look of a garden mole with the killer instincts of a rabid dog. I was on call 24/7: only ever a phone call away from being sent to doorstep a drug dealer or a naughty vicar. Whenever there was a dirty job to be done, I was there: fresh-faced and a little over five feet in my socks, I was simply less likely to be punched than my rufty-tufty male colleagues. A degree was irrelevant, though a black belt in karate might have come in handy.

After two long years, I defected to the BBC. Things were more civilised there: fewer doorsteps, more scruples. And, for the first time, I faced that tricky question: 'Where did you go to college?'

The textbook answer, of course, was Oxbridge. A redbrick university was just about acceptable, while a polytechnic, although beyond the pale, did at least show a certain pluck, an ability to pull yourself up by your bootstraps. But not to have a degree at all?

I quickly learned to change the subject.

However, the absence of letters after my name played on my mind. Going to uni as a semi-mature student wasn't tempting: I had a job most undergrads would kill for, and a mortgage on my first flat. And student grants had just been abolished. On a whim, I decided to try a course with the Open University. It looked like fun on *Educating Rita* …

When I read the small print, I couldn't quite believe it was going to take me six years to get my degree … but by that time I'd already paid. There was no student union bar named after Nelson Mandela, no crush on my lecturer (I never saw them) and definitely no grant. In place of a social life, my evenings were now filled with Criminology and Social History and Linguistics.

But what kept me going was the desire to wear a gown and have my family there to witness it – especially my grandfather, a former semi-pro singer who, at 86, could party for England. I specifically chose my final course, an oral-history project, to give me a reason to interview him on tape about his experiences as a soldier in World War II: I'd always felt his stories deserved their place in the archive.

In December 2001, I learned that I'd passed that last course, which meant I'd finally collected 360 points. And points mean degrees! I began to plan my graduation day – until a letter arrived from the OU saying that they'd changed the rules so that the journalism training I'd done no longer earned me points – so I'd have to study for a further year.

I'm not a believer in premonitions but something told me that I had to fight for my right to graduate. I composed a letter more important than any journalistic assignment. Eventually, the OU relented.

I chose the Royal Festival Hall on London's South Bank for my graduation ceremony: it seemed to embody the progressive principles of the people's university. My parents and sister travelled to London from Bristol, my granddad from Merseyside and my two closest friends also joined the party.

The enormous airport lounge-style floors of the Festival Hall were crammed with graduates of all ages, giggling like children as they queued for hired gowns. I know I wasn't the only one who felt disappointed that we didn't get mortar boards to go with them …

Next, we all posed for photos, with the same soft-focus background and the same stilted pose as all graduation photos adorning the mantelpieces of proud parents across the nation. Except the graduates clutching their fake scrolls at the Festival Hall had more grey hairs or laughter lines than the average 21-year-old.

The ceremony itself was both intimidatingly formal *and* moving, as we all took our moment on stage. I'd decided at an early stage in my studies that it wouldn't be enough just to get my degree. I *had* to get a First. After six years worrying constantly about my marks, my reward was to be at the front of the queue to 'collect' my BA.

Once it was over, we all went off to eat pizza and drink champagne. What I missed in having a group of fellow students to get drunk with, I made up for by being with the people who mattered most. And my grandfather did an excellent job of chatting up my friends … a mere 55 years his junior.

The un-posed photos from that day show me glowing: pride, the benefits of a university education – or simply relief at finally crossing the finishing line? Either way, in some pictures I could almost have passed for 21 rather than 34 …

Has my degree changed my life? Not really. By the time I graduated, I'd filled the gap left by the OU courses by writing my first novel … something which has ultimately had a much bigger effect on my life. But having those letters after my name at last has knocked the chip off my shoulder.

And it also gave me something far more precious. My grandfather died in 2003 – before my first book was published. So my instinct that I needed to graduate in 2002 had been right … And, as well as the memories of my big day, I have that precious tape of him talking about the best – and worst – days of his own life, fighting and singing his way through France and Italy and Greece.

I wouldn't swap that for a thousand degrees from the 'right' university.

James Haskell

England Rugby Player

Best day of my life – Saturday, 17 March 2007. The whirlwind adventure started a couple of months earlier with me sitting on the bench for Wasps, fretting about getting a first-team start; playing for the England Sevens team in Dubai and South Africa, running out against Ireland and Italy for England Saxons, to my full debut for England against Wales at the Millennium Stadium – all while still 21 years of age. I challenge anyone who doesn't believe in the magic of sport to rethink!

Little did I know that Monday, 12 March would kick off one of the most surreal and exciting weeks of my fledgling rugby career. I was on a high from the weekend game against Harlequins, which we had won after a fantastic second-half fight-back.

I reported for training on Monday, somewhat sore and slightly disappointed that I hadn't heard anything from England as to whether I would be involved in the build-up to the Welsh game. Although after the win over France I reckoned Brian Ashton would stick with the same squad of 22 players, I had hoped to be asked to attend training. After receiving some physio on a neck and shoulder injury I sustained in the Quins game, I was told not to train during the week. They told me I would have to wait to see what would happen about the coming weekend's game against London Irish. I was on my way back to the car park to return home when Ian McGeehan called me into his office and told me I had been called up to the England squad as Nick Easter had a neck injury.

Obviously with my own injury I was caught between a rock and a hard place: would I be able to train or even play if called upon? It was decided I was to travel down to the England camp but not to train on the Monday and to see how the injury felt the next day. I found myself in a degree of mental turmoil; obviously I was fully aware of the potential opportunity which awaited me but, conversely, if, through my injury, I would be unable to do either England or myself full justice, I determined I would bite the bullet and not play. I remembered the old adage my dad used to tell me: you never get a second chance to make a first impression!

Never underestimate the power of positive thought. On Wednesday, my shoulder felt much better and, having been passed fit to train at the end of the session, I was told I could very well be starting at either 8 or 6 against Wales if Nick's injury didn't improve.

Not knowing until the very last minute is probably one of the hardest things to deal with because it is not easy to get the mental side of your preparation right. If you are not actually sure you are going to be involved, while you can prepare by learning all the line-out calls and plays, you never completely feel part of the action if you are filling in someone else's shoes. All this coupled with the fact I had only played twice at number 8 in a premiership game!

The uncertainty continued for virtually the rest of the week but I prepared as if I was going to definitely start the match. Some pundits have alluded to England being a fragmented group but the level of professionalism, kindness and support shown to me by the rest of the players to help and encourage me to get to grips with all of the moves and plays in such a short time was amazing. Any questions I had, they would happily go through everything with me, and none more so than Nick Easter.

It was not until the Thursday morning that I discovered I was actually starting. I left my room early to go to breakfast and met Brian Ashton in the corridor talking to Nick Easter. As I passed by, Brian turned and offered his hand saying, 'Congratulations, you are starting number 6 against Wales.'

Naturally, I offered my thanks to Brian and my condolences to Nick and continued on to breakfast with my head spinning and my heart racing.

I was absolutely overwhelmed by the volume of messages of support and congratulations which I received from old headmasters, teachers, school chums family, friends, my coaches at Maidenhead Rugby Club where I started my rugby career and from the coaches and playing staff at Wasps, plus a whole host more. If you sent me a message and are reading this, then let me publicly thank you and say just how much your messages of support meant to me.

Saturday came upon me very quickly, which luckily meant I didn't have much time to dwell upon the challenge that lay ahead. Was I nervous? The answer funnily enough was no. I was more worried about letting down everyone who had been so kind to have rung, emailed, texted or written to me than I was about actually playing.

When I ran out with the rest of the team for the anthems, I couldn't stop smiling to myself; the atmosphere was like nothing I had ever seen or heard before. In fact, I thought to myself as I belted out the words to 'God Save the Queen', I want to do this time and time again. This is why I play rugby so I can experience occasions like this. It's funny, they say players out on the pitch don't really hear the crowd but the noise levels especially in the last 10 minutes were absolutely deafening, so much so you literally couldn't hear what the other players were saying to you!

While I enjoyed the game itself and without wishing to take

149

anything away from the Welsh who played very well, the result was a huge disappointment. Still, all things considered, I feel I acquitted myself reasonably well on my debut.

The capping ceremony was a very special occasion and one which will live with me for the rest of my life. The initiation ceremony less so! Every new cap has to drink a pint with every other member of the squad, 21 pints in all and of course some of the guys just love to spice up the beer a bit. Sunday as you can probably imagine was all a bit of a haze!

Michelle Heaton

Singer

My name is Michelle Heaton, or Scott-Lee, whichever works. I've been so fortunate to have lived my childhood dream for the past six years – to be a popstar was all I ever wanted to be. And with the job have come so many fantastic days it's been hard to think of just one. But one day seems to stand out more than the rest …

As a kid, I was always glued to the TV whenever *Top Of The Pops* came on. On one of the first shows I saw, Bananarama, Bros and Debbie Gibson were appearing. I was in total awe just watching them perform, dreaming that one day that would be me up there on that stage.

Ten years later, my dreams came true. Liberty X had just released our third single and a few days earlier we had been given the most fantastic news that we were the UK chart number one. So, we were invited to appear on *Top Of The Pops* the following week. Getting ready to perform on such a prestigious show was a daunting task: what do I wear? What should I do with my make-up? What about my hair? This show was everything to me and I had to look my best.

As we walked up the four stairs to the stage, my heart felt like it was going to explode. I set one foot on that glorious stage and was overcome with pride and satisfaction. Not only was I just about to perform on one of the world's most popular shows, but also my parents and closest friends were in the audience to share the moment with me.

The presenter took the mic, and announced to the UK the following words: 'Give it up for the UK's number one ... "Just A Little" by Liberty X.'

I began to feel a bit faint and the next three minutes and 30 seconds of my life were a big blur. All I remember is thinking, I'm on *Top Of The Pops* ... I'm on *Top Of The Pops* ... I almost gave myself jaw-ache from smiling so much!

At the end of the song, the crowd erupted into a mass of cheers. Tears of happiness ran down my face as I looked into my parents' proud eyes and looked at my four bandmates with love and admiration.

And, just when I thought this day couldn't get any better, the presenter took the mic again and said, 'We have a little surprise for Liberty X now.'

Suddenly, Richard Branson, our record-company owner, came on to the stage with five double-platinum discs for us all. OH MY GOD, OH MY GOD, OH MY GOD!

At that moment I was completely satisfied. I thought, if nothing else ever comes our way, it does not matter. What mattered was that I had fulfilled my childhood dream. And I was not only on *Top Of The Pops*, I had a double-platinum number-one single on *Top Of The Pops*! ... How cool is that?

Lauren Henderson

Author

I don't have one. Or at least, not one that's jumping up and down,
waving its hand and yelling, 'Pick me, Lauren! Pick *me*!' I wonder,
in fact, how many people can truly single out one perfect day: that is,
people who, perhaps, haven't experienced the long-awaited birth of
their first child, or been in the stadium, screaming, tears pouring down
their face, to see their team beat Man United 6–0 in the FA Cup
Final. (If that ever happened. Football isn't my specialist subject.)

It certainly wasn't my wedding day. That was raw, emotional,
terrifying and utterly draining. The night before, my fiancé had burst
into tears, stormed around the room and begged me to promise that
we'd never fight again. I wouldn't, but I hugged him till he stopped
crying and talked him down from the ledge. The next day, we
swapped moods: having had his crisis, my husband was composed,
positive, in a state of happy anticipation, while I woke up in a state of
extreme fear, my other emotions stuffed so far down they might have
been under a heavy glass cover. Marriage was suddenly scaring the
hell out of me. I knew my fiancé was the right man: I knew we had
to marry, so that he, as an American, could move to England with me.
But clearly, the idea of being a wife was paralysingly frightening to
me, and I hadn't faced this till the day it was due to happen.

153

I moved through the morning – brunch, hairdresser, manicure – as if I were in a drug-induced trance. When I was finally dressed, coiffed, made up and waiting to walk down the flower-strewn path in our friends' back garden that would be our aisle, I was so petrified I thought I was going to vomit. My maid of honour was stalwart: she grabbed my wrists, dug her thumbs into emergency acupuncture pressure points, and told me that if I threw up it was no big deal, we'd just wipe it up and keep going.

I didn't actually throw up. But I was in such a state that I forgot to take my bouquet with me, and I cried so hard all the way through the ceremony that, when it came time for me to read the poem I had planned, I accidentally spat my own tears, which had collected on my upper lip, on to the lens of the video camera. Repeatedly. Afterwards, I sat, shaking but relieved, for the rest of the evening, clinging on to my new husband as if he were a life raft.

So, not the best day of my life, by any means. Too much fear, too much panic. Maybe it was the day I met him: the perfect date, the perfect dinner, the walk home holding hands, the kiss at my door, the best first kiss I've ever had, closing the door behind me, knowing he was still on the other side, and standing there, pressing myself against it, eyes closed, feeling that I was the heroine in the most romantic of romantic films, near-delirious with happiness at having met him. And there were days and days of excitement straight afterwards, having left with a friend on a road trip from New York to New Orleans, receiving texts from him, each one lovelier than the one before. I remember running through a rain deluge in Charleston late at night, taking my shoes off so I could splash through puddles in bare feet, racing back to the hotel room to check my phone for messages, and reading one so romantic and funny and clever that I jumped up and down on the bed yodelling with happiness.

But I've had other wonderful days, not just romantic ones. Magical days with a group of girlfriends on a holiday in Sri Lanka, every morning waking up to bright sunshine, trees full of blossoms and chattering monkeys. In my memory snapshots, we laughed from morning to night. And the last day of my stay, I went for a massage, fell for the masseur and spent the night in his arms. That was a perfect day.

Or the one I spent skydiving in Florida, strapped to an off-duty SWAT cop, then drinking margaritas in a two-person bar swing with another girlfriend, laughing like drains, Cuban food afterwards in the balmy black velvet Miami night, the sea rolling into the shore, walking barefoot on the soft sand, salsa thrumming all along Ocean Drive, hot sexy little Latinos and Latinas, half-stripped, dancing on the sidewalk with hips rolling like oiled ball-bearings.

Or every day on holiday with my then boyfriend, now my husband, in a tiny rundown hotel on a cove in the Dominican Republic: nothing to do but sunbathe, swim, read, play board games, make love, drink bananakiris and try not to break any bones slipping on the marble floor of the bathroom, as the hotel was economising and wouldn't give us any bathmats. We have a photograph of ourselves in the bath, taken with a timed camera on the sink, and we're laughing so hard you can practically see our tonsils, because he dashed across the floor to get into the bath in time and nearly killed himself when his feet went from under him as he ran. I grabbed him and pulled him in just in time for the flash to go off, dragging him under his armpits like an emergency rescue at sea, hauling him up into the lifeboat just before the shark got his ankle. And then he accidentally kicked me in the crotch getting in, which made us laugh even harder.

Many lovely days. But perfect ones? A single, outstanding, perfect one? I don't know.

Maybe the perfect day is still out there for me. I know I can't plan it, or it won't be perfect. It will have to sneak up on me, take me by surprise. And maybe I won't even recognise it when it arrives, if it ever does: maybe the perfect day won't be the big showstopper we all picture when we imagine it. Maybe it's more gentle: not a wild explosion of fireworks, but a slow subtle infusion of happiness.

And, in that case, maybe I've had it already. Maybe I've had dozens of perfect days. Which would mean that I have dozens more to come.

I like that idea.

Lucy-Anne Holmes

Author

My best day was disguised as my worst. It wore gnarly teeth and a big beard and if it had been routinely searched it would have produced flawless fake ID saying, 'I am a bad, bad day.'

I am working in a hip-hop clothing stall in Camden Market. Not because I am hip-hop (I went to convent school in Buckinghamshire; I have a hyphenated name; if hip-hop is 'street', I'm 'rural byway'), but because my friend owns the shop and my friend is kind. She noticed that I hadn't done any acting work for months and offered me a job. Fearful of me turning up dressed as Zara Phillips, she instructed me to work wearing the clothing she sells.

This explains why, on the best day of my life, I am wearing an off-the-shoulder mini ra-ra dress, which looks like it's been made by someone who's taken too much acid, and wedge heels unsuitable for anything other than throwing at an ex-boyfriend's head.

I am also crying which isn't 'street' or conducive to sales. But I am alone in the shop and it is all I can do. This is because in this moment everything I have ever done and every decision I've ever made has proved to be wrong. I want to curl up in bed and listen to The Cure. But I don't have a bed. I share my sister's sofa with a smelly West Highland terrier. I want to cuddle the man I love. Except the man I love dumped me on Saturday, throwing me out of the flat we shared. On Sunday, I saw him out with another girl. I want to drive off somewhere but I can't because, while I was watching my ex-boyfriend smooch the pretty girl with big breasts, my car was being impounded. And I want to act but I can't act because I think my agent might have died.

Amid all this, there was one thing I was looking forward to. I was looking forward to driving to Sheffield on Friday to see a play. (If you needed further proof of my lack of 'street', there it is.) The play is directed by my favourite theatre director, a genius called Michael Grandage, and my favourite actor is in it, Derek Jacobi. It will be magical. Still, I can't go. It will cost £260 to retrieve my car and the train costs more than a flight to New York.

My expectations of today are lying somewhere beneath the earth's core. They can't get any worse, I may as well call my agent, I think … foolishly.

'Hello.' A man's voice barks. It's not boding well. My agent is a woman. I was right. She's dead.

'It's Lucy-Anne I …' I start.

'She's on holiday! Three weeks!' he bellows.

I should say, 'So no change there then.' But I don't. I went to a convent after all.

'Uh um …' I stammer but he's put the phone down already.

I sigh. I cry. I listen to ghastly hip-hop and fold T-shirts. My phone rings again. It's a number I don't know. I answer, even though numbers you don't recognise tend to involve someone wanting money.

'Lucy-Anne Holmes,' says a male voice. Bugger! An unknown number! The use of my full name! It's probably a court summons. I'll hang up now. But just before I press the red button I hear these words: 'It's Michael Grandage. My leading lady's lost her voice. I may need you to go on tonight instead. Now where are you?'

'Camden.'

'Perfect! I'll book you on the two o'clock train up to Sheffield from King's Cross.'

Blimey. It's 12.14 p.m. now!

'Actually no. We'll get you on the one o'clock train. But you'll need to get moving.'

I panic. What about my friend's shop?

I call her.

'You go, girl! Just lock up the shop. I'll sort it.'

I get the train with 42 seconds to spare. The script had been faxed to the ticket office. I read it on the train. It is poetry. Suddenly I am in 16th-century Spain in the middle of someone else's tragic love story.

I arrive at the theatre. I am laced in a corset and buttoned into an exquisite grey silk dress. Derek Jacobi appears in his dressing gown and practises hitting me. Then before I know it Derek Jacobi is in his costume hitting me in front of a thousand people. And the most handsome actor on the planet is wearing tights and kissing me. I pray I don't smell of my sister's dog.

We bow. As the audience claps, my favourite actor turns towards me and applauds me. The audience cheer.

I know now that not all the decisions I have made are wrong. That the reason I have no money and work in a hip-hop clothes shop is because I made the decision to be an actress. It isn't always easy but that moment repays the struggle tenfold.

Later in the bar I hold a cheque for quite a lot of money and directions to the hotel I've been booked into for the week. However, I'm too shy to talk to all the actors because of my ra-ra dress. I suspect they think I perform sex acts for money in King's Cross.

Michael Grandage approaches me. 'You were terrific. I can't believe you just came up here with the clothes on your back like that.'

'I don't normally dress like this. I was in a clothes shop and …'
I witter.

He just hands me an envelope and says, 'Cash … to buy some clothes while you're here.'

'Thank you.' I try not to cry.

'No thank *you*.' He smiles.

I watch him walk away. As I do I spot a rather handsome actor in the corner of the bar.

And I think he might be smiling at me …

Humfrey Hunter

Literary Agent & Writer

When Giles and I signed the publishing deal for this book, I was not planning to contribute a story at all. I had no idea what I would write about and, unless I was absolutely convinced I had found the perfect subject, I thought it would be better not to do one at all. It's a bit like how I've always thought of tattoos: I'd love to have one if I knew I'd be able to look at it with no regrets every day for the rest of my life. But, if I had any doubt at all, it would be better not to bother. And, as yet, I don't have a tattoo.

But, after reading the stories from our contributors, I felt I had to write something. The stories were so personal and so completely honest that I thought I owed it to them to give as much as they had. So, here it is.

Before I start properly, I am fully aware that you may think I am a nutter at the end. However, that doesn't matter because if you get this far into the book you must have already bought it. Also, my story is not about one day in isolation. I realise that means it doesn't match the title of the book but, hey, it's half my book and, if I want to break the rules, I will. So my story is about my whole life.

First, some background. My father died of pancreatic cancer in 1981, when I was four. At the time, my two sisters Rachel and Sarah were five and one and my mother was left to bring the three of us up on her own. I have no idea what this must have been like for her – more terrifying than anything I can ever imagine facing. But she never showed us any uncertainty or worry or doubt, even though I know now she must have felt all those things and much more besides. She just got on with looking after her children.

Throughout my childhood, I always knew I was slightly different to my friends because I didn't have a father. But, despite that, I never felt anything was lacking from my life. My mother gave us all the love, help and support we could possibly need. I never felt I missed out on anything at all and I do not have the words to properly express how much gratitude, respect and love I have for her.

Fast forward to Marseille, France, in March 1998. I was 21 and on a year out from university living in the city and working in a school in order to get my spoken French up to the highest possible standard for my final year. I was seven months into the year and, after going through some difficult times, I had made a breakthrough with the language. I'd spent day after day with French people for all those months and finally I was speaking the language fluently. It's a bizarre sensation – I literally woke up one morning and my brain had suddenly made sense of the thousands of alien noises it had been bombarded with over the previous few months and could now match them up with what it already knew and so use them quickly and effectively. I was so excited I would talk to anyone about anything. Random strangers, anyone. I didn't care who I talked to or what I talked about. This did get me into trouble once or twice as Marseille is a tough Mediterranean port city and sometimes not a forgiving place but those stories are not for this book.

One evening I walked down to the Vieux Port area in the middle of Marseille to get a taxi to my friend Kelly's house on the other side of town. Naturally, as soon as I got in the car, I wanted to start talking and to my delight I had a captive audience in the driver. I noticed there were some books on the passenger seat next to him so I asked what they were. Very happy to talk to me, he said they were about spirits – the souls of dead people rather than liquors. He said he had a gift, he could tell when spirits were around. I was fascinated and enjoying our conversation.

Then, smiling and calm, he said, 'Actually, there's someone with you now.'

For the first time in weeks, I was speechless.

The driver could see my stunned face in the mirror and tried to relax me. 'There's no need to be scared,' he said. 'You've lost someone close to you, haven't you?'

I don't believe in fortune tellers and their like. I think they're a bunch of shysters whose job is made easier because every person in the world has lost someone close to them. That means everyone has moments when they are vulnerable so 'you've lost someone close to you' is an easy and effective opening line to come out with when they're trying to fleece someone. But this was different. My taxi driver had nothing whatsoever to gain from me so when he told me all this I believed him. I did then and still do now.

'Yes,' I replied. 'My father died when I was young.'

The driver smiled gently. 'He's with you now.'

I felt numb. No matter how cynical I had been in the past, at that moment I believed this man was being honest with me. A hundred questions whirred through my mind. The biggest rushed to the front. 'How can I communicate with him?'

'You can't.'

'But what if I need advice? How will I be able to contact him? What can I do?'

'You can't do anything.'

'But what if I need him?'

'There's nothing you can do.'

I was getting frantic now. 'What if I need to ask him something?'

'When you need him, he'll be there.'

'But how will I know?'

The driver smiled again and paused. 'You'll just know,' he said slowly. 'When you need him most, you'll just know. He'll be there.'

I couldn't really speak after that and for the rest of the journey the driver would look back at me every now and then and just smile calmly and tell me everything was OK. And, weird as this sounds, it was.

At the end of the journey, he shook my hand, told me to take care and that the journey was free. I got out of the taxi and he drove away. I never knew his name and I never saw him again.

I stood still outside Kelly's house for what felt like hours as wave after wave of the most intense euphoria burst through me. I was overflowing with emotion yet there were no tears. For the first time in my life, the world finally seemed to make sense. It felt like something inside me slotted into place. I have no idea how or why but the way I felt when I got out of that taxi was unlike anything I have ever experienced, before or since, a kind of calm, content wholeness. As I stood there, I thought of my father, my mother, my sisters and the trail of events which brought me to that pavement on that road in that French city on that day. I was feeling my love for them all – particularly my mother, to whom this book is dedicated – with a newfound intensity and joy. I understood what I'd lost but I also saw clearly what I had in my life and why I was so lucky.

I am a committed atheist, I don't believe in fate and I believe my father's illness was the result of nothing other than a biological quirk. But, on that day, for the first time in my life, I was convinced that in some way he is with me and that there may be something in this world beyond the mere physical. I think about that moment every day and it gives me strength.

Steve Kemsley

Producer & Director

It was very sunny that day in June, the 18th, it felt as if the whole country was that little bit more alive and vibrant. Wherever I drove there were England flags fluttering in the wind as cars drove by, draped from the windows of thousands of apartments and houses. All the pubs had bunting, the country expected …

What on earth am I talking about? I'm talking about (one of) the best days of my life (so far).

There have been many wonderful moments, my wedding day, days abroad on holiday, my children being born, but it's difficult to isolate personal moments and refer to them as the best as they all have equal importance in my memory banks so I have chosen a day that is fairly generic but I have special reasons; that day was the day England took on the Netherlands at Wembley Stadium in an unforgettable encounter that culminated in our national team reaching the quarter-finals of Euro 96.

Now I am sure this day was special for thousands of us but I had a special reason. Since 8 April 1994, I was the official 'voice of Wembley'. I played all the music, created the atmosphere and was the 'announcer', the 'bloke on the PA', 'the DJ'. I enjoyed many amazing events at Wembley Stadium in the six years I was resident there, playing over 142 events and nearly eight million attendees but this day was special.

I got there early, as usual, before the turnstiles opened. I knew what kind of music I would be playing; I had already structured a playlist with the FA that went to all the other stadiums in the country but I always added my own personal touch. In fact, it was only days earlier that I took the personal and now much celebrated decision to play 'Three Lions'. It was after Gascoigne had scored that goal against Scotland. The sun was shining and, even though I wasn't supposed to play it, I looked at the assistant director of the tournament and said, 'You know what, if they fire me, it doesn't matter – I would have done it all, I'm going to play it.'

He looked around and saw the royal box was virtually empty. I pressed play ... The rest, as they say, is history.

Just so you know, the reason we weren't supposed to play 'Three Lions' was that Wembley was not an official home game for England; we happened to be the host country which didn't automatically give us home-game privileges and therefore playing that song might have been a bit biased! *Might* have been? I think (and I would) that it lifted the spirits of the entire country and I don't recall a football song being quite as popular as 'Three Lions' then became.

Anyway, back to the England vs. Holland game. What I failed to mention at this point is that I was also, as part of my day job, producing the official video releases for the tournament. We ended up making nine different titles in all, so not only was I DJing at Wembley Stadium, but immediately after the match I also ended up back in an edit suite watching the game again and editing down the highlights. If you ever have to pick one of those videos to watch, have a look at the *Three Lions Roared*; it brings back very happy memories indeed.

So there we were 76 thousand-odd people, half-an-hour before kick-off, a daunting throng of bright-orange shirts off to my right and a steady nervous atmosphere building. I decided (well before every other football stadium in the country picked up on the vibe) to play 'We Will Rock You' followed by 'You'll Never Walk Alone' and then 'Three Lions'. I have never heard 'You'll Never Walk Alone' sung by so many, so loudly. Even the Dutch fans joined in and for three minutes most England fans forgot about the special meaning the song has for Liverpool supporters, and the country united.

The game was, as everyone I am sure recalls, sensational. Shearer and Sheringham completely outclassed our Dutch opponents and the feeling after the match was one of total euphoria. The whole country seemed to be in a good mood. When I edited the highlights later that night at my studio, I virtually relived the whole experience.

People often ask me if that was the best match atmosphere of the tournament, but, in fact, it wasn't. The best atmosphere prior to a game was at the semi-finals against Germany. The expectation was colossal as was the atmosphere. Sadly, that day will always be tainted by the result and as such could never feature as the best day of anyone's life (unless, of course, you are German). So I had to pick the complete day.

I am a lucky boy – having Nick Heyward play at my 40th birthday, the bar mitzvah of my son at the Western Wall in Jerusalem, marrying my wife, her giving birth to our three wonderful children, seeing Duran Duran and Billy Joel at my brother's 40th, attending the original Live Aid, skiing fresh powder in Vale, Colorado – they are all incredible memories but we are only allowed to pick one for this book and for me it's the day we started to believe that 'football was coming home'.

Sophie Kinsella

Author

The best day of my life hasn't happened yet. But I'm fully confident it's on the horizon. I'm really looking forward to it, and have a pretty good idea of the way it is going to go …

I'll wake up fresh and energised. Leaping out of bed, I will discover that my hair is springing with salon sheen and volume. My waist will appear a few inches smaller than yesterday, and my complexion will be suddenly dewy.

The shower will run hot at once.

Flinging open my wardrobe door, I'll spot a new outfit I had totally forgotten about buying. And a new pair of boots.

Downstairs I'll sip a cup of tea, listening to the *Today Show*, in which not one interviewer will interrupt and not one politician will duck the question. An eminent scientist will announce the discovery of a substance which instantly dissolves landfill into organic slurry. Another scientist will reveal a revolutionary new source of energy. Of course, the top story will be Elvis's new single, following his reappearance from a commune in South America.

Perusing the paper, I will see the following headlines: MUFFINS DISCOVERED TO BE SLIMMING; CAPPUCCINOS INCREASE THE IQ.

The post will arrive, bearing a letter from the council regarding a recent parking ticket I was given. 'We are very sorry,' it will begin. 'We admit that our road markings weren't totally clear. Please accept this box of chocolates as a goodwill gesture.'

I'll head off to work, where my email box will contain only two emails, both from good friends. I'll write 3,000 words in an hour, and spontaneously come up with a brilliant new idea for a book. Which I will remember to write down.

At my Pilates class, my teacher will praise my posture. Clearly, all that hunching over the desk has been benefiting me.

On my way home, The Ivy restaurant will call. They will tell me they remember that I enquired about a table some months ago, and are just calling on the off-chance that I would like one tonight. For as many people as I like. As I'm accepting, I will receive three text messages from friends passing through London and at a loose end tonight.

As I arrive home, the builders working on my house will greet me with cheery smiles. It turns out that, due to unforeseen circumstances, the work will take a much shorter time than they planned – and be a lot cheaper too! The foreman will then offer me a cup of tea and praise whoever it was who worked on the house last time round.

My children will request broccoli for dinner. When I tell them they can't watch more than one DVD, they will shrug good-humouredly and comment on how fair life is.

Sipping a glass of champagne, I'll get ready for the evening. To my amazement, I will fit into the dress I bought in the sales thinking, One day I'll fit into this dress. My tights won't snag. My neighbour will pop round, wondering if I can make use of a pair of Christian Louboutins, size 39?

As we head out for the evening, my husband will present me with flowers and reveal he has booked a surprise trip for us all to New York. As we near The Ivy, we will receive another call – due to table complications, do we mind sharing a table with George Clooney?

169

After a riotous evening, we will emerge into a balmy London evening and watch the fireworks going off all along the Thames – to celebrate England's recent record-breaking gold-medal count at the Olympics (not to mention Tim Henman's surprise Wimbledon victory). We'll stroll for a while, before deciding to take a taxi home – whereupon one will pull up immediately. The taxi driver will tell us apologetically that he's feeling a bit hoarse – do we mind if he doesn't talk?

Karen Krizanovich

Writer, Journalist & Broadcaster

The best day of my life is the day I gave up.

Raised in a small town outside Chicago, I was horse mad. At the age of seven, I had saved 7,500 pennies to buy my first horse, a 22-year-old retired cowpony called Bandy. But, after a series of really awful nags, I decided at the age of 15 that I wanted a good show horse. Taking every dollar I had in the bank, I bought a tiny brown and black Quarter Horse called Jim Mac Too.

Mac was pretty. He was also pretty wild. He had two speeds: walk and blast-off. My parents did not see the point of hiring a professional trainer – what, were we *made* of money? – so I trained him the best I could, by asking people, reading and a lot of trial and error. A lot.

Training began at 5 a.m. every morning and went on for months, six days a week. Hours of riding shaped Mac into a good, smooth-moving horse – no longer a rocket with four legs.

But we had a problem: Mac was in love with his left lead. When they run, horses balance themselves with 'leads' – the correct order the front legs should move. If a horse is circling to the left, the front left leg is ahead of the other. To the right, the right leg is ahead. Nothing in the world would get Mac to take his right lead: he'd circle to the right, but on his left lead. This is the equivalent of a child running backwards down the stairs: sure, they can do it, but it is an accident waiting to happen. Anyway, show horses must take the correct lead. If not, in a large class, they'd be sent from the ring, beaten before they began.

So we worked and worked on that lead. Spring became summer. The show was coming up fast and still he showed no sign of improvement. The hot and sweaty morning workouts became displays of trainer/animal frustration. Mac did not understand what he was supposed to do. I did not know how to tell him. I tried every trick but nothing worked. He'd stride left left left and I'd go from anger, to tears, to silence, to despair. Mac became more tired, fed up, bored and puzzled.

One hot morning when we were out in the ring, circling the wrong way as usual, it came to me that maybe there was a life lesson in all this. Mac was not learning because I was not smart enough to teach him. Maybe he just wasn't the right horse. And I wasn't the right rider for him. Maybe I needed to see our limitations.

The summer sun was beating down hard from a cloudless sky. Even though it was early, we were both dripping with sweat. I felt sick thinking how Mac moved like a flying carpet in all ways except for that front leg.

Shaking my head, I relaxed in the saddle. Maybe, I thought to myself, I should spend the rest of the summer just enjoying my little brown nag without expectations. He was nowhere near as fancy as the other horses but he was shiny and healthy and fit, and he could stop on a dime and lope along like a deer. After all these months of dedication, training and care, I resigned myself that it was all for naught. We were failures. For the first time in my life, I gave up. I turned Mac to the right, headed for home.

It was then I felt his shoulder lift and move right. He'd done it. Mac had finally taken the right lead, one single stride in the right way. My joy knew no bounds, I leaped from the saddle, praising him and patting him. I took off the saddle and bridle as fast as I could and I walked him home, riderless. I carried the heavy western gear all the way, not him.

The day of the show came. Mac did his best. So did I. And we beat horses and riders who were normally better than us. Mac and I won rosettes and trophies and got our picture in the local paper: champions.

Little Mac is gone now but I still have the memories of that long dusty summer and the valuable lesson I learned that sometimes you have to give up to succeed.

Amanda Lamb

TV Presenter

The best day of my life started around 4.30 p.m. on Saturday, 12 April 1997 in the frozen-vegetable section of a certain well-known supermarket. Watching my best friend Ruby's knuckles turn white as she gripped the trolley and let out several expletives leading me to believe that her first-born child was on his/her way. The knuckle gripping was happening every three to four minutes and I remember reading somewhere that, if you gave birth in a supermarket, you'd get a year's free supply of nappies. I didn't think that would swing it, however, so we abandoned the trolley and made our way home. She still wasn't convinced it was actually happening. The baby wasn't due for another few days so at this point she'd put it down to something she'd eaten.

When she'd found out she was pregnant, she asked me if I would be prepared to be her birthing partner. We had already shared so much together that I was honoured and, if I'm really honest, a little bit scared too. I don't really do blood and pain, I have trouble watching an episode of *Casualty* but I threw myself into the spirit of things and started stocking up and reading as much as I could about what to expect. I already had my 'birthing partner' kitbag, which consisted of a flannel (for sponging down puffing, panting mother), lavender spray (for liberally spraying on anything in the vicinity to induce feelings of calm) and a copy of *Hello!* magazine (for me, I read somewhere labour can take hours if not days and I needed some light reading material).

Having arrived back at her house with her contractions showing no signs of abating, we gathered supplies and headed straight for the hospital. With the arrival of the aforementioned first-born due to happen very soon, things went into automatic overdrive. It's a very strange feeling to experience your best friend going through so much pain and not being able to do a single thing to help. The lavender spray did not, as I'd been led to believe, induce feelings of calm; if anything, I remember her screaming at me to stop squirting her with that ***** stuff or she wouldn't be responsible for her actions. The gas and air seemed to help, however – well, it certainly did for me and I think Ruby found it beneficial too.

Finally, at about 4.30 a.m., the midwife said the head was about to crown and asked if I wanted to see the baby coming into the world. Split-second decision … Of course I did. George Phillip Daniels entered the world at precisely 4.58 a.m. on Sunday, 13 April 1997 weighing 7lb 3oz. It really was the most amazing experience to date. Here was this tiny little human being ready to start his journey through this wonderful thing we call life. I remember them handing him to me while they looked after Ruby and there being this wonderful sense of peace and calm. I looked at him and said, 'Welcome to the world, little one,' and he looked at me as if to say, 'Who the bloody hell are you? I was comfortable in there,' and so it began, a bond that we will share for the rest of our lives and one that I am so very pleased and honoured to have.

Kate Lawler

DJ & TV Presenter

It began with a very drunken trip to Malaga Airport with my friend Emma. The sun was shining … We'd been DJing there and my friend Abi was driving us back to the airport to catch a flight home to London that evening. As much as I didn't want to get on the plane back to a cold and wet England, I was excited to be making the journey as my twin sister Karen was nine months pregnant and two weeks overdue.

I'd been out of the country working for the entire two weeks my sister was overdue but, as I couldn't do anything about being away, I was desperate for her to hold on until I got home! Knowing the baby could have arrived while I was away was a real worry for my sister and for me – seeing as I was her birthing partner!

My flight left Spain at 8 p.m. so I knew I'd be with my twin by midnight and as I boarded my flight I remember calling her and saying, 'You've waited this long, now just wait another three hours!'

As we touched down at London Gatwick, I turned my phone on immediately and as I was walking off the plane my phone rang. It was my sister's boyfriend Pete. 'Her waters have just broken, Katie!' he screamed down the phone.

I couldn't believe it. My twin sis had begun her labour, well overdue and just in time for me to be there. I was so happy.

My friend and I ran through the airport, grabbed our cases and jumped into a taxi to my house. As I arrived, my sister was having contractions, so I packed her stuff and Pete took her to the hospital. I wanted to go but they said there was no point until she was a certain point through her labour … So I went to sleep about 1 a.m. and had a very restless night. Between waking up every half-an-hour and checking my mobile for any updates, I was dreaming of all sorts, what sex the baby would be, christenings, mothercare, you name it!

I decided to get myself down to Farnborough Hospital at 9 a.m. and when I arrived she was still having contractions, but, as her cervix wasn't dilated enough, she couldn't begin the labour.

As a twin, Karen and I have always done nearly everything together. She is my best friend and we have such a wonderful relationship; I was so glad to be there with her and Pete at this time.

However, the labour was long and by 11 a.m. Karen was screaming the ward down and having such painful contractions she was nearly passing out. I've never seen anything like it; she hadn't even started pushing. Gas and air, holding her hand, telling her everything was going to be all right just didn't make me feel I was doing enough to help her. They gave her an epidural by 2 p.m. that day and it eased the pain, giving us time to rest and sleep a bit. The hospital room was small and uncomfortable so that didn't really happen. Around 7 p.m., I couldn't believe she was still only 8cm dilated, but we were getting there. At 9.30 p.m., she got to 10cm and by 10.30 she was pushing for her life, and me and Pete were each holding one of her hands. For the next hour, Karen cried, screamed, yelled, swore and panicked as she pushed for the baby to come out.

In the last half-hour of her labour, the baby got stuck and they warned they might have to give an emergency C-section. Karen was distraught, as she really wanted to do it naturally, so we went for it for the last half-hour, and at the stroke of midnight Louie Jake was born, weighing 8lb 4oz.

As they put him straight on her chest, his eyes were opening and he was waking up. Not one murmur or scream came from him, he looked so happy to be with his mummy on the outside world. It was so overwhelming and emotional. Twenty-four hours, one whole day, had passed and eventually my twin had brought her very own little boy into the world ... my nephew. I cried so much when I saw him and we were all so relieved that finally it was all over.

There were tears everywhere. I called my parents and told them the news. I ran outside to the waiting room where my big sis Kelly was waiting and we just hugged and cried together. I knew I was going to be godmother to Louie Jake at his christening, and holding him for the first time just 15 minutes after he was born was the best feeling in the world. I felt a sense of joy and amazement that my twin sister had made this little person and that he was related to me. Watching my sister, my best friend, give birth was the most amazing experience. It was, without question, the best day of my life.

Jason Leonard

Former England Rugby Player

The best day of my life would be playing a game of rugby with my mates. It sounds very simple so I'll explain it for you. In 1991, I played in a World Cup Final against Australia and I lost. Not a day goes by that I don't think about that Final and wonder, Could I have done something better? Could my teammates have played any better? If a certain pass had gone to hand, could we have won? Losing that Final is the biggest regret of my life. But I had an opportunity 12 years later, in 2003, to reverse that by playing for England in the World Cup Final in Australia, again against Australia. And this time we won it.

So was that second World Cup Final the best day of my life? No, it wasn't. Each and every time I went on to a rugby field, whether that was with the kids I grew up with in Barking or the club rugby I played at Saracens and Harlequins or playing for the Barbarians or England or the British Lions, those were the best days of my life – every time I walked on to a rugby field with my mates.

How I'd explain that is that in all walks of life people go through tragedy and they go through adversity, and as a member of a rugby team you share an all-encompassing commitment, friendship and solidarity. There's support for everybody. If I ever had to go through the gates of hell and stand in front of Lucifer himself, I know for a fact that my rugby teammates would join me and the scary thing is that I wouldn't need to say anything. They'd be there, right beside me. Not behind me but beside me, shoulder to shoulder, to face whatever would come, head-on, with me. What I find so amazing about that loyalty is that I wouldn't even need to ask, and if they needed me they wouldn't need to ask, I'd do the same for them. You put all that into a game of rugby and what you get is that, every single time you walk on to a field, you're walking on with your teammates who you will help and support through hard times.

That loyalty to me is everything about why I play rugby. That respect, friendship and camaraderie is everything to me. That's what kept me going for 16 years for England. When I wasn't playing for England, when I was playing junior rugby, like Joe round the corner – all he wants to do is play on a Saturday – it doesn't change. That's the one thing that doesn't change all the way through, whether you're playing for your Old Boys' fifth team or playing for England or the British Lions; that special rugby team loyalty is there. And it's there not only every Saturday during the game, it's there away from the game as well. If one of your teammates needs help or support, you'll be there. The respect that comes from that, the respect I have for my teammates, the respect that they have for me and for the opposition too, when they see a team that plays like that, they think it's a special team. It's used too often, too frequently and too lightly, but, when you're prepared to lay down your life for a friend, that is most probably the richest reward you could hope to achieve or aspire to in life. Rugby is a special game. It's still a game for all shapes and sizes, boys and girls play and there's even disabled rugby, so there's no social exclusion whatsoever but it's the team spirit that makes it really special.

In 2003, when the final whistle blew in the World Cup Final, the first feeling that came over me, like all the other guys, was relief. We'd gone through extra-time and it had been pretty nerve-racking. I thought I'd feel nothing but euphoria from winning it but I didn't. It goes back to the team ethos and your teammates and I was more chuffed for certain other people. I was more chuffed for Laurence Dallaglio, who's come through adversity, losing his sister, getting the captaincy then having that taken away from him. I was happy for him and I was happy for Will Greenwood, who a couple of years before had lost his child Freddie and during the World Cup had to go back to see his wife who they thought was giving birth early again. He then had to come back and carry on in the World Cup.

Then there was Martin Johnson who lost his mother just before the World Cup. So I was looking round and I wasn't actually happy for me. I was happy for everyone else, the guys who'd been dropped or missed out and then managed to get back in. The scary thing is I knew those guys were happy for me because I'd played in a World Cup Final 12 years earlier and lost, so they were happy that I got the chance to reverse that.

We were so close as a group of friends that not one person was taking this fantastic win for themselves. They'd done it all for their mates. That was the nicest thing about it. Even if you read the post-match interviews, that really came through. Jonny Wilkinson wasn't talking about him kicking that goal, he was saying he couldn't have done it if it wasn't for all the other players, like Matt Dawson passing him the ball and Martin Johnson taking the ball up or Lewis Moody and Steve Thompson winning the lineout before that. It comes back to the friendship you get in rugby teams. It's an unbreakable bond and in 30 or 40 years' time we'll still have that. We went through all that adversity and we won a World Cup and there's only a handful of people who've done that before us.

Lara Lewington

TV Presenter

One of the best moments of my life was the day I learned to swim, without panicking about my head going under.

For some people, this may seem the easiest thing in the world but, once the fear's set in, it's a challenge to overcome it. It took me years to stop being terrified of the concept of accidentally getting my head under water, then, when I did overcome it, came the most amazing turning point where the fear evaporated and I finally realised how everyone else seemed to find it so easy.

Since I was a kid, I've had a fear of water, possibly worsened by an incident in a swimming lesson at school. I used to hop on one foot while moving my arms in a swimming motion pretending I could swim, and, at the age of six, I hadn't worked out this was obvious to anyone watching. I was always the fat kid so I felt embarrassed to draw attention to myself in my swimsuit but also rather irrationally concerned that people would connect my not being able to swim with my being 'too fat', a suggestion that would have mortified me. So, one day, I was innocently hopping along when the teacher came and kicked my foot away, I went straight under, panicked, breathed in a lot of water and coughed and choked for a while. It was absolutely horrible and just the briefest moment of getting close to experiencing that sensation again terrifies me. Over the years I've had panic attacks in the sea or in swimming pools on holiday, which is rather embarrassing when you see toddlers leaping in fearlessly. I was once on holiday with a group of friends, who were playing around, being thrown in the pool and everyone was laughing. I had said please don't do it to me – but no one realised the level of fear I actually had until they did and I was in quite a state.

Obviously, I couldn't swim before the incident so I realise it can't be blamed entirely on my schooldays drama, but it certainly didn't help. After many years of trying to overcome the fear myself, I gradually learned to swim a little with my head above water. I would still hate to be splashed, as the water behaving in any uncontrollable way would send me into a state of completely irrational terror! But the real turning point came after much practice, and my boyfriend's very patient coaching, when I became able to hold my head under water without taking ages to psych myself up and still end up too scared to do it. From getting used to that came the ability to swim quite calmly, and even properly under water.

I knew how much better I'd got when swimming with my boyfriend's little sister and niece on a family holiday. They were both 11 at the time and I didn't want them to see me being scared in case my fear rubbed off on them. I just got on with it and swam half a length of the swimming pool under water. Realising I could hide my panic made me aware of how much better it was, as in the past I would never have been able to do so.

I'm still not the greatest swimmer, and I think I will always be a little nervous when I first get in the sea or a swimming pool after not having done so for a while, but at least now I know that, if you persevere, you can do things you never thought you'd be able to. There's no greater feeling than overcoming fear.

183

Rebecca Loos

TV Personality

My good friend Giles Vickers Jones has asked me to put together in words what the best day of my life has been. I find this almost impossible, as being a woman I am rather hoping the best day of my life is yet to come, when I meet my soul mate and future life partner or the day I become a mother, neither of which has happened yet.

So I look back on my very colourful life trying to pick a suitable day to share with you. A life which I am living to the max taking many risks, plenty of adventures; I've travelled the world, met all sorts of people from beggars to kings, learned to become a circus performer, survived on a deserted island with no food, no blankets, nothing for three months, had affairs, been in love, had my heart broken (a couple of times) and have broken hearts (lost count). In fact, most adventures seem to involve love and allowing love to take you over to the point where you don't care about right and wrong and you don't care about tomorrow – but, instead of writing about soppy love stories which we have all most likely at some point in our lives experienced, I am going to share with you a day when a childhood dream of mine came true. This day was Tuesday, 9 October 2007 in Barcelona, Spain.

As far as I can remember I have always loved cars, motorbikes and anything involving speed. My father's hobby has always been cars. He has raced Formula 3 and participated in many rallies including the famous Monte Carlo.

I was 16 when I begged my father to take me out of school and put me in a racing school, determined to be the world's first female Formula 1 racing driver. It didn't happen. I got many lengthy talks about how important A levels were and that racing is a man's world and how I would be struggling to get off the grid. So I had to erase all images of me standing on the podium at the Monaco Grand Prix in my Ferrari suit shaking a huge bottle of champagne and instead got stuck into my Spanish, French and English literature A levels!

I currently hold a licence to drive any car and any motorbike and have driven these as well as a range of tractors, quads and trucks. I've never driven a bus and to be honest never really had the desire to either! I've flown an ultralight plane but that is where it ends in terms of driving things in the air. On water I've driven the usual speedboats, and the usual water toys one rents for an hour while on holiday by the beach.

That is, until this October, when my Spanish agent called me up and told me that Martini wanted to invite me to spend a day on the Montmelo racing track in Barcelona to do a Formula 1 racing course with legendary driver Marc Gene! I almost dropped the phone, which was followed by a lot of jumping and screaming.

I packed my jeans, a T-shirt and my bright-yellow trainers, jumped on a plane to Barcelona and checked into a hotel for a good night's sleep. The next morning was to be my big day.

As I arrived at the racing track and met Marc Gene and the whole team, I was trying very hard to contain my excitement. We were taken upstairs to a classroom where Marc talked us through the day ahead. I was the only girl. Two of the big bosses from Martini were taking part, as were two football players from Barcelona FC and little old me.

Marc told us that, in order to familiarise ourselves with the racing track, first we were to do a few laps in a Ferrari 430 (one of my most favourite cars and one that I have only ever seen in person, never been in and most certainly never driven!). Containing my excitement was becoming increasingly more difficult as he went on. Following our laps in the Ferrari 430, we were to do about seven laps in a Formula 3 car and to conclude three laps in the Formula 1. He talked us through how the cars worked. I listened very carefully, eager not to miss a thing. Driving the Ferrari and the F3 was easy. The Ferrari has the gear change behind the wheel, levers you pull and push to change gear. This is now becoming more common in super and sports cars because it is a faster and more certain way of changing gears. A system I was already familiar with, so no worries there. The F3 is as basic as a racing car can get. You lie in the car just inches off the ground with your legs stretched out in front. There are three pedals as in a normal car and one wooden lever to your right, which you push once to go up a gear and pull towards you to go down a gear. Basic stuff and I knew I would have absolutely no problems there either.

The F1, however, is slightly more complex. Your position is the same, inches off the ground, but you only have two pedals: accelerator and brakes. The gears are tiny buttons on the steering wheel above which you have a row of round green lights that light up one by one depending on your revs – so you can only go up a gear when the third light is lit. And, as I learned later, one has to be going very fast indeed for this to happen.

There are more lights on the steering wheel and all sorts of complicated-looking things going on.

Class over, it was time to get dressed up in a bright-red catsuit (my dream was slowly coming true!) and head down to the racetrack. The cars were all lined up like racehorses in their cages eagerly waiting to be released to run as fast as they could around the track. The Ferrari 430 is a beautiful car and such a dream to drive. The only reason I actually got out of it after completing my laps was because the F3 and F1 were awaiting me.

As I slid into the ever so low F3 and sped off to take her around the track, I loved it more and more each round. A very easy car to drive and so much fun.

By now I knew the track well; I knew when to brake and when not and most importantly when I could put my foot down and go!

So they brought out the F1. This car suddenly didn't look much like a racehorse – instead it had transformed into a big black angry bull. I could see the smoke coming from its nostrils. Power is what this car resembles. Power and strength and if one isn't careful death. I loved it and couldn't wait to get in.

Once in the car, everyone was fussing over me making sure my helmet was secure, strapping me in with the safely belt, checking this and that (I felt quite stuck and trapped inside, as you can barely move your arms just enough to steer and that's it). It was also very hot.

Now during the class they explained that one of the most complex things in any F1 racing car is actually starting it and driving off without stalling. So I really didn't want to stall with everyone around watching, all cameras on me; all the boys and me had driven off perfectly, except for one who stalled and I had absolutely no intention of joining him!

The engine was running. The people around the car moved away to give my roaring bull the space it needed to take off. They signalled for me to put the car in gear, which I did, and then they signalled for me to drive off. I did so perfectly leaving the pit stop behind and entering the racetrack. When racing, you have to accelerate and go as fast as you can for as long as you can, brake hard just before the bend, take the bend and then accelerate and do it all again. So I did this, although at a speed I felt safe at and not one that would risk my life. All sorts of lights came on; I found it hard waiting for the third green light to come on to change gear because by the time it happened I was at the bend and had to brake, so I obviously wasn't going fast enough; however, I was going at the speed I felt safe at. This was important; I may be wild and daring in many things but I am well aware that there is a very thin line between crazy fun risk taking and danger. The latter is to be avoided because, once you cross that line, nothing but trouble lies ahead.

The engine is very loud and you can hear all sorts of mechanical clatter happening behind your helmet. Suddenly, a red light came on. I had a split-second panic, thinking I had done something wrong and the car was overheating followed by images in my head of flames and me stuck in the car being burned alive miles away from the team back at the pit stop. Shit! I forgot to ask how to get out in case of an emergency! I kept driving and nothing happened so, what with only one lap to go before this incredible experience was over, when I got to the straight stretch of the track, I put my foot down, screamed a loud 'Woooooooohooooo!' and went as fast as I could. Pure adrenaline!

As I drove back into the pit-stop lane, to sadly hand back my fierce bull, the smile on my face was the biggest in the world.

But it was over; my amazing day had come to an end. After many thank yous and kisses to everyone, I headed back up to the changing room to get out of my red racing catsuit. Guess what I passed along the way? The winner's podium! And yes I did stand on the number-one spot and imagine the crowds, the champagne, the feeling of winning a race. I am sure it was nowhere near the real thing but it felt good enough to me.

Without a doubt, this was one of the best days of my life.

Valentine Low

Journalist & Author

They are easy to remember, the big days in your life. Certainly, mine spring easily to mind: the day I got married, the day I got a staff job in Fleet Street, the day I went into Iraq with the British Army on the first day of Gulf War II, narrowly avoiding getting our armoured vehicle stuck in the mud as we made our amphibious landing and even more narrowly avoiding the landmines which we only noticed later, and which would have turned the most exciting day of my life into the last day of my life. The big days of your life; they are the ones you tell your grandchildren about.

But often it is the small days that afford the greatest happiness, inconsequential days where nothing much happens but everything just falls together perfectly. A day spent fishing, or walking in the hills, or playing football in the park – such things may only be simple pleasures, but they are the stuff of a life well led, and as plausible a candidate as any for the title of best day of your life.

Me, I spent the best day of my life planting potatoes. My wife and I have an allotment in West London, a patch of soggy clay surrounded on three sides by the car park of a sports centre. Charming is perhaps not the first word that springs to mind when describing its setting – try 'bleak urban dystopia', and then work down from there – but it's land, and it's ours, and, as long as the cabbages and onions keep coming, we are not going to complain. Often it can be hard finding the time to get down there – work does tend to get in the way – but somehow over the year Mrs Low and I manage to grow a decent selection of crops, from old allotment standbys such as broad beans and carrots to fancier metrosexual stuff such as rocket and Italian squash. And, of course, potatoes. In our part of London there is a thriving Irish community, who are well represented on the allotments, and I think that we would be swiftly drummed out of the Acton Gardening Association if we failed to grow a decent-sized crop of spuds.

The planting of the potatoes came on a glorious spring morning in the second half of March. It was a singularly fortunate combination of circumstances. Mrs Low and our son Orlando were otherwise engaged, our seven-year-old daughter Kitty had no pressing social obligations and the seed potatoes were crying out to be put into the ground. How better to pass the time on such a beautiful day than with a little light vegetable gardening? Kitty, being young and impressionable, seemed to think this was quite a good idea, not least because it would involve having the undiluted attention of her dad for a couple of hours.

Off we went to the allotment, father, daughter and half-a-dozen egg trays full of little baby potatoes sprouting away. Kitty was wearing her Wellington boots, and a rather fetching pair of child-size gardening gloves: when undertaking serious potato work, one cannot emphasise too much the importance of having the right kit. After a short negotiation, we reached an amicable agreement about the division of labour: I would do all the digging and ground preparation, while Kitty would do the potato selection and the writing of the labels. (Very important, the writing of the labels: you do not want anyone getting confused between the first earlies and the second earlies, or indeed the early maincrop and the late maincrop.) Other tasks, such as the measuring of the gaps between potatoes, and between trenches, were a joint effort.

Astonishingly enough, it all worked very smoothly: there is nothing quite like the enthusiasm of a little girl who wants to help her dad, and who feels she has an important role to play in the task in hand. 'Kitty,' I would say, 'I would now like half-a-dozen Charlotte tubers and an appropriate plant label,' and Kitty would duly pass the potatoes for me to put in the trench while she wrote out the label. We were, in short, a team; and while I have had many enjoyable days on the allotment – those rare occasions when Mrs Low and myself are there together instead of our usual habit of making separate trips are always a treat – I don't think I have enjoyed myself quite so much as I did that day. It helped that we spent the morning working in bright sunshine, and in fact it was so warm that I even took off my shirt for an hour or so. This may have been a bit of a mistake, for by the time we had the last potato planted I was sunburned, my shoulders and back a rather vivid pink. That doesn't happen often in March, I thought to myself, not in Shepherd's Bush.

Perhaps this all sounds a bit ordinary to be described as the best day of my life. I went to the allotment with my daughter; I planted some spuds; I got sunburned – so what? But that would be to miss the point. It is in such ordinary, deeply pleasurable days that true happiness is found. It is the difference between the time-pressed parent's desperate attempts to spend 'quality time' with their children, and simply doing stuff with your kids, regular everyday things which don't sound particularly special but are the real foundations of family life.

I do, however, have one regret about that idyllic Saturday morning: it is that the one-time Education Secretary Alan Johnson wasn't there to see us.

He would have been ever so proud. Mr Johnson was not in the job at the time, but when he was he launched the Government's new parenting strategy in which he said that parents should be encouraged to bond with their children by working together on an allotment. He also mentioned something about visiting sports grounds, playing music and taking photographs as possible alternatives, but I think that my eyes glazed over at that point.

'The involvement of fathers is crucial,' Mr Johnson said. '[It] is associated with children's better educational outcomes, school attendance, behaviour, higher educational expectations and better social and emotional outcomes.'

I like to think that, in 40 years' time or so, when Kitty goes to collect her Nobel Prize for medicine, or possibly nuclear physics – I don't think she has decided yet – she will tell the world that she owes it all to the day she went to plant the potatoes with her dad.

Ewen MacIntosh

Actor & Comedy Writer

I don't remember much about the day. I was at work as usual. Although I'd moved to London to write and perform comedy, it certainly wasn't paying the bills, so I was working as a supervisor for a market-research company. To be honest, the job was OK. I didn't enjoy it as much as I used to because I had got as far as I could without taking a permanent contract so I had nothing to aim for. The reason I didn't take a permanent contract was so I could leave quickly if a good acting job came up, but after a year in the big smoke nothing much had happened and I was getting frustrated.

The worst thing about working 9 to 5 in London was always, for me, the rush hour. When I worked for the same company in Edinburgh, I would take a bus into work and it would take 10 minutes. Trying to get from Clapham Junction to Farringdon every day was a very different prospect and involved a lot of getting crushed and standing in queues – not the greatest of hardships but when you feel like there is no end in sight it can be fairly soul-destroying at times.

I would get the occasional call from my agent to go to an audition and there was a bit of money coming in from the writing but all in all I was starting to wonder if moving to London was maybe a rash decision.

I remember that it was the lunch break and I had a message on my phone to call my agent, which I did. She basically asked me if I wanted to do six weeks' work in the office. Now, the thing with agents is that most of them assume that absolutely everyone knows absolutely everything about the minutiae of what is going on in the world of film and TV casting/production.

I didn't. I thought that she had taken pity on me after so long without any acting work and was offering me the chance to do work experience in her office. Maybe I could meet the odd director or producer coming in for a meeting … I could perhaps make coffee for some of the more successful actors and get some tips from them. But I would basically feel like a pathetic failure as my lack of success was rubbed in my face every day.

These were the thoughts rushing through my mind as I tried to find a suitable response. I think I said something along the lines of 'What would it involve?' desperately trying to buy some time while I thought of a way to get out of it.

'Well, they're looking for people with a background in improv comedy to play some of the supporting roles' came the reply.

And then it dawned on me; she wasn't asking me to come and do work experience, she was asking if I wanted to take a small background part in a TV show that, let's be honest, nobody except a handful of people in the industry had heard of: a show called *The Office*.

Penny Mallory

Rally Driver & TV Presenter

A forest somewhere in Cumbria in 2003.

I drove down the forest track knowing that at the very least this was going to be an extraordinary day. I was a little nervous, which was strange, as I'd done this kind of thing loads of times before.

The gravel road led me through huge pine trees until I got to a clearing where the M Sport Ford World Rally Team had set up various trucks and awnings, with mechanics busying themselves around a Ford Focus World Rally Car.

All World Rally cars are exciting – but this one was a very special car. I clocked the car's registration straight away, and it clicked – I had driven this car in the Network Q Rally of Great Britain back in 2000, and became the first woman in the world to compete in one. A huge honour and privilege. Today the driver was former World Rally Champion Colin McRae.

Our mission was to film me sitting alongside Colin, while he drove like a man possessed around the gravel stage. I was going to ask him abut his driving style and technique and he was going to talk and demonstrate his skills. Sounds simple and exciting. Once filmed and edited, it would form part of Colin's *Pedal to the Metal* DVD which would be on sale in a few months' time.

First things first – grab a coffee and catch up with the film crew and mechanics. Between them all, they had to make sure the car was all in perfect working order, then rig the car with cameras. We needed a camera pointing at his feet (it's quite something to watch the clever footwork of these drivers), one pointing at me, one at Colin, one facing forwards looking at the road ahead and one final camera that would catch the 'sideways' action – which would make the really spectacular footage. Rally drivers spend a great deal more time at 90 degrees to the road than they do facing forwards.

I had known Colin for probably 12 years – from way back when I started rally driving. Our paths had crossed many times over the years, and of course I had interviewed him hundreds of times while presenting *The World Rally Championship* for Channel 4.

We could hear Colin landing his helicopter in a field not far away. We all thought, Flash git, but no one said it out loud.

Saying hello and catching up with Colin was easy. He was a very laidback guy – always taking the piss, laughing at everyone around him and occasionally taking the piss out of himself. He was relaxed and in a good mood. Great start.

I have been lucky enough to have driven lots of rally cars, and have sat next to some of the world's best rally drivers, but this was going to be something extraordinary.

Imagine a car that is stripped bare of every non-essential item, there's no soundproofing, no carpets, no stereo, no electric windows. Bare metal everywhere which means it gets really hot inside. Left-hand drive. Sequential gearbox (like a motorbike) and gear changes can only be made on full revs, without the clutch.

WRC cars have to be as lightweight as possible and be as well balanced as they can be. 0–60 seconds takes less than four seconds. Top speed is only 120mph but there aren't that many opportunities to be completely flat in top in a forest. And, if you get to be flat out, the huge brakes will stop you on a sixpence. It's as close to an offroad Formula 1 car as you'll ever get. Awesome.

This is a Ford Focus WRC – but nothing like a road-going Ford Focus. Only the rear-view mirror is shared with both models.

Belted and buckled into our racing seats, Colin set off down the stage. He blurted out, 'What a piece of shit this is … I can't drive this all day … what a heap of junk!'

And there was me thinking it was the best piece of machinery every built. Clearly, his current WRC car had moved on and evolved into something far more easy, responsive and quick to drive.

Wow, this man has talent, I thought. It felt like we were never going to get through the next corner alive, but a tweak on the handbrake, an adjustment on the wheel and we were heading down the road, chatting away about his driving. It was like being on a merry-go-round ride for eight hours. Sideways through impossible bends, flat out down the hill, doubting if the brakes could ever stop us in time for the next corner. Colin McRae was one hell of a natural driver, and amazingly was also able to multi-task by answering all the questions I fired at him as we sped through the trees.

How much fun can a girl have in a day? It got better. Once filming was done, Colin asked if I'd like to jump in his helicopter – he needed to pick something up from his brother, Alistair. I didn't need to think hard about that one, so, as we lifted into the air, my face was still beaming. Not only was this man a genius behind the wheel of a car, but he was also one hell of a pilot. Unbelievable guy.

The day Colin died in his helicopter on 15 September 2007 was one of those days I'll never forget. I had had the privilege of not only knowing him, and working with him, but also driving and flying alongside him for that incredible memorable day, laughing and joking and having a ball. At least it's all on DVD so everyone can enjoy it.

God speed, mate.

Chris Manby

Author

I can't pretend the day started out in a particularly promising way. I'd taken the train down to my parents' place in Warsash on the Solent the previous evening, freshly heartbroken and crying all the way from Clapham Junction. When Dad brought me a cup of tea at half-past eight, I'd already been awake for hours, going through the things the man I'd loved and so suddenly lost had said to me and trying to work out if there was anything to be saved. When Dad said we were going to spend the day looking after my five-year-old nephew, my feelings were mixed. I adore my nephew Harrison but I was worried that he would pick up on my unhappiness and it would make him nervous or upset.

Dad has never been one for long, analytical conversations in the wake of disaster. His take on my love-life traumas had always been dismissive or comedic (such as when Mum and I were discussing a break-up and Dad ran in from the garden carrying a toad. 'Kiss it,' he said. 'It may be your last chance.'). This time, however, Dad seemed to understand that my heartache would not be assuaged with a joke. So he suggested something completely different.

'We're going crabbing,' he said.

Crabbing?

'Yes. Fishing for crabs.'

He showed me the kit: a bucket, a couple of bamboo sticks accessorised with those little net bags you get in boxes of washing-powder tablets ... and some lightly rotted fish-heads begged from the fish counter at the supermarket the night before.

My sister arrived with Harrison. Though it was May, the weather was atrocious and Harrison's body-size was doubled by a puffa jacket. We walked down to the harbour and out on to the jetty. The tide was fairly high. It was a grey day and the wind was strong. I made Harrison sit down on the jetty, afraid that the wind would catch his puffa jacket and sweep him out to sea. He sat down cross-legged beside me and watched patiently as Dad filled the net bags with the fish-heads and weighted them down with pebbles. We dangled them over the edge of the jetty, letting them sink right down to the sea-bed. And we waited. And waited. It started to rain.

'Have we got one yet?' Harrison asked roughly every 10 seconds.

We would pull the net bags out and see nothing but dead fish. But, eventually, we got a nibble and after that there was no stopping us.

The first crab was as small as a 10-pence piece. The same brown as the mud it lived in. Later there were crabs as big as Harrison's fists with shiny shells, red legs and splashes of neon green. We caught dozens of them, shaking them from the nets into the bucket where they roiled, snapping their claws indignantly at the thought of the fish supper out of which they'd been cheated.

After an hour or so, during which the light drizzle only got heavier, we took the crabs we'd caught halfway up the beach and released them. The real fun of crabbing is seeing them running sideways down to the sea. Harrison whooped with delight as they skittered on past him.

We walked back to see Grandma. En route Harrison held my hand and told me about a television programme he'd seen in which a builder went into one of those portable loos, a Davlav, only to find himself hoisted up into the air by a crane. Harrison was tickled by that. And I was tickled too by his retelling of the tale.

About a month later, disaster struck. Harrison, his little brother Lukas and their mum, my sister Kate, were getting ready to go to the library. As they rushed to leave the house, somehow Harrison's thumb was caught in the front door and practically severed. He was rushed to hospital in Portsmouth for emergency surgery. My sister later told me that, as Harrison was being wheeled into the theatre, the nurse explained how the anaesthetic would work.

'You'll just have a nice dream,' she said.

'I'm going to dream about going crabbing with Granddad and Auntie Chris,' he told her.

Thank goodness the surgery – almost three hours of it – was a success. A year and a half later, you can hardly see the scar.

Hearing about Harrison's exchange with the nurse reminded me how precious life is. The best days aren't always birthdays and weddings. That grey afternoon on a jetty with two of the most important men in my life will always be one of my favourite memories.

James Mannion

Journalist

O n reflection, the best day of my life was probably my wedding day. That's really what I should be writing about – and as far as Mrs M is concerned that's *exactly* what I've done – but seeing as this book is in aid of Sporting Chance Foundation it seems only right and proper to tell you about the best day of my *sporting* life. One grey day at the Old Wembley seeing Aston Villa giving what is biblically known as a 'good old-fashioned humping' to the much fancied Manchester United in the Worthington Cup Final.

The year is 1994 and via the most painful of semi-finals – vs. Tranmere, which went to penalties and caused me to leave a game early (well, a slowly updating teletext page) for the first time ever; I left the house cursing my father for getting me involved with this team and this unbearable stress – Aston Villa were at a Wembley Cup Final for the first time in over 20 years. OK, it wasn't the FA Cup but the Worthington/Milk/Coca Cola (why so many beverages?) Cup is still the League Cup by another name, and, despite an illustrious trophy-filled past that included a glut of Championships and even a European Cup, it was my first chance to see us lift some silverware and to visit the hallowed Twin Towers.

The day began as all good footy road trips should – with alcohol.

Myself and various members of my Villa-supporting family loaded up the car with crates of four-packs of varying flavours – only for the whole lot to be consumed before we had reached Spaghetti Junction. This lead to the second tradition of away days – peeing in a moving vehicle. (We'll move on, but let's just say denim, car seat and plastic bottle met urine with varying degrees of success.)

Not before long, though, talk turned to what we thought our chances were for the forthcoming game of two halves. Sure, we had a promising team of League stalwarts (and an even more promising collection of moustaches) with the likes of Kevin Richardson, Earl Barrett and Sean Teale – but could we really hope to stop a rampant Man U side who contained the likes of Cantona, Giggs and Keane? These guys were on the brink of achieving England's first ever 'Triple' and both Saint *and* Greavsie fully expected them to do so. We were to be a minor footnote in their glorious reinvention.

Well, as a man much better paid than me once put it, football is a funny old game – and, as soon as the teams emerged on that March date, I had a funny feeling we might just get something. There was the fact that all the radio reports we'd been absorbing on the journey down had suggested the neutral viewing footy audience were anything but. In fact, there seemed to be a building collective national wish that we stop Man United in their tracks. This was confirmed by the four or five Londoners who stopped me to shake my hand on the walk to Wembley – identifying me as a Villa fan from the replica shirt I was wearing over a baggy hoody top and voluminous Stone Roses-sized jeans (I looked like a moving Isosceles triangle) – and to ask that we 'put one over those red bastards'. We were suddenly surfing a wave of public popularity that hadn't happened outside of B6 since *Crossroads* had disappeared from our TV screens. Buoyed up by such a groundswell of good feeling, our boys seemed to emerge from the tunnel walking slightly taller, chests puffed out slightly bigger and facial hair bristling slightly bushier-y. Add to this the fact that United were wearing a very strange third kit of canary yellow and lime green, and the Mighty Reds all of a sudden looked more like Not So Mighty Swizzler Lollies. However, when all was said and done, they still had – on paper at least – by far the strongest team.

Thankfully, then, we were playing on grass not paper (ho ho) and from the first toot of the ref's whistle we were all over them. Never before had the strike partnership of Dalian Atkinson and Dean Saunders looked so dangerous, never before had the gloves of Mark Bosnich look so big in goal and never before had Eric Cantona been subjected to so much sixth-form-humour-based abuse from a long-haired reprobate from Birmingham. You see, I had taken it upon myself – seeing as I was about 100 rows from pitch-level and therefore out of kung fu range – to 'weaken' the talismanic Frenchman's hold on the game by ensuring that every time he was in touching distance of the ball I would cry out at the top of my lungs the choice phrase 'Encoulez Le Poulet!' For those of you without GCSE French, I was suggesting, quite forcefully, that Eric was having 'relations' with a feather-coated farmyard animal. The more my friends and family giggled at this outburst, the more they were encouraged to join in – and soon a minor percentage of the Wembley crowd were heard screaming the phrase every time Mr Cantona got near the ball. Subsequently, he had a shocker. Where once he would caress the ball to a teammate, he shinned it into touch. Where before he would thread a pass through the eye of a needle on to the toe of a goal-bound teammate, he shanked balls off backsides and hit linesmen and mascots. He was firmly in my pocket and no amount of collar raising and Gallic hand-on-hips protesting was going to change that. (Incidentally he wasn't the only person to be negatively affected by my clever and caustic comments. The woman standing behind me? One, Mrs Cantona, of course. I'm sure it's no coincidence that Eric was 'encouraged' to quit British football not long after that – the image of a Brummie shouting barely literate swear words must have lived long in the memory …)

We owned Man United that day (and there aren't many teams who can say that) – and even the suspected late red surge, fingernail biting and clock watching didn't materialise when Andrei Kanchelskis decided to handle the ball in their penalty area, getting himself sent off and giving us our third goal from the spot. It meant we could enjoy every minute – and we did. We sang, we cheered and – come the final whistle – we shed a tear of joy. Aston Villa had won 3–1 and the evil footballing empire had been thwarted. Of course, of the two managers, Sir Alex Ferguson would have the more profitable footy future but, for that one brilliant, best ever day, we were on top and all was well with the world.

Sharon Marshall

Journalist & Author

This is going to come across as shallow. I know I ought to write about doing something incredibly brave and selfless for charity. But sod it. Let's be shallow instead.

My best day so far was the day I snogged Morten Harket, the lead singer from A-ha.

OK. Technically it wasn't really a mutual snog. He was more of a passenger. If I'm being strictly honest, I suppose I assaulted him really. But it happened a while back now and he still hasn't sued. So I'm classing it as a snog.

Morten had been a 20-year obsession. Ever since he appeared in *Smash Hits*, pouting with cheekbones, tight jeans and hipbones.

A week later, every girl in my high school class knew the words to 'Take On Me'. We universally hated the girl in the comic-book-style video because she got to kiss Morten (even though he was only a line drawing at the time).

And we all loved Morten. We loved him even more than David Hasselhoff. The Hoff was torn down off the bedroom walls. Morten went up instead.

He stayed there for years. We all went to see the Bond film *The Living Daylights* just because he sang the theme tune. We wore leather

205

shoelaces round our wrists. In an act of politeness, we learned how to spell the names of his bandmates, Magne Furuholmen and Pål Waaktaar even though we weren't really that bothered about them.

And, in 1986, they did a UK tour. Inexplicably, my parents didn't want the 14-year-old me getting on a train to Sheffield to scream at a popstar and tell him I loved him. Everyone else in class had the sense to lie and invent a sleepover, and off they all went.

They made banners with Morten's name on, which, for courtesy's sake, carried small mentions for Mags and Pål. They queued at the stage door to give in their handwritten marriage proposals which the security guard swore he'd pass on.

There was one girl called Lisa who said Morten had blown a kiss in her direction during 'Take On Me'. She didn't shut up about it for months. Cow. I hated her.

I carried the hurt for 20 years. Until Guilfest, summer 2006, a large field in the middle of Guilford. A-ha had re-formed and they were headlining. And this time I was ready. I was a TV journalist and I had a press pass. This time nothing was going to stop me.

What happened next was shameful, pathetic, juvenile and no way for a grown woman to act. I didn't think about any of this though. I just thought, I wish Lisa could see me now.

I flashed the press pass at reception, and demanded an interview with Morten Harket.

'Do you have an appointment?'

'No.'

'A camera crew?'

'No. But I've got a press pass. And I just need two minutes to do a very important interview for this very important daytime programme I'm working on. It's urgent.'

They went off to ask him. Twenty minutes later, they came back. He said that, if it was a genuine interview, I could meet him after the concert: 'As long as he's not going to get wet.'

In my 15 years of interviewing celebrities, this was, and still remains, the oddest response I have ever had to an interview request but I didn't argue. It must be a Norwegian thing, I thought. He will not, I assured them, get even the slightest bit damp.

Twenty minutes passed and then I was waved through to his dressing room.

Mags and Pål were on a sofa outside. They stood up and looked hopeful. I decided this was not the time for politeness, blanked the pair of them and opened Morten's door.

He was waiting. By candlelight. A clever move. As, by candlelight, he still had the pout, the cheekbones and the hipbones. (Unlike David Hasselhoff who I met last year by full stark, studio light and who turned out to be disappointingly old and full of phlegm in the flesh.)

No, Morten was candlelit. And Morten was still perfect. And Morten was much, much closer to me than he'd been to anyone in my class that night back in Sheffield in 1986. And he was expecting me.

As I promised a genuine interview would emerge from our meeting, I will print my exclusive chat with Mr Harket in full.

Me: Hi. Can I kiss you?

Him (slightly startled): Where do you want to kiss me?

Me: Here, in your dressing room! [I know I know, silly cow. I should have answered 'the lips' or 'your hotel'. I was overcome and still worrying about the Norwegian water thing.]

Morten gives me brief kiss on cheek.

Me: Thank you. I love you. I have been wanting that for 20 years. I kissed you every night on my bedroom wall. You feel so warm. Can I have an autograph? Will you write something saucy? [Hope you're reading this Lisa by the way!]

Him: Saucy? I don't write. I do perform though.

Morten puts his hand on my bottom.

Me: Oh God!! Oh God!

207

At this point I'm afraid I lunged. He tried to duck but was not quite fast enough. Maybe his reflexes aren't what they used to be. Or maybe he just wasn't expecting a middle-aged daytime TV presenter to assault him.

I have a photo of us together. I radiate happiness. He looks terrified. And slightly distorted from where I'm grabbing his face and trying to force him in my direction while he shouts towards his PR for help. I think we sort of look like a couple though.

Whatever. I've done it. I beat Lisa. I've touched him. I've kissed him. I told him I loved him. I got closure.

I told you it was shallow. But it's still my best day so far. Cheers, Morten.

Lisa Maxwell

Actress

The best day of my life is unquestionably the day my daughter Bo was born. It was a Sunday afternoon, I went into labour and thought, Oh, I don't really want to be feeling any of this, so I went to the hospital and had an epidural. Fortunately, I had an anaesthetist who had a raging hangover and didn't want to keep popping back to top me up so she gave me a whacking great dose of it. That bit hurt and I think I swore 25 times in half a second. Then I settled back into the hospital bed, watched the MTV Awards and ate chocolate oranges. Eleven hours later she was born, my perfect little girl, 6lb 13oz, no stitches, just blissful from beginning to end. Obviously the technicalities of the birth are not the thing that made it the best day of my life. The fact that my baby girl was given to me and arrived on the planet is what will always be the most special thing I've ever had the luxury of experiencing. And every birthday since – she's now eight years old, so eight birthdays – have reminded me of what was the best day of my life and will always be.

It was very straightforward. We decided we were going to try for a family and two weeks later we were pregnant. I was doing a show called *Boogie Nights* at the time at the Savoy Theatre with Shane Richie who is a dear, dear friend and subsequently godfather to Bo. I had to wear very tight lycra hotpants for that show and the thought of having to hobble around until I was six months pregnant filled me with horror. So I made the decision to leave the show early and spend some time with my partner. It was a big decision but you have to get your priorities right – family is more important than jobs. Lo and behold, two weeks later, I was pregnant. It was a very easy conception and a very easy birth and actually it's been quite an easy childhood really. She's been an absolute sweetheart! I hope there are some more special days to come but until now that's the best one so far.

Martel Maxwell

Journalist & Presenter

'Hello, editor's office.'

'Oh hello. It's Martel.'

'Hello, Martel. Again.'

Nervous laugh. 'Hi, I don't suppose there's any news?'

'Not since last time you called.' The tone of the editor's PA wasn't nasty, more incredulous.

Looking back, the audacity of this 22-year-old girl calling from Dundee was something else. I had phoned the editor of the *Sun* – who had just made the top-ten most powerful people in the British media – three times a day since my interview a week earlier.

I'd made the final 20 candidates for the newspaper's first graduate traineeship. Two would be chosen from the thousands that had applied.

Six months before I had returned from another interview in floods of tears. Not because it had gone badly – it had gone rather well. I was terrified I'd actually get the job and become a trainee criminal lawyer in Glasgow. Because, through months of work experience after graduating, I knew the future was less *LA Law* and more getting shoplifters off so they could reoffend after lunch. Less lowering my voice for dramatic effect to a hushed jury hanging on my every word, more bringing a packet of B&H to my client in Perth Prison who was up for horrific child abuse.

The thought of that for the rest of my life was insufferable.

And, so, I sent my CV to national newspapers, because that, I decided, was what I wanted to be. A journalist.

Making the final 20 for the *Sun*'s traineeship made me realise I had to make the final two. It was my way out, my big chance. This was it.

The first half of my interview at Wapping HQ in London was with Rebekah Wade, the then deputy and now editor of the *Sun*, along with journalist-turned-lecturer Linda Christmas. Next to Christmas, Rebekah was good cop. She was also rather striking, with her mane of untamed red hair and undeniable charisma.

Notorious ball-breaker Christmas said, 'Everyone else has more work experience at newspapers – this is clearly not what you really want.'

(She – allegedly – asked one candidate how he expected to physically get himself to a breaking news story when he was so fat.)

'I do want it. I've never wanted anything more. I've just completed work experience at the Scottish *Sun* and had stories published – that's not on my CV.'

I sensed Rebekah liked this.

Afterwards, she walked me to the editorial floor where a sign advised: 'Walk tall, you are entering *Sun* country.'

I did. I knew this was where I wanted to be, where I could hold my head high and be part of the biggest and best.

The editor David Yelland was not what I expected. Having read *Stick It Up Your Punter*, I imagined all *Sun* bosses were like Kelvin Mackenzie, all Fs and Cs and hands banging on tables. Yelland was reserved, bespectacled and bald.

'Martel, you're up there with the top-five people I've seen today. If you don't get this, I'm sure you will do well.'

'David, I'd rather be the worst you've seen than just miss out. Being third isn't good enough. I have to be first or second and I've never wanted anything more.'

The audacity.

And so here I was calling the editor's secretary to see if a decision had been made.

'Martel, I'm afraid you are going to have to be a little more patient. I will call you as soon as …' Her voice trailed off and I heard a man in the background.

'Is that Martel? Put her through.'

'Oh, David would like a word with you.'

Cue dry mouth, clammy hands, pins and needles in my left buttock.

'Martel, the standard was exceptionally high.'

Bugger. B*llocks

'But I'm delighted to say we chose you as the *Sun*'s first ever graduate trainee.'

'Really?'

'Yes, are you happy?'

'I'm so happy I might wet my pants.'

He didn't laugh. It didn't matter, I had the job.

Now, I don't want you to think this is the happiest day of my life because friends and family are not dear to me. They are.

But getting the *Sun* job heralded the start of a new exciting life. Looking into my future and thinking, Is that it? was the worst feeling I've experienced because life is short and I want to lick the lid off of it. Changing my future was terrifying, exciting and worth it.

Two years later, after training at City University, reporting on features, news, sport, cars and Page 3 in London, Manchester, Glasgow and Sydney, Yelland called me up at 3 a.m. (I was in Australia, so it was no doubt a perfectly sensible hour in Wapping) to tell me he would like me to join the *Sun* as a staff member on the City desk.

I told him I'd been banned from doing maths at school. He didn't seem to mind.

After a spell, I ended up doing what came more naturally, as a showbiz reporter, otherwise known as The Best Job in the World. Asking celebrities cheeky questions at yet another free bar? How I miss it.

I've been with the *Sun* for eight years – more recently in Scotland as a columnist. If I felt as passionately about a boyfriend after that length of time, as lucky to be with him, as eager to see him every morning, I'd be married by now.

Along the way, I've done all manner of things for the job. I walked down the Kings Road in London wearing only my bra and pants in December, visited the North Pole, replaced a Page 3 girl after making the final of TV talent show *Popstars* and waited so long at a premiere in Leicester Square to meet Tom Cruise I wet myself.

A madness, but by jove a grand madness.

Jake Meyer

Explorer

When I was 14, I set myself the challenge of trying to climb the 7 Summits, the highest mountain on every continent. When I was 15, my father and I welcomed in the Millennium dawn from the summit of Kilimanjaro, the highest mountain in Africa, and the first of my continental highpoints. To share this wonderful experience with my father was both an incredible start to the Millennium and also to my 7 Summits aspirations.

Five and a half years later, on 4 June 2005, my breaths came in short, rapid gasps as I knelt exhausted in the snow. None of the six other continental highpoints I had climbed on my global mountaineering journey could have prepared me for this. My legs were burning from the lactic-acid build-up. My lungs were screaming, trying to draw in what little oxygen there was in the air and my heart was pounding so hard I thought it was about to burst from my chest. My head torch cast an eerie white glow over the frozen ground in front of me as I struggled to clear the ice that was rapidly accumulating over the exit valve of my regulator with my thickly gloved hands.

I was high up in the Death Zone on Everest's rocky and exposed North-East Ridge. With only 30 per cent of the oxygen found at sea level, our bodies were struggling to survive in the bitterly cold and extremely treacherous conditions. The weather on Everest in 2005 had been one of the worst on record as the upper slopes of the mountain were assailed constantly by the ferociously high winds of the jet stream. For weeks we waited patiently for the conditions to abate. On day 64, the weather window, which we had been praying for, finally materialised. The supplementary oxygen cylinders on our backs would give us a few precious hours in which to make a desperate last-bid attempt to reach the summit, but ultimately it was up to us to find the physical and mental strength to drag our beleaguered bodies onwards and upwards.

Having left the relative safety of our tent at 10 p.m. the previous night, our small team climbed through the inky darkness of the night for what seemed like untold hours. We heaved our way up snow-filled couloirs, and gently crept along knife-edged ridges. The wonderful cold silence was broken by our own ragged gasping breaths and the crunching of our boots in the snow or the cringing shriek of our crampons as they scratched across rocks underfoot. We passed old oxygen bottles embedded in the snow, and abandoned ropes lying snaked over vertical rock bands like unkempt creepers obscuring damaged fortifications. We were regularly reminded of our own fragility and mortality as we passed bodies of climbers who had made the ultimate sacrifice in the quest to fulfil their goals and dreams. Their corpses were a grim reminder that attaining the summit is not success itself; safe return, summit or not, is the only true success.

Eventually, after eight hours of struggling towards the summit, we climbed the crest on to the final summit ridge. A hundred metres in front of us lay the object of our pain and suffering, the reason for the literal blood, sweat and tears that we had poured into this expedition. We started walking carefully along the ridge towards our podium. Despite our complete and utter exhaustion, we attacked the final straight with renewed vigour. This was it, the final victory parade.

Ten minutes later, we stood on the top of the world: 8850m/29035ft above sea level. The gateway between the earth and the heavens. The ground around us dropped 15,000ft in all directions and above us the sky felt close enough to touch. Below us the sun rose lazily from the curved horizon, basking both Nepal and Tibet in its warming orange glow. Only the most majestic and prominent of the world's mountains emerged from the cloud cover, in meek honour to their sovereign Everest and her conquerors. Cho Oyo, Shish, Makalu and Kanchenjunga all lay in humble admiration at a discreet distance, and Lhotse and Nuptse sat bowing at her feet to the south. At this I just burst into tears. Tears of joy, tears of liberation. The myriad of emotions: elation, exhaustion and relief came flooding out. Suddenly everything had been worth it. It wasn't about the past hours, days or even weeks of hardship and adversity. It was about the five and a half years since I had shared the Kilimanjaro summit dawn with my father. The ultimate goal of the 7 Summits was now complete and with it came the pride of having attained exactly what I had set out to do all those years before. It was a beautiful and poignant moment; to be the highest humans on the earth. It truly was the best day of my life.

Jamie Murray Wells

Entrepreneur

If anyone had told me three years ago that I'd be running a multimillion-pound company, I'd have thought they were having a laugh. I was only 21 and still an English student at the time.

But the business I started back then, with £1000 of my student loan, has become that company. From the humble beginnings of my parents' front room with a couple of mates as my workforce, Glasses Direct went on to secure £3 million of venture-capital funding on Friday, 13 July 2007. Unlucky for some – but not for me. In fact, as it turned out, this was the best day of my life.

It all started in the spring of 2004 when I needed some new reading glasses while studying for my finals at the University of the West of England. I was shocked when they cost £150 so I decided to investigate if I could sell them more cheaply. I discovered customers were being ripped off. One ophthalmic laboratory admitted frames only cost about £7 to make. It wasn't rocket science – if I cut out the middle man and sold glasses from £15 online, I'd still make a profit.

So Glasses Direct was born and things took off really quickly – by August I was roping in friends to come over to my parents' house at three in the morning to help me process orders. I'd sold 8,000 glasses in two months and soon enough I'd raised £100,000 investment from family and friends.

Within 18 months I'd secured another £700,000 via Angel investors, Dragons' Den-type backers. I was hugely inexperienced in business so I knew I needed to surround myself with brilliant people. From David Magliano – the brains behind easyJet's marketing – to ophthalmic surgeon, David Spalton, they were all keen to come on board.

Things were going great guns and, by the end of 2006, we were selling 150,000 pairs of glasses a year and making a real impression on high-street opticians. But we'd come to a crossroads. Either we continued on Angel money, aiming for 1 per cent of the optical market over three years, or we went for venture-capital investment becoming a billion-pound international company.

Finally, on New Year's Eve, on my way to a party at my local pub in Gloucestershire, I decided to bite the bullet and follow my dream. Failure was frightening but not trying was worse.

For the next six months, I worked 24/7. I persuaded the board it was the way forward, appointed advisers and then started mapping out Glasses Direct's future. The financial model alone took 100 edits.

Finally, by June, after hours of meetings, presentations and tours, we had an amazing offer of £3 million from two major venture capitalists. One was Index, who previously backed Skype and Betfair, and the other was Highland Capital, the US fund behind Etoys.

It was like my Dream Team of investors, the ultimate partnership. The next few weeks were spent on due diligence, where my company was literally turned upside down to establish any potential problems.

It was incredibly stressful as by then I knew if they got cold feet, or there were any issues, our reputation would be discredited and we'd have to start from scratch.

Finally, Friday, 13 July was earmarked as the day the contracts would be signed. I woke up that morning feeling nervous but excited as it seemed it was just the formalities to go. The date also struck me and I tried not to dwell on its negative connotations!

At 8 a.m., I had a breakfast meeting at Le Meridien, Piccadilly, with some guys from Highland, but all I could stomach was orange juice. My offices were still in Wiltshire, so at 9.30 a.m. I headed to one of my investor-director's offices, Al Gosling from Extreme TV, to make some calls and wait before I cracked open the champagne.

It seemed like a done deal but then, at around 10 a.m., everything started quite literally falling apart. I spoke to some of the existing investors and our lawyers and discovered a last-minute legal complexity was causing problems. It was to do with the very fine detail of the deal but I was told, unless it could be sorted in the next couple of hours, everything would be off.

In disbelief, I sat with my head in my hands. Since we'd launched I'd appeared in lots of newspapers, particularly as I was such a young entrepreneur. Inevitably, that meant certain editors would be following our progress closely and any delay in an announcement would be hugely damaging to our reputation.

But in my heart I knew it could still happen, so I dashed to my lawyers' office at the Gherkin skyscraper in central London in a last-ditch attempt to make it work.

Finally, with literally minutes to go to our 1 p.m. emergency board meeting, the lawyers indicated things were back on. It was a nervy waiting game and, instead of the planned celebration lunch at the exclusive top-floor restaurant, I ate half a takeout ham and cheese sandwich from Pret at my desk.

Amazingly, that afternoon, thanks to my advisers and lawyers, it was all signed off and, by 6 p.m., I was holding a cold glass of champagne. It was an incredibly emotional time. The first people I phoned were my parents.

That night, after I left my team, I headed to Club Opal on Gloucester Road to a friend's birthday party. I was ecstatic but the day's events also felt so far removed from my social life which is just like any other 24-year-old's. No one wants to sit around discussing work so I just hung out and had fun, like any other night, just with more champagne. Somehow, though, that made the day even more perfect.

Since then, Glasses Direct has gone from strength to strength. We're forecasting sales of more than £10 million this year and there are talks of a worldwide brand rollout.

And as for me? I took a well-deserved safari holiday to Kenya with some mates. You've got to be a workaholic to get where I have but I never forget life is about having fun too.

Lembit Öpik

MP

There have been many outstanding days in my 42 years on Planet Earth. The first day was the most *important*, although I do not remember it. And it is true that, since then, in the tapestry of chances and glances which gives our evolving adventure its depth and texture, a smaller number of days have stood out as notably positive. The day I began going out with my wonderful girlfriend … the day I got my motorbike to work again … the day I first flew solo … the day I scored 21 on a television programme called *Mastermind* … the day I walked again after breaking my back … So many days on memory's carousel, slides in a show, snapshots of joy or dread or agony or hope – of what I *thought* a life less ordinary …

How easy it would be to tritely choose one of those. What a luxurious conundrum to wrestle with – to machinate over individual incidents. But to do that is to miss the wood for the trees. 'Best.' Ordinary? I realised only recently that 'living an ordinary life' is not a 'failure of a life' – but a failure of attitude. The extraordinary thing is being here in the first place, experiencing *anything* and having the unfathomable good fortune to be aware of it. I'm amazed I notice that, whatever these things that happen to me, they are happening to *me*. If you see it like that, the best days aren't many. The best days are *all*. Terminally ill people who reassure their loved ones know this. People who go to pieces in traffic jams do not.

When I was six years old, I fell out of a tree on to a post. The injuries nearly killed me, but after a lengthy recovery I lived to climb another day. In my teens I crashed my motorbike five times and my bicycle once – each accident an antidote to my petulant disregard for the laws of physics.

I nearly got myself killed in a foolhardy fundraising hitchhiking expedition with my old friend Clive Banks on the M20 near Dover. Then there was the time when I found myself pounds from bankruptcy, but recovered thanks to pennies from heaven, blessing my lucky stars that providence was a better banker than I was. And each lesson occurred on a different day. Each a rite of passage, a red letter day of learning. Tell me how I should choose between them! Does doing so not elevate one scene above the whole play?

It's not that I think we're prisoners of destiny. Far from it. I believe we have a big say over our path. But I sense that the purpose of each day is closely linked with the whole experience of why we're here in the first place. Whether you're at work, in hospital or down the pub, it's all got a purpose.

Of course, it's natural to recall one moment or hour or dawn-to-dusk episode which was a supreme time of joy. Yet joy is like a kettle boiling, the contents turning to boisterous steam, the heating element at risk of burning out if allowed to burn too long. Happiness is not so vulnerable – more like a lake, warmed deeply but slowly by the sun, and thus unperturbed by the temporary antics of an occasional storm, or thin ice on winter cold days, for the warmth within cannot be stolen, unlike steam, whose character is to dance and laugh and leave. No, the peace which comes with happiness is only snatched for moments by the fun-seekers.

And yet, for all this protestation, the publishers press me for a best day – 'for the sake of consistency' – which I read as 'convention'. Well, if it makes them happy, I will name my best day. It was the day I saw a miracle. A small cure, in truth, but observing the healing power of someone's hands was intriguing and reassuring beyond words. I think the event was something to do with a cosmos we don't fully understand. A power keeping silent vigil over species everywhere, intervening in moments of extremis and calm – two sentiments in almost ironic resonance. And, yes, what I saw *was* a real miracle – as it seemed to go beyond physics. The person *really* got better. She is better to this day. I marvelled at a power which has neither pride nor vanity but simply form. And it reassured me that my relative importance is just as slight as I'd suspected: equal to any other sentient being, but infinitesimal in the grand scheme. It's reassuring to know you're expendable. That was the day I began to put my mistakes into perspective.

But you see, even here I've just cheated! I disguised an outlook as my best day. I confess, I can't really offer a single frame from the moving images of four decades without sneaking in a message.

So I apologise to the publishers ... but with little sincerity. In their hearts even they know the meaning of life is the journey itself. And in your heart you know it too. If you look at it like that, since nothing you have done can be relived, the best day of your life is today, here, now, this present moment when you consider what your senses tell you, and remember that the future, as ungraspable as the past, is never ever attainable in the *present*. The best day can only be the authentic one which is *being* lived: the one I have today.

Mark Parker

Illusion Designer & Magician

'You woke up this morning, Got yourself a gun …
The day I went out drinking with a mafia hitman's son.'

A few of you may recognise that as the opening line of lyrics for the brilliant HBO series *The Sopranos* … Being in the entertainment business I often rock in late at night after a long drive, having had the car windows open, freezing, only to get home and find I can't sleep … One of my favourite shows since its birth on TV has been *The Sopranos*.

My story happened in September 2005 when I was invited to work at a trade show in New York at the Jacob Javitt Centre which is a massive show/conference venue. Over the years, I had worked and taken holidays in the States but had never for some reason been to The Big Apple and, at my then 36 tender years of age, a bit of me was a tad excited in a childlike fashion about going. Landing at JFK and seeing the Manhattan skyline for the first time is really smart as hell, I don't care who you are, and it's only really at this point your mind tells you, 'I'm here in New York.' Then, before you know it, you are surrounded by the immense buildings of Manhattan island, getting excited at the steam bellowing out of a drain cover, seeing Macy's and even a rusty old pulldown fire escape, surrounded by the bustle of the brash New Yorkers going about their daily business … I loved it.

The next morning I went down to the Javitt Centre as I was in town a few days before the show started to get the lie of the land. After convincing the large bling-covered security girls I meant no harm, they let me in for a look around the hall I would be working in. Exhibition halls are like carnage before a show starts – wood, metal, people, rubbish, dust and all sorts of crap lying around – then, the night before, it's all cleaned, carpeted and, as if by magic (no pun intended to those who know me), it's all ready with stock- and brochure-filled 'booths' as they are called over there.

Anyway, I found the 'booth' space and met the union-approved guys that were erecting the stand ready for the show. Like music to my ears the banter is fab. Dwayne (who we will talk about later), a tall pony-tailed guy with an American-Italian look about him; Little Dan (the head), as they called him for some reason, although I nicknamed him Dan Dan the Hologram man as he kept vanishing then reappearing beside me like the shopkeeper from *Mr Benn*; Mikey, who just doesn't give a damn about anyone in a really funny way; John, who was half-Irish and just sat back and loved the laughs; and then there was Al, a wiry 6' 5" ex-mob guy, who was once dragged out of his marital bed at 3 a.m. by the FBI as part of a massive swoop on mob crime – as you can imagine his stories were fascinating, the sit-downs with mob bosses, the FBI taking covert photos, the hijacking of trucks after tip-offs, etc. etc., all the stuff we see on TV; this guy had lived the life, got caught and now had a normal job. These were proper New Yorkers.

I got talking to Dwayne about all sorts of stuff, and I told him how hilarious it was for me hearing all his crew bantering New Yorker style, especially as I love watching *The Sopranos*.

He casually said, 'That's a great show. I only live 10 minutes away from the actual club which they use to film the Bada Bing scenes for the show.'

'Get outta here!' (I was getting in character by now!)

'I'll take you if you like.'

Well, he didn't have to ask twice, I was made up. We agreed that, once the show was over, it was game on.

I worked on the stand for the few days the show was on entertaining possible customers for the UK company I was hired by, showing them all product-related magic effects … well, it beats working for a living! All the time I was thinking of my Bada Bing visit.

On the last day of the show, Dwayne rocked in just as it closed, true to his word. Top man. By now, two other guys were joining us – Rupert, an old pal of mine who was involved in the stand design, and the client's American agent Alex, a great guy but I don't think he has ever walked the dark side of the force on a night out, so he was also intrigued to see the Bada Bing, being a *Sopranos* fan himself.

We all jumped in Dwayne's blue Ford Cougar, smoking and laughing as we went through the Lincoln Tunnel into New Jersey. Dwayne drove like he had just robbed a bank and Alex was in the front experiencing a white-knuckle ride as we sped up the wrong side of massive American trucks before darting into our exit road at the last possible moment. We were getting close!

The club we were heading for was called the Satin Dolls, a lap-dancing bar, and they basically just change the signs for filming *The Sopranos*. Dwayne explained all of this as we screeched into the parking lot. It was exactly like it is in the show. In we went past the monster-chested doorman and I stood there and took it all in. It was awesome – the massive rectangular bar with the pole-dancing chicks in the centre. I'm in the Bada Bing, unbelievable.

Now it's time to drink and soak up the Bing experience. It started with beers, then Jagermeister bombs, vodka … it was getting messy. After a few token lap dances – although I never understand what all the excitement is about, it's an expensive tease – I got talking to

Dwayne. I asked him about his surname 'Kuklinski', and he explained that his father was Polish and his mother Italian.

I casually joked that with a name like that he could have been in *The Sopranos*.

He half smiled and said, 'Mark, we have been getting on and having a few laughs, etc. I'll tell you something.'

I'm thinking, What is he about to announce? Is he a mob guy? Just killed someone? I was drunk and intrigued …

It was none of those things, but it turned out his father was a man named Richard Kuklinski, more widely known as the Iceman, the mafia hitman with over 200 killings to his credit. Look that name up on the internet, it's scary stuff.

The penny dropped pretty quickly for me because as it happens I had seen a documentary about 'inside the mind of a mafia hitman' and I quickly realised who his father actually was. At the time, his father was in Trenton State Prison for his crimes and wasn't due out for parole until he was 120!

Picture the scene: I am half wasted in the Bada Bing talking to a guy who turns out to be a famous mafia hitman's son … I'm almost in *The Sopranos*.

I couldn't help but ask him what it was like growing up with a mafia contract killer for a father. He explained that his family always knew he was a criminal but never about details. They were either totally skint or had bundles of cash around, that's just how it was. Dwayne was 17 when his father was actually convicted and it all came out in the press about his activities. The Iceman title was given to him after he had killed a guy and stored the body in an ice-cream-truck freezer for a couple of years before burying it. The thinking was that the time of death would be difficult to place when it was found, but apparently it was wrapped so well when the police actually found it there were still particles of ice in his heart … hence the name Iceman.

Dwayne is a top bloke and, from what I saw, seems unaffected by his past and we still keep in touch.

After we left the Bada Bing, not forgetting the sad purchase of a T-shirt and a group picture outside the club, Dwayne announced it was time to head off to a proper bar, so he could also have a drink and leave his car.

Ten minutes later, we pulled up into a darkened parking lot where the only visible bit of life was a door with a sign above it saying: AXIS BAR. In we went, no windows and all we could hear as we entered was some screaming thrash-metal music trying to escape the confines of the building ... tattooed bikers in leather waistcoats, rock chicks, black painted walls and dark murals, people lying drunk under tables ... it was a world away from the West End of London, my kind of place.

Dwayne is a regular and there was no bother, but he said, 'If you get any trouble let me know and I'll have a word.'

In fact, they all turned out to be great laugh. I was showing them all close-up magic while off my face and then destroying them with my drunken cocky no-fear pool-hustling skills on the pool table. Having spent most of your school life in a snooker hall potting balls into the massive American pockets makes you look like a genius out there.

In between more meister bombs and Jim Beam, it was getting messy, but all credit to Alex, who was keeping up with us all but staying close to everyone just in case.

More drinks later, I noticed Dwayne talking to this shortish guy that had walked in who shall remain nameless. Dwayne introduced me to this mini version of Stallone and whispered to me, 'This is about as close as you will get to the real *Sopranos* tonight; he has just been given an 18-year-old girl for a year as a thank-you for a "favour" he did for the mob.'

I get along with most people but this guy was hard work, very much the standoffish type with heaps of attitude but he was sort of chatting and asking questions, then he announced, 'Do you guys want to go and see some more girls?'

A collective drunken yes later and we all fired off to another place called Shakers. This place was a mini version of the Satin Dolls with lots of dancing semi-naked girls and chrome poles. Mini Sly looked more at home here and it was very apparent that every male customer in the place did not want to make eye contact with him or any of us for that matter – I can only assume that they were assuming we were connected with this guy somehow, which was quite funny really as none of us looks anything close to being gangsters.

More drinks and banter ensued but, at this part of the night, I felt, as wasted as I was, that the little mafia man was starting to test us new boys a bit. He would order lots of shots and insist they were drunk – that's like giving a cat milk in my book, ask Mr Greening! So I must have passed that one with flying colours, but I was aware he was playing games a bit.

The girls who dance in the centre of the bar have this thing where they get down and walk around to you … wriggle their sexy little behinds at you and you tuck a couple of one-dollar bills into the said thong. Now Mini Sly would do that and then deal out about 50 single bills across the bar, look to half-imply that it was for us new boys, but then stand back and watch to see if we actually took it … pretty poor darts in my book. I piled his money up to one side and used my own; I didn't know if he was offended at the time, but felt it was the best call to make. It's funny how, no matter how messed up you are, you still manage to grab some sense when you really need it. It didn't ruin the night but the tone had started to change certainly.

It was about 3 a.m. and Dwayne was as drunk as the rest of us by now but somehow he still managed to organise a limo-type cab to take us three back to Manhattan, bless him. A $100 cab ride later, we all ended up in McDonald's in Times Square all drinking coffee and reflecting on the night's events. Alex said he had just seen a side of America he didn't know existed. This was certainly one of the most unique nights out I had ever been on.

When Giles asked if I would submit a story about one of the best days of my life, the most recent without question was the birth of my youngest son Fenn four years ago but all that midwife and baby talk isn't the best of reading. So a slight twist on my best day and probably night!

Charlie Parsons

TV Producer

How do you pick out the best day of your life when every day is a good day? I haven't had a child, a miracle recovery from a fatal illness or an amazing wedding ceremony and I'm a very lucky person.

My big career lift-off as a TV producer happened with *The Big Breakfast*, a daily morning show that went out on Channel 4 between 1992 and 1999.

The day we won it was a pretty cool day.

I and my two partners, Bob Geldof and Waheed Alli, had been working damned hard to get what was at the time the biggest commission Channel 4 had ever given. We were the underdogs – no one thought we had a chance. We were a small TV production company making a controversial Friday-night programme called *The Word* but were looked down upon by our more serious and centrally placed rivals. People didn't really expect us to get any other commissions let alone something as long running and important as the breakfast show. Earlier that year, 1992, I had even gone to a special seminar on breakfast television organised by the Royal Television Society where pundits and experts from all over the world said that the only possible way of doing breakfast TV was to do it in the

232

traditional way with sofas and news – as it was already being done on BBC and ITV. Our idea was not like that: I wanted the show to feel and smell radically different, not to come from a studio or to have the fake autocue-read 'good mornings' existing shows had, but to seem real, from a real house and with no autocue, with an emphasis on positively cheering up the mornings – like the old Steve Wright show was on Radio 1.

To pitch, we sent Channel 4 a 'taster' tape in a special comedy cornflakes box, with a chart of facts and figures replacing the chart of daily vitamins provided and pictures of the proposed presenters at breakfast replacing the cover. The tape featured all sorts of nonsense including Paula Yates hoovering to the music and in the style of Queen's 'I Want to Break Free'. Even though we felt we still didn't have a chance, Channel 4 decided to put us in the running. They made us present a lot of further information, running orders, ideas, and so on. After dozens of meetings, where enthusiasm and attention to detail impressed, we got into the running to do one of the two real-time pilots that would decide the commission.

Channel 4 had set a ludicrously tight deadline to pitch, pilot and make the show. It would have been tough had we just been making a studio show but our show was so ambitious it involved doing a two-hour studio show every morning from a real house kitted out with cameras, lights and all the paraphernalia of a real studio. The pilots were in July. The breakfast show went on air in September. We had to work on the pilots and the show as if they were both happening. In practice, it meant finding a temporary house for the pilot (we found one in Forest Hill, London) and a real house which could be the permanent home for the show by August: it would need to be kitted out and get all the required planning permission. We actually had to apply for planning permission for three houses, as we couldn't be sure we would get our idea through the bureaucracies of local councils.

And so to the day of the pilot: the night before the show, our chosen female host had a last-minute panic attack and decided she didn't want to do it. Her dad rang the office and, if the director hadn't answered, he would have left us a message; she was well known but the offhand manner in which she dropped out made it clear she didn't think we had a chance of getting it. On the spot with less than six hours till we 'went live' and very little choice, I asked a researcher who was working late on a very serious music and arts documentary in the office to present the show; she would have to do two hours of live banter, with virtually no preparation, but sportingly she agreed. I can't believe even now that I did this.

By contrast, good fortune had meant that Chris Evans, who was signed to another company, was able to do the show at the last minute. My pitch to him consisted of no detail, just my telling him it would be brilliant.

And we were off.

'Good morning, it's 7 a.m. I'm Chris Evans.'

'And I'm Danielle Lux.'

'And you are watching *The Big Breakfast.*'

We did it two days in a row. Afterwards, exhausted, exhilarated and excited, we all lay out in the garden of the borrowed Forest Hill home and drank a lot – we knew we'd done well. But we weren't sure we'd won.

The pilots had been broadcast live to the studio of Channel 4. One monitor was at one end of the vast room; the other was the other end. We heard on the grapevine that the whole Channel 4 commissioning executive was clustered round our show intrigued, fascinated and surprised. But it was not until three weeks later that we heard.

I was in Cannes staying with some friends in a villa. These were pre-internet and pre-mobile-phone days. I literally had to go to a phone box on the beach and phone in to get the result. We had won it. Our hard work had paid off. We deserved it, honestly. But we had not expected to win: although we felt our show was shining, you can't take anything for granted, especially in the world of television. Of course, the work was only just beginning – we needed to secure deals with our presenters, confirm the house and the equipment and organise a million things. But these were all exciting and brilliant challenges ahead. This was the start of a little television history. Did we celebrate in Cannes that day? You bet we did!

Marie Phillips

Author

A mountain gorilla is not a creature you meet by chance. There is one mountain gorilla on earth for every 10 million people and they are severely endangered. Not only that, they tend to hang out in places like the Impenetrable Forest, on the border of Uganda, Rwanda and Burundi.

'Impenetrable Forest': there is a clue there. You are not about to run into a mountain gorilla in the Costcutter on Newington Green Road.

Ten years ago, when my sister was working for an NGO in Uganda, my parents and I went with her to the Impenetrable Forest to track the mountain gorillas that live there. At the time, there were 300 gorillas in the Forest – numbers have since increased to 340, the result of much hard work by conservation groups, aided by the increased political stability in those countries. Five family groups of gorillas have been habituated to humans, allowing a very limited amount of tourist contact: one small group a day, for a maximum of one hour. Our group that day consisted of my family plus one couple who were staying at the same camp. We assembled at dawn at the edge of the forest, nervous and excited. We were in no doubt that our visit to the gorillas was to be a very special occasion indeed.

Gorillas do not nest in one place, but roam around their territory sleeping wherever they please, so they can be pretty hard to find. There is no useful path that leads you to the gorillas, no handy rendezvous point. You go through the forest, and I mean through. A guide at the front hacks his way in with a machete and you follow as best you can. Be prepared to leave long strands of your clothes behind, hanging from the thorn trees, along with your hair and skin. What the gorillas leave behind is shit. To find the gorillas, you follow a trail of shit through the jungle, as well as the odd terrifyingly large footprint. You hope that they have shat a lot, and in nice, locatable lines. There is no guarantee that you will see any gorillas at all, let alone up close.

We hiked for several hours through the forest, hoping not to encounter anything else that might choose to congregate somewhere impenetrable: deadly snakes, for example, or guerrillas rather than gorillas, a real risk at that time. But we were in luck. Around lunchtime, we emerged into a clearing, and there they were: a large family group, consisting of a silverback, some females and some babies, having a little rest.

Gorillas are big creatures and need a lot of leaves to keep them going so they eat all day, aside from a noontime break and it was just at this break that we had found them.

The gorillas didn't seem too perturbed to see us emerging from the trees, far less perturbed than we were to see them. We knew we were coming; we had prepared for this moment; in fact, we had been drilled in the rules of gorilla watching: no loud noises, no sudden movements, don't feed them, don't run away from them and never ever make eye contact with a silverback – as if you would wish to. It's like challenging Mike Tyson to an arm wrestle. We had seen gorillas on TV and in the zoo. But this was nothing like what we had expected.

First thought: gorillas are huge. If they didn't want us here, they could just scrunch us up and throw us home. Second thought: gorillas are wild. This is their home, and we are trespassing or, rather, they are letting us in. Third thought: gorillas are intelligent. I could see them watching us, assessing us, inapprehensive but quietly curious. The guides made a kind of humming sound as we approached the group, something which approximates a happy, unthreatening gorilla noise: the gorilla equivalent of waving a white flag or passing a tray of canapés.

In return, the gorillas made a low grumbling sound, which, apparently, is a tolerant welcome – holding out a hand to shake/taking a vol-au-vent. It was a familiar noise: yes, by coincidence exactly the same stomach rumble I get when I'm nervous. The couple in our group thought they could hear another gorilla; my family knew better.

Once we had observed each other from a distance for a while, humming, grumbling and rumbling, our guides beckoned to us: they had found another gorilla, a young female sitting in a nearby thicket. We approached. Closer. Closer. Closer. We were only a few feet away. We stood, we watched. We looked into her eyes (a lady gorilla will allow this liberty). Did I imagine it or was there some recognition there? I had seen animals in the wild before, but it was always a question of 'us' and 'them'. I have never identified with a lion or a hippo. This gorilla seemed to be one of us. Not different but the same, a family member, thinking, feeling. 'Goodness,' breathed my father, 'she looks just like my mother.' Which is what we were all thinking, I was just glad that he said it first …

It was the most humbling experience of my life. I'd always taken for granted that as a human being I was special, better, above the animal kingdom and apart from it. But, if that gorilla was one of us, we were one of them. And it was not their wars, their expansion, their incursions and their pollution that was putting my species at risk.

We only stayed there for an hour but it changed me, my perception of who I am and where my place is in the world: not at the top of it, that's for certain. And, to this day, every time my stomach rumbles I think about the gorillas: how they welcomed us, and what we owe them.

Natalie Pinkham

TV Presenter

The best day of my life? How is it possible to single out just 24 hours for such a grand title? It is therefore a choice that I have made years on – based on the glorious benefit of hindsight; it was a day that I now look back on as one which offered a catalyst for personal growth – one which was pivotal in the way I want and choose to see the world. It was 17 March 2004; the day of The Jarrod Cunningham SALSA fashion show.

Jarrod Cunningham was a professional rugby player and was married to my good friend Carrie. He was diagnosed with Motor Neurone Disease (MND) on 14 June 2002. Following several long dark months of introspection, Jarrod had something of an epiphany, realising that he needed to turn things around, and do all he could to find the good in his seemingly desperate situation. He began to champion the merits of self-belief and the power of the mind to achieve all you set out to do; in doing so, he quickly became one of the most inspiring people I am lucky enough to have met.

After a brainstorm in their Middlesex flat, Carrie, Jarrod and I decided to pull together a committee to produce a fashion show to raise funds and awareness for this little-known and desperately cruel, debilitating muscle-wasting condition. Carrie's background is modelling, mine is television and our other great friends, Stacey Dawson and Elly Richardson, are a professional dancer/choreographer and an aspiring fashion designer, respectively. While none of us had any experience of putting together, marketing, selling and delivering a show, we decided (with the morale-boosting input of Jarrod) that anything is possible with our combined skills, plus a bit of imagination and application.

The response to our requests for support was overwhelming. City law firm Norton Rose injected some much-needed cash to kickstart things. Couture fashion designer Lindka Cierach and London jewellers Boodles offered stunning dresses and dazzling diamonds to light up the catwalk. Brands across the board supplied everything from underwear for the racy section of the show(!) to chocolate for the guest goodie bags. An eclectic mix of delectable models and dancers gave their time and energy for the cause; rehearsing three times a week, late at night, in order to accommodate everyone's 'day jobs'. A whole range of celebs backed our plans, with, among others, BBC's Craig Doyle, *GMTV*'s Ben Shephard, tennis star Annabel Croft and Radio 1's Edith Bowman, Mark Chapman and Colin Murray, plus a whole bevy of beauties from the world of sport all agreeing to strut their stuff on stage.

We decided the tickets should go for £30 each; but we under-estimated the interest in the show – we sold out in less than two days. Then in what felt like no time at all the evening was upon us. It was a chilly spring night. Scantily clad, roller-donning, half-made-up models raced around backstage, as the venue – Cafe de Paris in London's West End – quickly filled up. A buzzing, packed nightclub offered the perfect setting to launch Jarrod's message – one of energy, self-belief and resilience in the face of adversity. Heart-warmingly, it felt like the whole world was ready to support my friend in his plight to change the common perception of a terminal diagnosis.

The dancing, modelling, showboating and pouting to perfection

240

went down a storm. Rapturous applause encouraged even the most reluctant of amateur models into the limelight. Jarrod's newfound self-awareness coupled with his unwavering determination to fight the odds was received incredibly well when he rounded off the evening with a 10-minute speech about the emotional and spiritual rollercoaster he had been on since receiving the life-changing news a little over 18 months earlier. He explained, to the captive audience, that it was his wish to 'try to give people confidence and belief in themselves. I try to be calm, especially when others are not. I try to teach discipline and work ethic, and ask questions so they learn from their own answers. I listen.'

Jarrod was racked with self-pity in the early days following his diagnosis – and yet he metamorphosed into a person who touched so many lives. He became convinced his path was preordained – facing up to and challenging the pitiful outlook about MND forecast by Western medicine became his raison d'être.

Jarrod died in the summer of 2007. I felt a crushing, physical pain when I heard the news. It was like the illness had somehow won. It had taken someone from this world who we all still needed, who could still have such a powerful impact on people's lives. But then I realised that it was actually the power of the human spirit which had triumphed. Jarrod's message had truly been heard; otherwise why else would so many offer their time, energy and resource for free to make the fashion show such a memorable night?

My parents have always encouraged me to be the best I can be in whatever I do, on every level, from the most menial jobs to life-defining work and decisions. Mum helps me to reflect on the direction my life is taking by drawing up a questionnaire on an annual basis. I don't have to show her or anyone else my answers – but it helps clarify my thoughts on life, at regular intervals. One of the questions in December 2004 was 'What were you most proud of this year?' and my answer is one that I am more than happy to share – it was my involvement in Jarrod's fashion show. What was essentially such a simple event made me sit back, take stock and realise that kindness, helping others, a sense of togetherness, self-belief and instilling self-belief in others are what life is all about. All those human traits were in abundance that night. Jarrod's message was reflected in the faces of the crowd – hundreds of faces, all willing us to make a success of the evening.

Certain things take me back to the night. Christina Aguilera's song 'Fighter' triggers goose bumps over my entire body, and I am sure will do for years to come. Most poignant: the words 'Thanks for making me a fighter'.

Major Owen Pritchard

Royal Welsh

It was spring 2004 and the war was won, the peace wasn't lost and the bombs and mortars came more out of a sense of obligation than any desire to see you dead. I was 26 and about to reach the end of a six-month tour as the intelligence officer for Basra City and my successor had recently arrived in theatre.

My replacement, Ben, had touched down about a fortnight previously and his battle group were due to take over in just under a week. He was clearly a good operator and was actively demonstrating the kind of enthusiasm that I had long since forgotten; indeed, he was already beginning to sweep twice as clean. Having spent the last week shadowing me, he had taken over the post proper that day and so relegated me to a back seat for my final few days in Iraq. No more responsibility therefore meant a change in my prioritie; out went concerns over detailed reporting, accurate briefing and predicting future threat, and in their place came the big three: getting a tan, not getting killed and getting some TLC from our blond MO (a medical officer is a military doctor attached to a unit – in our case a 5' 10" blonde named Claire). Unfortunately for me, achieving all three would be far trickier than I'd anticipated.

Your final few weeks in theatre are hard for everyone. For the majority of the tour, most soldiers succeed in putting aside the fear of those things that they can't control and instead focus their mind on the details that they can. The last few weeks, however, become much more confused; your mind mixes up all the excitement you feel about going home with the increasingly acute knowledge that you're yet to get there. Although I was more of a desk jockey than your average tom, I was still anxious; indeed, working in intelligence (albeit at a very low level) meant that I knew not only the location of every past roadside bomb but also all the best that were yet to be. Therefore, as going out the gate meant only the sharp-sightedness of fear, I instead decided to spend the day in camp … working on my tan.

By this point in the tour, we had moved from the old Baath Party Headquarters to the Shat Al Arab Hotel. The hotel stood on the west side of the Shat Al Arab waterway and was no doubt quite grand in its day. Unfortunately for us, its day was well gone and now it was no more than a derelict shadow of its former self: no running water, a rampant smell of raw sewage and nearly a thousand soldiers sleeping and working in rooms fit for only a few hundred guests. In its defence, however, out of the hundred or so locally employed civilians that worked there – many of whom were undoubtedly spying for the variety of militias looking to one day replace us – there was an old man (a soldier back in '91) with little in wealth but honour who, together with his rather more sedentary son, made and sold the most fantastic of all ice creams.

The day's morning brought little; a lie-in long enough to smile but not so long as to get noticed, shortly followed by a quick bit of exercise. (The camp gym never invited a long stay, housed as it was in the old hotel conservatory – there's nothing like a glasshouse when the other side are throwing stones.) I then popped in to see Ben, but he was busy – the poor man no doubt deserved a much better handover – and had lunch flirting with doctor, but she was paged away. As this left me to consider my other priorities, after a quick visit to the old Iraqi soldier to sate my pistachio habit, I, Discman in hand, headed to the roof.

My intention was to use about half-an-hour of the midday sun before swapping sides – I've never been much of a sun-worshipper but my vanity had got the better of me and I was determined to go home with a tan. I took off my top, hitched up my shorts (to what can only be described as a rather unsightly 'wedgy') and turned on some tunes – it is my experience that, at this point in any account of modern military life, the writer rarely listens to anything without either politically charged or emotionally poignant lyrics – I dozed off to English Beat's 'Mirror in the Bathroom' and woke up two hours later to The Violent Femmes, and with an arse as red as Mars.

Determined not to publicly humble myself further, I tried to find the most clandestine way back to my room. My intention was to quickly cover up as much of my now glowing self as possible and lie low till the morning (rumour has it that under the Army Act 1955 you can still be charged for sunburn). Unfortunately for me, this would mean a surreptitious scurry through the third-floor lines while hoping that A Company were all out on patrol. So I crept down the fire escape, through broken doors and along the A Company corridor until I was at the top of the stairs to where I lived. This, though, was where things went awry. As I hit the landing between my floor and theirs, I heard from both above and below me the full cadence of South Welsh Infantry in expletive-laden banter; I was surrounded by swearing soldiers and stuck.

Deciding to grin and bear it, I headed down the stairs for my room on the first floor. It was on the next landing that I became somewhat confused – back in 2003 helmets and body armour were not the norm on British army bases, nor for that matter were helmets often used on patrol – but yet instead of meeting unequipped, accommodation-bound soldiers I encountered a purposeful patrol dressed to the nines with eyes that, due my inappropriate attire,

245

showed less than the usual deference to my rank. Realising that none of them knew me by name, I took advantage of my anonymity and enquired about their heightened state of dress. The answer took me somewhat by surprise, even if the condescension didn't: 'Because of the mortar attack, sir.'

'Sorry,' I replied, 'when did this happen? I've been at the gym for the past couple of hours and you can't hear the sirens over there.' Officership is nothing if not the art of bluffing.

'Twenty minutes ago,' came the corporal's voice back, slightly less rich in scorn.

'Thanks, sorry to keep you,' I mumbled before giving them the right of way.

Twenty minutes ago – I couldn't help but laugh as I thought of my bare red arse cheekily smiling at the sun while all around me mortars vainly fell – maybe a tan wasn't quite as important as I'd thought. Still smirking, I darted back to the sanctuary of my room and hid till the day had passed.

Now I know that, for many, sleeping on the roof through a mortar attack would not constitute the best day of their lives, but as we all know vanity and 80s music have always had a great deal to answer for, and, given that 1) tanning has never been one of my priorities since; 2) I survived it; and 3) that evening I received some much-needed medical attention from the MO, I can with all honesty say it was one of my life's more memorable ones.

David Quantick

Journalist

No one single day has ever quite got it together to be an entire day of being best. Some of them have had absolutely brilliant starts and then gone to pot at remarkable speed. I have had good bits over the years, many of which don't overlap, time-of-day-wise, so I'd like to put forward a sort of composite best day of my life. A montage best day of my life, if you like. And it would probably go something like this …

My dad wakes me up and tells me I'm late for school. As I arrive just in time for the first lesson, I realise this is a dream and wake up – and I don't have to go to school for hours. (This was an actual dream and was my favourite for several years.) Breakfast is my secret favourite, cornflakes with cream of the milk and, owing to some recent cooking on my mum's part, actual cream.

Now time passes and it is Christmas morning. I run downstairs and under the tree are various Action Man-related items and (possibly from a later era) a lot of *Simpsons* videos. As I unwrap them, I fast forward in time to another happy moment. It's the 1980s and I am living in a vile bedsit in West London, hating my life, but – here's the postman – and a letter from the producers of the then hugely popular comedy show *Spitting Image* telling me that they like one of my sketches and are going to use it. From this day on, I am a comedy writer.

Forward again now to a small town in America where I am standing in a church and – hey! – it's my future wife. After the wedding, our limousine driver – who is now also my father-in-law – drives the limo at 90mph the short distance from the church to Karen's parents' house. We barely have time to wave at the guests before the G-force pins us to our seats.

Still laughing, I discover I am in a record shop buying a copy of the *New Musical Express*. I have a review in it. I walk out of the shop, reading and reading … and nearly walk into my driving-test examiner. It is the beginning of the 21st century and, despite tons of driving lessons, I am probably about to fail my driving test for the fourth time. But – hurray for fast forwarding! – this time the examiner tells me I have passed. 'You're joking,' I say, but she isn't.

Now it is the evening. I am in town having a curry with my friends Simon and Andy, and later we will go to the pub. Brilliantly, however, at the same time I am also at home with Karen. We are having a DVD night and somehow watching hundreds of great movies – *2001*, *The Long Goodbye*, *Time Bandits*, *All About Eve*, *Zoolander*, and a host of others.

And so – after a slightly bizarre late-night snack of Christmas pudding and port – to bed. It has been, if not the best single day of my life, certainly the greatest hits of the best day of my life. I'm happy with that!

Heidi Range

Sugababes Singer

To tell you about the best day of my life, we have to start on a train journey from Liverpool Lime Street to London Euston. I know this doesn't sound particularly exciting but please bear with me. You see, on this train journey, like many others before it, I was staring out of the window. But, instead of watching the industrial North and the cars and the fields and the sheep whizz by, I was playing out a music video in my mind. A music video starring me!

This video wasn't being filmed; it wasn't tipped for the top of the charts. Hell, there wasn't even a song yet. But a girl can dream, can't she? My dream finally did come true on 4 May 2002. Sugababes' single 'Freak Like Me' entered the charts at number one and, to tell you the truth, it was even better – in fact much, much better – than I'd ever dreamed of on the train from my home town to the capital city that afternoon. I had flown back from Thailand to Liverpool that day and my mum was throwing a party at her house. Red, white, green and orange were the colours reflected from the light, not of the living-room décor or of the balloons and banners that had been hung around the house but of the many bottles of red and white wine, champagne and beer and vodka that stood side by side in the kitchen. What a night we had in store!

As it goes, what a night had to be put on hold for half-an-hour as

249

the many drinks we had lined up on the kitchen units were no good without coke, soda, juice, etc. Me and my sister volunteered to drive to the local shop while my mum finished laying the dining table with sandwiches, cheese, sausage rolls and other party food for my family and friends. Me and my sister got into my mum's blue Fiesta, put on our seatbelts and turned on the ignition.

As we were about to pull out on to the road, we heard the radio DJ announce that Sugababes were tipped for the number-one spot in the charts later that day. (Now don't get me wrong, I along with my friends and band members hadn't been getting ahead of ourselves presuming we had our first number one – we had received our official call earlier that day to confirm that we had done it!) Driving down the road with my sister where I had lived since I was four years old and listening to my song on the radio full blast while we were singing along at the top of our voices and crying with happiness is a treasured memory that I will never, ever forget. The day was spent with the people I love, my family and friends who had known my dream my whole life in our house.

I don't remember the exact time the announcement was made, somewhere between 6.30 and 7 p.m. I suppose, the lapse in checking the time was due to my excitement for what lay in store as well as quite a few glasses of champagne by now! We were all gathered round our radio, which was playing at full volume, party poppers in one hand and topped-up glasses of bubbly in the other, beaming smiles on every face from my baby cousins to my two nans as we waited for it to become official.

And there it was in glorious Technicolor on Radio 1: 'Freak Like Me' by Sugababes was top of the charts, number one. Everyone screamed, cheered, hugged and cried, laughed and danced and, yes, it really was the best day of my life.

Dan Rookwood

Journalist

The best day of my life began at a urinal in Istanbul. Of course it did.

It was while watching everything go down the drain – not just several bottles of beer but my engagement ring savings, relationships with my girlfriend and boss, and, hell (in the overly emotional heat of the moment), My Entire Life – that I had an epiphany. A Eureka! moment. Up until that point, it was up/down there as the worst day of my life.

It had started 40 hours and £2,000 previously in Los Angeles. I was there to interview a Hollywood star for my magazine and then to enjoy a holiday with my girlfriend, Sam. The day before my interview, I got a text message in the middle of the night. I saw that it was from my younger brother, Joel, and my heart leaped. It simply read: 'Got u a ticket!' I've still got that text message on my phone.

I didn't get back to sleep: I lay awake wondering how I was going to explain to my girlfriend and to my magazine that I was catching the next flight to Istanbul to go to the European Cup Final between Liverpool and Italian giants AC Milan.

One of my most vivid childhood memories from growing up in Liverpool is being allowed to stay up with Joel to watch the 1984

European Cup Final when Liverpool beat Roma on penalties, thanks to goalkeeper Bruce Grobbelaar's famously wobbly legs. I was five, Joel was three and our support of Liverpool FC was crystallised into an obsession that night.

Sam didn't understand, nor did my editor. But there was nothing rash or foolhardy about my decision. In fact, there was no decision to make. I'd waited 21 years for this.

Of course, so had every other Liverpool fan and there were close to 80,000 of us making our way to Turkey so finding a last-minute flight was complicated and expensive. I made it via Paris, London, Frankfurt, the money I'd be saving for a diamond and a lot of luck. When I arrived, my phone wasn't working; no one's was. But, in among the red sea of 30,000 Scousers that thronged Istanbul's Taksim Square the night before the game, pretty much the first person I saw was Joel. It was a hell of a night. It made me proud.

Once the game kicked off, however, everything went horribly wrong very quickly. By half-time, we were 3–0 down to Milan and it should have been more. A record thrashing was on the cards. It was embarrassing. People all around me were in tears; a few were even leaving. It didn't feel like a football match. I went to the gents. It was while thinking about what I was pissing away that I began to laugh. It was either that or cry. The bloke standing next to me began to sing. '4–3! We're gonna win 4–3! We're gonna win 4–3! We're gonna win 4–3!'

It was then that I had my moment of clarity. I didn't for a second think that we could turn the game round, but I was determined that, come what may, we were going to make the most of it, put a proud fight.

As I returned to my seat, 45,000 Liverpool fans were singing the most deafening, nerve-tingling rendition of the famous Liverpool anthem 'You'll Never Walk Alone' I'd ever heard. Louder, even, than after the decisive semi-final second leg against bitter rivals Chelsea at our own home ground of Anfield. Somehow we'd taken over the ground. Three-quarters of the Ataturk Stadium was swaying with flags. It was collective grieving. Milan's end was silent, still, awestruck.

And then it came, the golden sky at the end of the storm that we, with hope in our hearts, had sung about at half-time and a million times before; the hour that has gone down in history as the greatest comeback in the history of the game. There's no point me trying to give a suspense-ridden account of what happened next. Everyone knows the story, and I really couldn't do it justice. To come back from 3–0 down to draw level and then win on penalties ... it's beyond my expression. If Shakespeare had been stood next to me, he'd have snapped his quill and just shaken his head in disbelief. If this had been a film script, the actor I was due to interview on Sunset Boulevard that day before would have rejected it on the grounds of being too far-fetched and schmaltzy.

It was actually too much for me. When Liverpool's talismanic captain Steven Gerrard grabbed the game by the scruff of the neck by heading the first goal back early in the second half, I went so ballistic I actually thought I was having a heart attack. That's not hyperbole – I'd been diagnosed with a heart condition a year earlier. Clearly, I wasn't the only one: we counted five ambulances rushing around the athletics-track perimeter of the pitch to the Milan end during that second half. So, when Vladimir Smicer scored the second, the place erupted but I deliberately remained as calm as I could. All around me was the Pictionary definition of frenzy. We were going to do this.

In my comparative calm, I remember thinking of Michael Owen whose ashen face I had seen at Anfield following the semi-final victory over Chelsea. He had left Liverpool the previous summer to join Real Madrid because it was 'his one chance to join a big club and win the European Cup'. Surely there could be no one on earth more gutted than him right now. Not even the Milan fans.

For an extra tug of the heartstrings, the inevitable equaliser came courtesy of a Xabi Alonso rebound after he'd seen his penalty saved. I cried my eyes out. The rest of the match both lasted an agonising eternity and was over in a blurred flash. I don't remember too much of it – not even the decisive penalties. Strangely, though of course I have the DVD, I have never watched it. I don't want to corrupt what memory I have of actually being there; seeing it through wide, welling eyes – eyes which are once again streaming with tears that splash on to my keyboard as I write this.

I know that whatever happens – marriage, kids, marriage of my kids – I've already had the best day of my life. Some people might find that a sad admission and a depressing one, to know that it will never be better than that. I don't. For the rest of my days, that hazy, red-tinted memory will sustain me. I was there in Istanbul.

Simon Rouse

Actor

The obvious one would be the birth of my daughter but I'm not going to go down that road. Apart from that, the best day of my life was when I was 18 and got a place at drama school, Rose Bruford, a very good drama school, where Gary Oldman went. There was some opposition from my parents to my doing it. I'd been to the National Youth Theatre a couple of years before and I wanted to go again but they wouldn't let me as I had to study for my A Levels, which I said I'd do but I never did.

Acting was the only thing I was interested in. It was something I could do and enjoyed. Like most kids, I was in love with the idea of it as much as anything else. All the clichés, getting to meet girls, becoming famous and all that stuff was part of it. I think most actors are like that when they're kids. Then, when you start doing jobs, you realise what it's about.

So I won a place at the drama school and I was very excited about it. When I won this place, my parents didn't really want me to go. They wanted me to go to university. I hadn't studied very much for my A levels; I just mucked around and misbehaved. They were very worried about it, I think, not knowing what I was going to do. I got a minuscule grant to go to Rose Bruford. I remember I hitched down to go to drama school to save money on the fare. I had this huge trunk sent down as well.

At drama school there was a scholarship awarded each year for the best actor in the year. It meant that your fees were paid for the whole course and that included money to live on. People were always talking about it and everyone was up for it. It would come up in conversation and then people would forget about it, then it would come up again later. And I got it. That was the best day of my life. It was the most fantastic day. The principal called me into his room; I'd already been suspended once that term for falling asleep during a lecture and I thought I was going to get it in the neck again. The principal, Norman Benedetti, whose real name was Norman Bennett, would you believe, said, 'I'm very happy to say we've decided to award you the scholarship for your year.'

I was so over the moon. At that age, 18, when you get those things, the physical feeling of excitement and joy is amazing. You never feel like that about anything again in your life. Those feelings you have when you are a teenager are just so intense. I wasn't allowed to tell anybody until it was announced at a meeting in front of the whole college in the afternoon.

He'd told me in the morning and I remember I left his office and ran down to this little private spot at the lakeside and I could hardly breathe I was so excited. I rang my parents and it was like I had been validated for having made this choice. I was always slightly worried that maybe I had let them down and I shouldn't have been there.

But it was like someone saying you're in the right place, you made the right choice. To be able to ring my father up and tell him he didn't have to worry about how I was going to get through the course or getting a grant from Yorkshire Council because for the next three years everything was paid for. It was the most glorious day. Then they announced it in front of the whole college and it gave me loads of plus points. That was a fantastic day.

Raphael Rowe

Journalist

To understand the best day of my life you have to know the worst days of my life which began on 19 December 1988. It was about five in the morning when I was suddenly woken by loud muffled voices coming from the downstairs door to my flat. I leaped out of bed and started to pull on a pair of boxer shorts and a T-shirt before making my way to the stairs leading down to the voices which were now a lot clearer as my ears and mind woke to the shouts: 'Armed police.'

I stood open-mouthed at the bottom of the stairs as masked men pointing guns at me screamed: 'Is there anyone else in this flat?'

I shook my head indicating no before they ordered me to turn around and walk towards the door backwards. Once there they grabbed me. Minutes later I was in the back of a police van with two plain-clothes officers looking at me like I was some kind of species from another planet. Dazed and shocked, frightened and cold, that moment was only the beginning of a 12-year ordeal that will stay with me for the rest of my life and those close to me.

I was 19 years old. I had been arrested for murder and robbery. I was convicted and sentenced to life imprisonment with two other boys. I was told by the trial judge I would serve a total of 54 years.

But I was innocent. I didn't commit the robbery or the murder. I was wrongly arrested, charged and convicted. But in the end I was held in prison for 12 years.

On 17 July 2000, aged 32, the Court of Appeal quashed my convictions and those of my co-defendants and I was set free that day. It would be simple for me to say that was the best day of my life and at that point it was. But as my days of freedom became months and then years I have been able to cherish moments that are truly the best days of my life because I never thought I would ever have the chance to have a life after 19 December 1988.

At the time I was wrongly arrested, I was seeing a 16-year-old girl called Nancy. Like my family and many others, she was caught up in the whirlwind of the dreadful situation in which I found myself. She stuck with me right through the trial and for a short time after but, as I was buried in the prison system and she had her whole life ahead of her, it was only right she got on with her life.

I never forgot her in all the years I was in prison. At the beginning, many had turned their backs but she never did. A month after I was released, I made contact with her for the first time in 12 years. I just wanted to say thanks for supporting me and believing in me. Although she paced up and down the platform of a train station, unsure if she was doing the right thing in meeting me after all that time, she did board the train. We met at London Bridge.

My years in prison had been tough. Apart from the brutality and mental torment I suffered, I missed all the experiences teenagers turning to adults gain to prepare them for life. I had never loved and was so guarded I didn't think I could ever love or allow someone into my life after losing the sense of trust.

But I'd always trusted Nancy. After a few hours catching up and allowing our chemistry to flirt, I asked Nancy for her number. To my surprise she refused saying it wasn't a good idea, although she agreed to take mine. We parted and for a moment I wondered whether I would ever see or hear from her again. Then my mobile rang. I hadn't quite got to grips with mobile phones as they didn't exist when I went to prison. When I did manage to answer it in time, the second time it rang, it was Nancy giving me her number. That led to our getting together again.

I went on to become a reporter on the BBC Radio 4 *Today* programme and am currently working as a reporter for the BBC TV *Panorama* programme. Within a year of working for the BBC I took a risk. I travelled to Afghanistan soon after the war on terror had torn the country to pieces in search of the so-called most wanted terrorist. Soon after, I was in Sierra Leone meeting rebel soldiers and then in Beirut interviewing Interpol's most-wanted diamond smuggler who I'd secretly recorded admitting to me that he was smuggling a million pounds' worth of blood diamonds a week.

I've met and have received Christmas cards from Sarah Brown and Gordon Brown, the Prime Minister, and I have met many inspiring individuals from around the world, which some people might consider to be the best day of their lives. But what led to the best day of my life was meeting Nancy at London Bridge a month after my release from prison.

And in May 2004 the best day in my life started. A day I never expected to happen. It was the day Jay Joseph Rowe was born. Our son. It was followed by our marriage in Jamaica in 2007 and the news that my wife Nancy Rowe is pregnant with our second child as I write.

Emma Samms

Actress

I t is, of course, almost impossible to figure out what has been the best day of your life. I've been very fortunate in my 47 years of life to have had a great deal of wonderful things happen to me and enough catastrophes to appreciate them.

The obvious choice for best day would be the birth of my first child. The exhilaration of having successfully produced a life from within oneself is almost impossibly joyous. Yet, if I had chosen that day I would have been given so much grief by my second child that, without doubt, I must choose another.

So I will choose a day of introspection. A day when I had time to think and time to appreciate.

It was before I had given birth the first time. I had just moved back to England from the United States having lived there for the past 13 years. I had yet to pack up my worldly belongings as I was going through a divorce so I was travelling light with only two suitcases.

I was also travelling light in the emotional sense. Only weeks earlier, I had been starring in the television series *Models Inc* and the pressure of that daily grind – learning lines, starting work at 5.30 a.m., dealing with the press – had suddenly evaporated. I had no schedule, no responsibilities except the one to hand, which was getting a load of laundry done.

I was staying with a childhood friend in his small flat in Clifton, Bristol. When he went to work I would wander the Georgian streets, marvelling at their architecture and character. Years of living in Los Angeles had left me with the American tourist's ability to gawp at anything older than 50 years of age.

I had volunteered to do the laundry that day. My friend's flat, being crammed into the ground floor of an old Georgian townhouse, had no room for a washer or dryer, so I loaded up the laundry bag, threw it over my shoulder and headed for the launderette.

It wasn't a warm day but the sun was out. I was wearing a coat but I still felt the cold chill of an English autumn day and I revelled in it. Los Angeles has sunshine and little else. Having grown up in London where even the slightest whiff of sunbathing weather produces, seemingly out of nowhere, an ocean of deckchairs and their slumbering, reddening occupants, I was shocked to realise that one can get used to sunny weather and actually take it for granted.

There's no easy conversational opener in LA because the weather is nearly always the same. There's no social advantage to having a suntan. There's not even the classic hairdresser's line of 'So where are you holidaying this year?'

More importantly there are no obvious seasons to mark the passage of time in Los Angeles.

So, as I carried my laundry bag, I felt the freshness of the smog-free air, I noticed the warm red hues of the leaves and I stepped over conkers on the pavement. I spotted one conker so perfect and ripe, still sitting in half its prickly shell that I couldn't resist bending down, releasing it and feeling the smooth, shiny roundness of it in my hand.

As I walked along the street I was filled with the joy of my simple task – to do a load of laundry. It suddenly occurred to me that months before I had been sitting in the back of a limousine looking out through its tinted window and had seen a woman carrying a large load of laundry and I had felt terribly sorry for her. Yet here I was, carrying a similarly large load of laundry and not worthy of a moment's pity.

It was quite thought provoking, to say the least.

After I had reached the launderette and was watching the clothes slosh around in the machine, I reflected on how snap judgements or generalisations are dangerous things. Who would think that the person in the limo could have been more miserable than the one carrying the laundry bag?

I realised that getting to be the one in the limo didn't mean you also got to be happy or fulfilled.

I felt safe in that launderette. Safe from all the stalkers that anyone in the public eye accumulates, safe from the paparazzi and safe from other people's opinions. I wasn't worried about my lack of make-up, whether people would listen in to any conversations I was having or comment on my clothes. I knew that no one would ever recognise me there and, even if I did look 'A bit like that girl off *Dynasty*', it would never occur to anyone that it would actually be me.

So I was loving the fact that I wouldn't be recognised, yet isn't that what I thought would be so cool all those years ago when I started out? Didn't I think that fame would be a buffer to all problems?

I re-evaluated my life that day. From the cosiness of that launderette with its enforced waiting time and lack of distractions, I came to the conclusion that a successful career isn't enough. I gave myself permission to slow down.

I have since moved to the Cotswolds and live in an ancient house which is perpetually being renovated. I have two glorious children and a wonderful partner. My work is just that. I work to pay the bills but nothing more. I turn down any jobs that take me away from my children and my real life for any appreciable length of time. If I feel the need to be creative I write or paint.

And I am happy. Happier than I have ever been and I thank goodness for the length of the gentle cycle of those washing machines in that launderette in Bristol. It gave me the time to realise that sometimes the only way to realise that a dream isn't for you is to live it and come out safely on the other side.

Paola dos Santos

Yoga Teacher & PR Consultant

'Wow! You're off to work on a project in Nicaragua with street kids for a few months … sounds scary.' My brother was worried about me. 'Sis, are you sure you should be going out there on your own without firm plans? And are you sure it's safe to be getting a ride from a friend of a friend of a friend of a friend at the airport, along windy roads in the middle of the night? Are you always going to be mad?'

My brother may have thought I was mad but it didn't feel like that to me. Instead, it was exciting. I'd known I wanted to work with young children not as fortunate as the kids in the West for years and to be able to do it in a part of the world I'd fallen in love with over a decade earlier was an amazing opportunity.

When I got to Nicaragua, I did get picked up from the airport by some bloke and his farmer friend – in a 40-seater bus. And I was the only passenger. My brother would have been beside himself but they were fine. And so we drove to the beautiful town of Granada which was to be my home for the next two months. It's a beautiful city on the shores of Lake Granada with the kind of stunning views out to sea you'd expect from that part of the world. But, like many parts of Nicaragua, Granada is also extremely poor. Over the past few decades, the country has been pretty much destroyed by a series of brutal wars.

So that was where I ended up spending two months. The school I chose to work at was open morning and afternoon and the rules were strict. The little men and women who wanted to attend had to arrive on time or else there was no entry. For those who did come along, food was the reward. There was another rule: anyone who had drunk alcohol or sniffed glue that day was not allowed in. Abuse of those substances was rife and the school wanted to take a stand against their effects.

As you can imagine, the children were temperamental, angry, lost and abused but also cheeky, smart, comical and bright. But, above all, they were just children craving attention and compassion. Some lived in very basic accommodation, some on the streets and most were working the streets, shining shoes, selling chewing gum or simply begging. Attending class would often get little-man Juancito or louder-than-life Adonis into trouble because it meant less time spent flogging their goods and providing for the rest of their family.

From day one, I knew it would be difficult. I quickly realised trust would need to be built up over weeks not days. Fights often broke out, chaos dominated the classroom and the boys could be lewd and horrible (I speak fluent Spanish so could understand everything they said). The environment was difficult but making even small progress with any of the kids was an incredible feeling.

Looking into their eyes and just comparing them to my younger cousins or siblings could easily have brought a tear to my eye and, later, when I thought about what had happened, often did. But at the time I couldn't let that happen. This was their reality so I had to get over myself and crack on.

Throughout my time at the school, we were always thinking of how we could realistically pull off taking the group on a day trip somewhere. Easter was coming up and we decided to try to get permission from all the parents of the kids (those that had parents, anyway) to take them to an island not too far from the mainland. We would arrange food, entertainment, music and the kids could kick back and enjoy the swimming pool. The island of choice had a local feel rather than one overrun by tourists so we knew we would not cause too much of a spectacle. We had 21 kids in total and I managed to persuade a couple of travellers to come and help out – big strapping boys from Australia and the UK strong enough to carry three or four kids each on their shoulders in the pool! So we had 10 volunteers and we were set.

Despite living close to the water, some of the kids couldn't swim. They'd clearly never been on a boat before but, even so, the initial fear that took over their faces as we crossed the water eventually disappeared. It was amazing to watch – these kids were on an adventure and you could see they were bursting with anticipation and excitement.

Watching Juancito bite his bottom lip and then throw a smile my way on that boat journey was worth every mosquito bite, minor earthquake and vulgar remark I'd endured over the months. Eight-year-old Juancito's drunk father who often came looking for his son (or rather his son's money) at the school was now far, far away. The uncle or brother who abused their niece or nephew was far, far away. We were heading off into a day of carefree fun with no baddies in sight.

The food was consumed ferociously, we danced to music, played games, won prizes and, my word, did we play in the pool. Five hours of pool action and there were still screams for 'More! More!' at the end of the day. Standing in the swimming pool's rather murky water being splashed and hugged was a release not only for the kids but also for me. I know it was only one day and that putting a tiny sticky plaster on a social problem as big as street kids doesn't solve anything in the long term but above all I knew these were good memories for these beautiful children and why shouldn't they have good memories too? We hadn't taken them to somewhere opulent and out of their reach; we were on a small island, in a local restaurant and swimming in a dirty pool and yet, from the expressions on their faces, you'd have thought they were in Disneyland.

Tony Schiena

World Karate Champion
Actor

In order to describe one of the best days of my life I would need to start with one of the worst. In 2002 I had left Los Angeles and returned to my home town of Richard's Bay South Africa. My sister had been battling cancer and I wanted to spend time with her, so I went home. I had spent a few months with my family and my sister when I decided that since I had been pursuing an acting career in Los Angeles, maybe I should head to Johannesburg which was only a one-and-a-half hour flight away from my home and try the same. After all, I needed to earn some money.

I started having meetings and auditions and I wasn't training and started to drink quite a bit. But only the year before I had won the World Traditional Karate Championships and captained the US Karate Team to gold. Anyway, an interesting audition for Adidas came along. It paid a substantial amount and required a lot of athletic and gymnastic expertise. The audition was an obstacle course of sorts. It was all going well until I had an accident, jumping off a platform and landing on solid, hard, ground. I was rushed to hospital, all the while striking my upper thighs to try get pain away from my ankles. I had fractured both of them and couldn't walk. I was wheeled onto a plane to London where I underwent surgery.

And so I was laid up in a hospital bed at the time that I was meant to be defending my World Title. I went from wheelchair to crutches. I spent my days at physio and swimming, trying anything and everything to get strong again. It was at that time that my dear friend Ciro Orsini introduced me to Armand Assante, Emmy award-winner and multiple times Golden Globe nominee. He was in London to prepare for a role and I was training hard and recovering. We hit it off and started working out together. Armand asked me to join him in Liverpool while he was filming so we could continue to train. I took him up on his offer.

In Liverpool we continued to train hard together. Armand had to progressively lose weight for his role, playing a cop dying from cancer. A week into the shoot, the studio fired the director and dumped a week's worth of footage – that's approximately a million dollars worth. They then hired the seasoned veteran director, John Irvin and the next morning he fired ten actors. That's when Armand looked at me with a serious expression on his face and said, "Here's your shot. Sink or swim." I had never acted professionally before.

The first scene of the "new film" involved my character, a C.I.T.U. (Computer Investigation Technology Unit) cop on a crime scene searching for web-cams conversing with Armand's character, a tough, disgruntled cop, who was giving me a hard time.

And there I was, filming it. 'SILENCE, TURNING OVER…' – the thirty-man crew dead silent…my heart beating faster than if I were to fight a World Championship final with one arm. 'ACTION!' Sitting on my haunches, carefully investigating the crime scene, dialogue flows to and fro between Armand and me. But Armand keeps cutting me off. After the second time, the continuity girl comes to me with her script, pointing out how many lines I missed. I then proclaim to her that I'm trying but Armand keeps cutting me off. She then decides to hastily relay what I had said to her, to Armand. Armand then comes over to me and states that 'I need to put it out there or lose it.' So here I am sitting on my haunches, my ankles aching like crazy, my 'buddy', not doing me any favours and here we go again, 'ACTION,' and finally, 'CUT.'

Armand walks over to me, looks at me seriously, I'm trembling inside, he puts his hand out, 'Congratulations, that was good, I mean it. That was good.' I stood there shocked. My life as a fighter had ended. I had become an actor. One of the happiest days of my life.

Alice von Simson

Journalist

I've been lucky enough to have enjoyed a very happy life so far, packed with wonderful experiences and even more wonderful people, so it is hard for me to pick just one day as the best of my whole life. But, if I sit down, empty my mind and think about it really hard, one blissful day of pure, unadulterated happiness does stick out. It was the sort of day that changes your life forever and makes you think that, at that moment, if someone were to come and take it all away, it would all have been worth it. Yes, that day I achieved what some people search for their whole lives and never find – Nirvana.

And what happened on this marvellous and magical day? I hear you ask. Well, I'll tell you. I was volunteering in Hawaii at the time for a programme that took disadvantaged kids out of school for a week and let them focus on just being kids again. My job was to teach sports, nature classes and team-building and to lifeguard for them when they were using the pool. Throughout the week that they stayed with us, I was their counsellor, friend, teacher and mentor. I watched them learn, grow and gain confidence that they never thought they would have. But, despite what you might think, this had very little to do with the best day of my life because, on that particular day, we didn't have any kids staying with us at all.

No, watching a bunch of little tykes learn to play football was perfectly pleasant, I'll admit, but it was absolutely nothing compared with the day that the US Marine Corps came to use our pool. Those of you who have never had the privilege of seeing 50 wet marines in their swimming trunks will have no idea of the levels of ecstasy that I experienced on that day but let me tell you honestly that, if God had reached his hand out of the sky and told me that this was my last day on earth, I would have died a happy girl.

Preparations for the marines' visit had started early on. The kitchen staff had set up a vast barbecue, the gardener had been working overtime, mowing the sports field and raking up leaves, the pool had been cleaned, the windows washed and a banner hung in the entrance hall proclaiming 'A Big Ohana Welcome to the USMC!'

As the appointed lifeguard for the day, I too had a lot of things to prepare. I awoke at the crack of dawn to wash my hair, rub on scented lotion, apply make-up and carefully pad the requisite red swimsuit with a pair of sport socks and half a roll of toilet paper. It's lucky that no one started drowning that day, because a quick dip in the pool would have turned my chest into papier-mâché! It looked good though and that, I told myself, was what was important.

With the basic preparations complete, I had just enough time to do a quick inventory check before I was expected at the pool. I needed a water bottle to sip languorously on, sunglasses for undercover perving and a whistle to attract attention. *Dear God, let there be some weak swimmers*, I prayed as I mounted my rostrum and waited for the men in uniform to arrive.

Luckily for me, it was a particularly hot Hawaiian day and there was barely any wind. After the long drive, the servicemen were hot and sweaty. All they could think about was ripping their shirts off and diving into the pool, which, coincidentally, was all I'd been able to think about for the last 24 hours too.

I was not disappointed. One after the other, they divested

themselves of their clothing and leaped into the water, until it became a seething mass of rippling torsos, buzz-cuts and gleaming white teeth. I didn't know what to do with myself. They all had those American names that you hear in the movies, Chad, Rob, Buck, Buddy, Rover, whatever, I didn't care. I could barely speak, finding it hard enough to remember my own name let alone theirs.

Like all good things, though, it was over far too quickly. Gleaming pecs were towelled off, shirts pulled over bulging biceps and my boys were ready to be bussed back to their base. Waving frantically, I watched them pull out of the driveway and only just managed to resist the urge to chase the bus down the road like a mad collie dog. When the last of the dust had cleared, I lay back on the grass with a rattling sigh and thanked God for sending the Marine Corps to me.

Now I know that there will be worthier stories in this book; people captaining their national team to victory, winning OBEs or witnessing the birth of their first child. Some of the contributors may even have saved a life or at least changed one for the better. These are all admirable things for which I applaud them heartily, but if I am totally honest I don't think that meeting the Queen, winning the Ashes or even giving birth to my first child could give me any more pleasure than I got from supporting the troops that day in Hawaii.

Grub Smith

Writer & Broadcaster

I had been making travel programmes for five years. But they were not the sort of TV shows that try to sell you a holiday destination, the ones which feature clean, smiling presenters walking down a golden beach, admiring an old church or sipping a cocktail on the hotel balcony. No, my brief was to land in a different country every week and then complete a variety of stupid, shameful challenges.

More often than not, these involved eating disgusting local food (cockroaches in Mexico, dung beetles in Africa), getting extremely drunk or taking my clothes off for comic effect. It won no BAFTAs.

But the worst thing about it was that we were always taking advantage of our hosts. They had been fooled into thinking I was some kind of Michael Palin figure, visiting their homeland to film a wry but respectful travelogue which would boost the tourist trade. But, in fact, we were just after cheap laughs. If there was a racial stereotype or a national quirk to take the mickey out of, we did it, figuring that we'd be safely back in Blighty before they ever saw the programme.

It took a disaster to change our way of thinking. We were in Papua New Guinea, on our way to visit a remote tribe called the Mud People. They had lived isolated in the jungle for many centuries, and had only been discovered by anthropologists in the 1970s. They got their peculiar name from the fact that they wore no clothing, choosing instead to daub themselves with mud and twigs. In the right hands, an encounter with them would have made for moving, eye-opening television. But our plan was to line four of them up, play a tape of the 70s pop group Mud singing 'Tiger Feet', and then giggle as I tried to teach them the dance steps.

Happily for the sake of international relations, we never made it to their territory. A terrible storm blew up in the tropics, a typhoon which hurled sheets of rain down on to the roads. There was no tarmac out here, just rough soil paths cut out of the forest, so very soon the way was impassable. Our car became wedged in a soup of mud. Night fell. The lightning flashed. We were miles from anywhere.

Worryingly, our driver informed us that we were also in bandit country, where robberies at gunpoint were common. Half of me assumed he was winding us up, and that he'd be starting on the ghost stories next. But then a torch shone from up ahead. A figure was approaching our vehicle through the lashing rain.

We tensed. Unarmed, we stood no chance. A tap came at the window, and reluctantly the driver wound it down. He spoke to the man with the torch, and then translated. The intruder was driving a lorry full of food and medical supplies for his village but had become bogged down. Would we help him?

Outside, the mud was a yard deep. There was no way my director and I fancied stepping outside of our dry back seat. But then, from somewhere, I thought, What the hell? Let's give someone a nice impression of Brits on tour for a change. With a new gung-ho attitude, I leaped outside.

Immediately, one of my shoes was sucked away from my foot. It disappeared into the quagmire with a ghastly slurp. My other one lasted two steps, and after that my socks were easy pickings. I was also soaked by gallons of rainfall. But, for some reason, this all just made me feel happier. And, when we finally reached his lorry, and saw how many heavy crates we would have to carry, it just made things better.

For four hours we carted the supplies to the top of the hill. Then, with much slipping and falling over, we pushed his lorry up a hastily made path of stones and logs foraged from the jungle. As in a cheesy Hollywood movie, the dawn was breaking as we reloaded the last of the boxes and waved him goodbye.

I'm not saying the experience changed me for good – I still made some very rude remarks about Germans when we got to Berlin the next week – but it certainly felt good to give a helping hand to someone I'll never see again. They say virtue is its own reward, and in this case it might just be true.

But, if you ever find yourself in Papua New Guinea and happen to see someone wearing a muddy pair of vintage Nike Air Max, do tell the thieving bastard I want them back …

Phil 'The Power' Taylor

Darts Player

I'm sure I'm not going to be like everyone else in the book because the best day of my life was when I left school. I hated school. I couldn't see the point. My friends left about a year before me and they were all out working and earning money and I was sitting there for free! As soon as I went out of the gates, I thought, Right, here we go. I left school on the Friday and started work on the Monday. I was 15 and a half at the time and I thought, Sod this sitting here for nothing – I could be out earning money!

I liked being out earning money as soon as I first did it and still do. I'd had a taste of what it was going to be like three or four months earlier. I worked in my summer holidays, earned about £60 and bought myself a little moped and did it up. I stripped it down, stripped every nut and bolt. I even cleaned the piston, that's the kind of person I am. I used to go riding round on it and loved that moped. I left nothing to chance, I had to get everything right, no stone left unturned.

School wasn't all bad though. I liked certain subjects, like lessons with Dave Moore, one of my teachers who's still a friend now. He could make two flies walking up a wall sound interesting. But some lessons were just dictations and that made it boring.

I did carry on with education after I left school, though, and I enjoyed that. I went to college on what was called day release back then to study

275

engineering and I really liked it. I went for about seven years, from roughly about aged 20 to 26 or 27, one day a week. And I was top of the class! I was second from bottom when I was at school then top of the class when I was working. I was an engineer and studied toolmaking. I was interested in it and knew I was learning something which would benefit me, which was what I didn't like about school. I would have liked school to have been a bit more about skills for life. I really think they should teach a bit of that, such as tax or VAT.

I've always worked hard and it's the graft that's got me where I am now. I was in Glasgow this week and at teatime the traffic was chock-a-block with people coming home from work. All the buses were packed and I remembered sitting on a bus like that on my way home from work, crammed in with everyone else. I'd hate to go back to that now. That's what I appreciate about my life now. I've just got back from Glasgow and I'm going to do a couple of hours on the practice board before I go to bed tonight. You've got to do that. You've got to remember where you came from because you can get complacent if you do well. But as I've got older I've started appreciating what I've got more, my career and all the rest of it.

I was 28 when I started playing darts. I played for fun for a couple of years and then turned serious in 1990. I won the World Championship that year. I did it to earn money. I was working three jobs then to earn money to keep the family going. I used to work 7.30 a.m. until 4 p.m. then come home. I was a sheet metal worker so I used to do cars as well. I'd weld them and do MOTs so I'd have people waiting for me at home for me to do their cars. I'd come home, put my overalls on and go into the street and repair cars for people. Those days are gone now, people don't do that any more. Then I used to work behind a bar on Thursday to Sunday and I'd fit the darts in around all that. Those days made me what I am. I'd do it again if I had to. I wouldn't like it but I'd do it. So the best day for me was when I could get out there into the big wide world. I loved that day.

Brian Turner

Chef

Actually I'm going to be greedy; this covered three days and culminated in the best day of my life. I had a phone call from the offices of *Ready Steady Cook* to ask if I would be prepared to do an item on the *Children In Need* programme on BBC TV with a team of the boys who turned out to be Antony, Ainsley, James and Tony. We phoned each other and had no real idea what was going on or what we had to do but, hey ho, always game for a laugh and to help such a great charity, we all agreed spontaneously. I had done *Children In Need* four years earlier and loved it, but boy was I nervous! But I was confident we could cope with whatever they wanted us to do. So, on the Wednesday of the show, we all met in the rehearsal rooms in Wembley, and laughed and joked as one does with boyish bravado but I know we were all asking the same question: What are we going to do? Soon the time would come, we had two hours to discuss, start and then the following day four hours of rehearsal; then the big day, so what was it?

I forget the lady's name – sorry – but someone from 'up there' at the BBC stood in front of us, thanked us and told us we were to do 'The Full Monty' live on television!

Sudden realisation: we were going to strip and I was standing next to Ainsley! I think not, so I quickly moved! 'Well that's it,' said Nicky, who was to 'rehearse', choreograph and train us in just two and a half days, 'let's get on with it.'

We were made to listen to the music – Tom Jones's 'You Can Leave Your Hat On' – watch Nicky move lightly around the floor, pretend to strip and listen to those immortal words: 'That's all there is to it!'

What?! Wednesday in a room in Wembley, laughing and falling all over the place, Friday, BBC1, White City Television Centre, a live audience and millions watching on telly, taking our clothes off in time to music? 'That's all there is to it!' You must be joking.

However, we rehearsed. Thursday, we rehearsed and we got better, but the best day of my life was still to come. The day came and we went into rehearsals, the routine was getting better; Antony was still useless, Ainsley still big, James hadn't been on *Come Dancing* and it showed … and Tony and I were still there.

The day was a fun day, Nicky was a delight and really worked hard to give us confidence; we rehearsed the afternoon and then had a break. Now it was time to think about what we were doing: all our faces were drained, people were everywhere, the presenters Terry Wogan, now Sir Terry, and Gabby Roslin said hello and there were so many stars, we were gobsmacked; even top-of-the-bill Barry Manilow said hi! We tried not to be starstruck but I'm not sure we succeeded.

So now we had uniform fittings and a full dress rehearsal – how frightening is that? There was a large empty studio just waiting to be filled. The orchestra tuned up and we rehearsed taking all our clothes off and remembering where to put the hat at the last minute.

My youngest son Ben arrived to keep me company and to keep my pecker up (can I say that?!), and he kept saying, 'Look, Dad, they're from *Corrie* and they're from *EastEnders*.'

Was I bothered? I never even noticed them. I was mentally rehearsing my steps and moves.

We kept rehearsing; 'Just one more time,' someone would say and off we went. All through the whole thing, Nicky was great and promised she would be in the audience doing the moves so we would know where we were at any one time.

We were due on at about 10 o'clock-ish but things kept getting put back; the public were paying fortunes to see us do it, and the total kept mounting. I remember someone saying we had passed the million-pound mark, the fastest, at that time, raised on TV for charity. Why did all these people want to see us take our clothes off?

'Time to go' came the call. One more quick trip to the toilet, and this is it!

We waited offstage, the lights went down, we took our positions (I'm trembling now as I write this), Terry made the announcement, the lights went up, the girls screamed, the music started and off we went; it was a machine, we moved to the music, all in time, except Antony.

Those three minutes went on forever, the final bars, no clothes and just a hat to cover my modesty. The crowd went mad, the presenters loved it and we collapsed offstage. What a day!

Barry Manilow finished the show and then came to tell us we were stars. He was so kind, we did it again in the bar; more drink and we did it again!

The rest is just a memory, five cooks, a great charity and a unique moment in my life!

Giles Vickers Jones

TV Presenter & Author

My grandfather, Papa, was a tough old sod, set in his ways, grumpy, opinionated, but he always made me laugh, maybe because I share a lot of those traits! The thing about my grandfather was he was always very black and white. I mean, I remember one time misbehaving, probably being a little cheeky, I could only have been six or seven. My grandfather was having no backchat. He marched my brother Guy and me to the end of the garden and told us he'd never met such horrible little children and to buck up our ideas and stop behaving like spoiled brats or else! He was the kind of man to call it as he saw it.

He was such an eccentric he had his shed at the end of the garden like a lot of men but his resembled a NASA workspace. He could make everything, even building a steam engine on a piece of wood the size of a mouse mat. As he got older, he needed a stairmaster, you know like the one Thora Hird used. Not content with the gentle, safe climbing speed, Papa, as a former electrician, rewired it so a cat couldn't outrun it up the stairs. It used to scare my nan to death – the thing was like something out of Alton Towers. He was such a unique guy.

Growing up, I was a lot closer to my grandmother, Nan, because she's like all nans should be: jolly, interested in your little lives and very loving and, wow, what a roast dinner! That said, I was close to Papa but not until I was an adult when I understood that he was a really caring good guy. There's one specific moment, just a conversation that I had with him, which was a day I always remember. It cemented our relationship and culminated in our joint efforts and the day that changed my life.

During the last few months of uni, I realised that being a graduate of French and business, albeit good to have on your confidence CV, wasn't much needed for the path I was deciding to take. While at university, I, along with my ex-girlfriend, went on a BBC game show called *The Other Half*. It was one of those many throwaway shows that are churned out for Saturday nights. Anyway, the one thing I remember was watching the presenter Dale Winton interacting with the audience, the producers and the guests, and witnessing first-hand what a great time he was having. There and then, against the grain of my life, having been at military boarding school, having played rugby and studied at university where I barely watched more than four hours of TV a week apart from the prescribed dose of *Neighbours*, I decided I wanted to be a TV presenter. I was 22 or 23 and so fairly late in the game and with no links to TV whatsoever. All my family were military; what was I going to do?

Fast forward six months after uni and I had a very small agent and, more importantly, a little understanding of the business I was trying to enter.

I'd discovered that, to make it as a presenter, I'd need a showreel, a video of me on camera. With no experience, I'd decided to film my own mini TV clips and piece them together. The obvious choice was to ask my grandfather to help, as, ever since I was a little boy, he'd made tapes of the family birthdays and so on. He was a proper techno geek – even his indicators in his car spoke to him. So Papa and I would chat every few days over the phone plotting the making of my showreel. We researched shows like *Wish You Were Here* (mental note: they are walking and talking), sitting down on a sofa (relaxed like on *GMTV*) and doing quick interviews with strangers like *Streetmate*. With our rough storyline plotted out, off we went for the funniest couple of days, me and my 73-year-old grandfather, walking stick in hand, and his sturdy Sony Camcorder. In London we filmed an interview with a celebrity – thanks, Eric Knowles, what a great guy; he even gave my grandparents a couple of vases with caricatures of his face and they still have them in pride of place. We did walking and talking outside the local chemist and quick vox pops in the Reading Sava-Centre. Watching my grandfather chase behind as I asked inane questions, himself an ex-military ex-Harrow pupil, wondering why I didn't get a proper job, was golden.

We finally cut together a tape and we were both firmly proud of what we had achieved. I went back to making cocktails in restaurant chain Frankie and Benny's, listening to swing music looped and looped for six-hour shifts (the thought of Vegas sending shivers down my spine) and Papa went back to *Top Gear*, his shed and rugby on TV.

The next few months saw me do a variety of jobs working as an actor on the Royal Opera House stage, doing promotional work and eventually modelling. The modelling gave me some fairly sensible money and the chance to live in London and pay my way.

But please don't think for any minute I'd put that trusted showreel in the drawer labelled failed ambition. Every day I'd chase work, chase various contacts, call the BBC, pester other presenters. A lot of doors were closing; I mean. I'd had no presenting experience, so why would anyone employ me?

Then a bit of light shone my way. An audition for a digital-TV channel came through my model agency.

'When is it?'

'Tomorrow! What are you doing?'

I was getting my hair styled and coloured for L'Oreal and doing a catwalk show! I was going to miss this big opportunity.

The whole time I was there, knowing that I'd missed my audition, broke me. I never let on even when we won our hair show, even though my hair felt a little flat. A little dramatic I know, but I was genuinely gutted.

As soon as I'd finished my job, I tracked down where this audition was being held and more importantly who was the producer. It turned out that the woman auditioning people was also a model who I had met at a model casting two months earlier. I had given her my trusted homemade showreel at the time and nothing had come of it. Anyway, it didn't matter right now. I had a name and I had an opportunity if only they hadn't chosen anyone. The night couldn't end fast enough. The very next morning I had decided to call her at 9.30 so jumped in the shower. When I came out I had a missed call. It was her, the presenter/producer. Could this be fate?

Like a boy to porn, I couldn't move fast enough and called her straight back. She said that they had chosen someone yesterday but suggested I swing by. I ran there and finally met up with everyone: the producers, the presenter, the cameraman and the editors. It looked bloody exciting and a chance for me to become a presenter. I could almost taste it. Although they had chosen the other presenter, I suggested I come along and help out on their shoot, maybe do a couple of links (presenting to camera) with them. It went so well and I got on with everyone.

When I went back to their offices, I was once again crestfallen, as the presenter they d chosen was heading down that afternoon. I did what turned out to be 'my break', working for the dating channel. I offered my services for free for three months, which I knew would mean a return to Frankie and Benny's and making cocktails at nights but I didn't care. They said yes. I signed a contract and I was now a presenter!

I got straight on the tube, thinking how my life would change and what this would mean. I got through the door and the first thing I did was dial Nan and Papa's, and give him the chance to say in a very minor way we did it. This was the best day of my life: I got my first TV presenting job and shared it with him. He was so proud and right up until he died in May 2007 he was the first person I called if I ever got any presenting job and he couldn't have been any more supportive if he tried.

RIP, Papa.

James Walsh

Lead Singer with Starsailor

When I think of the best day of my life, many things spring to mind. The day I got married, the day my daughter was born and the day I watched Liverpool beat Chelsea in the FA Cup semi-final at Old Trafford of all places! As a musician, though, I think meeting The Rolling Stones is as big as it gets (apart from meeting McCartney but I guess that will come one day). Following on from our support slots with U2 in Paris and Cardiff, we really didn't think it could get any better until we got the call from our agent that we were chosen to support The Rolling Stones. The story doesn't end there though. We played a number of gigs with the band before the fateful day we were allowed to cross the barrier into the land of the Stones!

The day we got to meet our heroes was Wednesday, 19 July in Hanover, Germany. I remember we played our own set first and went down a storm. It is always daunting playing with a band like The Rolling Stones. They attract such a hardcore audience that it is almost impossible to make an impression. Imagine you are 60 years old and you have waited 30-odd years to see your favourite band! The support band would have to be extra special to make an impression, so we were very happy with the response.

Post-gig, we were met by a female member of The Stones' entourage. (Don't ask me what she did – there were fucking hundreds of them. Charlie Watts even has an Espresso Tech!) She then ushered in 'The Shabeen' where we awaited the arrival of 'The greatest rock 'n' roll band in the world'. Incidentally, 'The Shabeen' is Keith's idea and you are likely to see many of his old mates knocking about in there prior to the show. We had to wait a bit as Mick Jagger likes to run for a good while before each show.

Then, finally, we were taken into the corridor and stood outside the dressing rooms as Mick, Keith, Charlie and Ronnie came out to greet us. The actually meeting was very brief but memorable, Mick said he bought our first album, Charlie was very quiet and polite, Ronnie kept laughing and spoke very highly of Mark Collins from The Charlatans and I couldn't really understand a word Keith Richards said, which I guess is what you would want from him. A quick shot was taken by the band's official photographer, then they went on stage.

We rushed round into the audience and heard the first chimes of 'Start Me Up' with beaming smiles on our faces. It was one of those moments where you think, Isn't it great being in a band? After the Stones finished, when they had long gone back to their hotels, we stayed at the venue and got absolutely bladdered! We then thought it would be a good idea to go down to their dressing-room area and steal as many dressing-room signs or any other bit of Rolling Stones-related stuff we could find.

The perfect end to a perfect day.

Clare Wigfall

Author

To tell you the truth, the story I'm about to tell you is not really about me. It's about the kids I met that summer afternoon. They were what made it one of my best days. Seeing them step out of their everyday lives and into their imaginations. Seeing them smile.

The story begins in a sleepy village in the Czech mountains. The kind of village where families drive battered old Skodas and cut wood in the summer to feed their stoves in the winter.

What makes this village stand apart from others is the large brick building dominating the central square. We pulled up that day in its shadow, and as we did tiny faces appeared at the tall Victorian windows, peering between the net curtains and staring at us as we unloaded the car: we'd come to the district children's home.

I looked up and waved and, within a second, like frightened mice, the children disappeared. The suddenly blank windows of the imposing building made me anxious, reminding me that we didn't know what to expect from the day.

You see, when I was 10, I helped out at my junior school fête on the face-painting stall. I loved it so much I started my own face-painting company a year later, even though at the time, of course, I wasn't much older than those whose faces I was painting. Many years after that, when I found myself living in Prague and spending too many hours alone at my writing desk, I decided to start up my childhood company once again.

I have always been artistic, but, for me, face painting is something special. It's a bit like magic. When you paint a face, you can see the child before you literally transform. It's not just their appearance that changes, but their whole personality. They *become* something else – a princess, a tiger, Spiderman, a butterfly. Their imagination comes to life.

But today was going to be a new experience. Our usual clients were wealthy expatriates, children from privileged homes, children in frilly party frocks, children whose brightly wrapped birthday gifts would pile up as their guests arrived.

The children we were about to meet had been abandoned, or orphaned, or removed from neglectful families; most would spend their whole childhood in this unfriendly-looking building.

In their short lives, they'd suffered in ways we could hardly imagine – sexual abuse, neglect, violence, crime. A number of them, we'd been warned, suffered from severe behaviour issues and their reaction might be hostile. Most had never seen foreigners before. Nobody knew how these kids would respond to us.

The children were already waiting patiently when we came into the meeting room. They turned in their seats and stared. They were scrubbed clean in faded hand-me-down clothes and house slippers. It was hard to tell the girls from the boys because all of them had their hair shorn close to their heads. Many were Roma gypsy children, with beautiful black eyes and dark hair. The youngest of them was only three, the oldest almost 18.

They watched as we unpacked our paints, staring quietly as if we were from another planet, but there was something in the air that we couldn't miss – an electric buzz of excitement. It gave us encouragement.

Three boys were called up first – early teenagers, the sort who at a

287

normal party would reject face painting as babyish. They sat down shyly and, when we handed them our face-painting books so they could choose a face, we realised something: these kids had never in their lives come across face painting before. They didn't know what it was and had no idea what they were supposed to do.

'Pick a face,' we urged. 'Which one do you like?'

'Spiderman,' said one of them eventually, uncertainly and with a hesitant smile. The other two quickly echoed.

That was when we began to work our magic. To their surprise, we swooped the colour across their faces and, as the transformation began, they relaxed and smiled. They started to giggle. The giggling was infectious. They pointed at each other and began to shriek with laughter. Others flocked around. 'Me next! Me next!' they shouted, dancing on their toes with excitement.

We painted, and painted, and painted. Near the end, a young girl sat down before me. She'd been bobbing at my elbow for a while, changing her mind every minute as to what face she was going to choose. '*Pejsek*,' she now told me – doggy.

For me, the very best moment when you're face painting – *every time* – is the moment when you hand across the mirror. In the reflection, you see the child's face light up as they catch a first glimpse of themselves. However many faces you've painted, however tired you are, when you see that smile you can't help smiling too. I looked at that little girl, with her shorn hair, and her hand-me-down clothes, and no mother or father to love her, and as I did her smile stretched into a grin, a wide gap-toothed grin, the biggest and best grin you could imagine. It spread right the way across her painted doggy face.

'I'm a dog,' she said in an awed whisper. 'I'm a dog!'

And at that moment it was absolutely true. She'd stepped out of her life. They all had. We'd let them loose in their imaginations.

To my delight, she gave a woof and tumbled away with the other dogs. The cats purred contentedly. The spidermen spun webs from their wrists and climbed up the walls. The princesses danced in their silk ball-gowns. The tigers roared and disappeared into the jungle.

And the glittering butterflies, perhaps they were the most achingly beautiful. They flapped their tissue-thin wings and lifted into the sky. Higher and higher they went until they were little more than tiny specks against the blue, fluttering in the summer sunlight.

Eddie Young

Businessman

L ooking back now, I see that what started as a pretty normal day
in my working week changed my thoughts on life forever. It
was a driech day in Glasgow. It was raining and I was stuck in traffic
on my way to an eight o'clock meeting. I feared it was going to be a
pretty boring couple of hours, and so it turned out.

After the meeting and deeply depressed about how boring and dull
my work was, I jumped into the car to go to present a charity cheque
to a local children's hospice. A number of us had collected monies
through various activities over the previous year and it was now time
to go along and present our collection to the trustees, one being a
rather famous actor who will remain anonymous at the moment.

To be honest, at the time, the thought of going to the hospice and
meeting the sick children wasn't top of my wish list of activities for
the day. The fact that I am totally chicken-hearted made me certain I
would struggle to cope with the situation.

On arrival, I bumped into an old friend as soon as I got out of the
car which made it much easier to walk up to the entrance. We were
greeted by a few ladies who were handing out soft drinks and taking
our coats. What I would have done for a stiff one to ease the pressure!
Anyway, we walked through to the main reception area to see in front

of us a mixture of people from local minor celebrities through to nursing staff, all mostly adults and visiting children.

We stood and had small talk with a couple of others for 10 minutes or so. And it was then that this little angel walked into our group and bold as brass introduced herself to us all. Her name was Amy and she immediately took over the whole conversation and became the centre of attention. My initial reaction to her was one of surprise as her attitude seemed really positive and very bullish. I thought she must be here as a visitor.

Then it was time, we were third to present our monies: a quick walk up on to the makeshift stage, a couple of photographs and it was over. Good, I thought, I can now chill out a bit.

Moving back to the group, I noticed the little one had gone, I assumed back to her parents, and we started chatting again. It was then the shock came. A male nurse had joined us and he was telling the others about Amy's plight and the fact she was terminally ill. He thanked both of us as we came into the group and said that without our type of help the hospice would struggle, which is a bit of a joke in a society such as ours.

He then went on to tell me about the little one, how she had been there for a couple of weeks. Her story was particularly sad because her mother was a single parent and was struggling to cope on all fronts, working to earn enough money to survive while looking after the little one. He said that this was not unusual and that the hospice was mainly here to help children like her.

Again, as with her first entrance, Amy appeared as if from nowhere, smile as wide as the Clyde and booming with confidence. The next 30 minutes of chat and laughter changed my view on life forever.

I thought, Wow, what an attitude to life she has – she is so positive, always looking on the bright side, eyes full of life and energy, constantly chatting, smiling and laughing out loud as if she had not a care in the world.

Time went quickly as it always does in a fun situation and soon it was time to leave. Amy again laughed all the way to the door with us, being the centre of attention right to the end. Her way, I suppose.

As I walked back to my car in a state of shock, her enthusiasm for life and laughter had made me feel better in an hour or so than I had felt all year. Suddenly all the problems of work and life had disappeared because I saw they were pretty insignificant compared to her issue.

Driving back alone, my heart, though happy, felt sad knowing Amy probably wouldn't see Christmas only six months away or her next birthday. But one thing I did know, which gave me great heart, was that every day she had would be lived to the full without remorse or sadness.

The fact that she had accepted her problems without the baggage you assume would go with it was amazing. She was the most upbeat, positive and in-your-face person I had ever met and she still is to this day.

The day that had started with boredom, sadness and a sense of fear had turned into a life-changing experience which we can all learn from.

So, when you are having one of these long-knife nights or a day that seems to be getting you down, think about little Amy, as I do, and the rest will fall into perspective.

Is it strange that we may only appreciate what we really have when we are losing it? Amy had an attitude for life like no one I have met and if we could all feel like her I think our daily living would be so much easier.

Three months later she was gone. I heard she was still positive to the end. But why should that surprise me!

Acknowledgements

Putting this book together was difficult at times but, more than anything, it was fun. Each time we received a story, it felt like we were unwrapping a Christmas present and we feel hugely lucky to now have this book you are holding to show for our efforts. As you'd expect, we have to thank a few people.

First and most importantly, thank you to everyone who contributed a story. Without you there would be, quite literally, no book at all so we are profoundly grateful. We were amazed at how open and honest everyone was, even some people who are complete strangers to us. The stories are heart-warming, inspiring, hilarious and, in several cases, moved at least one of us to tears. We are extremely proud of the resulting book, which is entirely down to you, so thank you all very, very much.

In particular, we'd like to thank the contributors whose stories went into the proposal which got us a publishing deal: Phil Greening, Alan Carr, James Corden, Lara Agnew, Paola dos Santos, Ewen MacIntosh, Lewis Crofts, Mike Gayle and Ann Daniels. Special thanks also to Chris Manby, who very kindly put us in touch with some brilliant writers and never quite realised how valuable her contribution was. And to all those who helped us get stories, thank you. You know who you are.

Then there is Cass Pennant, thank you for publishing our book and for having enough faith in us to make it all happen so quickly.

Finally, we'd each like to say something separately.

Giles: Humfrey, God bless your ability to allow me to do all the work but, wow, that man can get you working! Humfrey, I jest. What a great guy to do this project with; none better, more patient or more talented at self-motivation. Then we have Ottie and the rest of my family who have always supported me and the various showbiz friends who will be hugely grateful that the book is now finished and I'm going to stop hassling them. Thank you all.

Humfrey: Giles, thank you for being a constant source of energy, amusement, friendship and for having the good grace to acknowledge the indisputable fact that I'm the better squash player. Oh, and for coming up with the idea for the book and then labouring under the sad illusion that you were doing all the work. Mustn't forget that. Secondly, my friends (in particular Oli, Charlie, Ross, Sean, Pally, Tom K, Dan A, Brad, Josh and Nick) for their generosity over the past couple of years, which has gone way above and beyond the call of duty, and last of all my sisters Rachel and Sarah because if I don't mention them they'll kill me.

That's enough gratitude for now. We hope you enjoyed the book.

Giles and Humfrey